THE ETHICS OF ONLINE RESEARCH

ADVANCES IN RESEARCH ETHICS AND INTEGRITY

Series Editor: Dr. Ron Iphofen FAcSS, Independent Consultant, France

Recent Volumes:

ADVANCES IN RESEARCH ETHICS AND INTEGRITY

Series Editor

Dr. Ron Iphofen *FAcSS, Independent Consultant, France*

Editorial Advisory Group

Professor Robert Dingwall *FAcSS, Dingwall Enterprises Ltd and Nottingham Trent University, UK*

Dr. Nathan Emmerich *Queens University Belfast, UK*

Professor Mark Israel *University of Western Australia, Australia*

Dr. Janet Lewis AcSS, *Former Research Director, Joseph Rowntree Foundation, UK*

Professor John Oates *FAcSS, Open University, UK*

Associate Professor Martin Tolich *University of Otago, New Zealand*

ADVANCES IN RESEARCH ETHICS
AND INTEGRITY   VOLUME 2

THE ETHICS OF ONLINE RESEARCH

VOLUME EDITOR

KANDY WOODFIELD
Samaritans, UK

emerald
PUBLISHING

United Kingdom – North America – Japan
India – Malaysia – China

Emerald Publishing Limited
Howard House, Wagon Lane, Bingley BD16 1WA, UK

First edition 2018

Reprints and permissions service
Contact: booksandseries@emeraldinsight.com

British Library Cataloguing in Publication Data
A catalogue record for this book is available from the British Library

ISBN: 978-1-78714-486-6 (Print)
ISBN: 978-1-78714-485-9 (online)
ISBN: 978-1-78743-446-2 (Epub)
ISBN: 978-1-80043-175-1 (Paperback)

ISSN: 2398-6018 (Series)

INVESTOR IN PEOPLE

This volume is dedicated to the members of the #NSMNSS community across the world who continue to push the boundaries of social science and internet mediated research by sharing their experiences and challenges as technology continues to transform how we live, and understand, our everyday lives.

CONTENTS

ABOUT THE AUTHORS

Wasim Ahmed is a Doctoral Researcher at the Information School, University of Sheffield. His PhD looks at understanding pandemics and epidemics on social media platforms. He has many years of experience in social media research working on a number of commercial and industry projects across academia, government, industry for companies such as Manchester United. He has published peer reviewed articles on social media, and has delivered a number of prestigious talks across the world. He runs his own analytics blog, and regularly posts on social media research for the LSE Impact blog with a readership in at least 136 countries. Wasim has an interdisciplinary background with an MSc in Information Systems, and a BA in Philosophy.

Peter Bath is Professor of Health Informatics, Head of the Information School, and Head of the Health Informatics Research Group at the University of Sheffield. As Chair of the University Research Ethics Committee (UREC), Peter was responsible for the review of University of Sheffield's research ethics policy, which included new policy on the ethical issues relating to social media research. Peter is the Principal Investigator of the 'A Shared Space and a Space for Sharing' project, a transdisciplinary project examining how people in extreme circumstances share information online. He is supervising a number of students who are utilising social media data as part of their PhDs. Peter has published over 200 papers/abstracts, including 116 articles in peer-reviewed journals.

Libby Bishop is currently working 80% at GESIS-Leibniz Institute for the Social Sciences in Cologne (Germany) where she is the Leader of the Data Security and Data Linkage Team in the Data Archive. The team is enhancing capacities for the Secure Data Center, including remote access to sensitive data and curation of new forms of data such as social media. With her 20% at the UK Data Service at the University of Essex (UK), Libby is a Manager in the Research Data Management section. She has expertise in the ethics of re-using data and informed consent. She also develops and delivers training on legal and ethical issues in sharing big data and on secondary analysis of qualitative data. During 2017, she is leading the Legal/Ethics strand of a CESSDA (Consortium of European Social Science Data Archives) Research Data Management project.

Pete Burnap is Reader in the School of Computer Science and Informatics, Cardiff University. He is an applied computer scientist with a principal focus on data and computational methods such as machine learning to model Web-enabled human and software behaviour – contributing to the academic fields of Social Computing, Web Science and Cybersecurity. His research outcomes, which include more than 60 academic articles – stemming from funded research projects worth over £8million, are organised and disseminated via the Social Data Science Lab, within which he is a director and the computational lead.

Jenna Condie is a Lecturer in Digital Research and Online Social Analysis at Western Sydney University, and a World Social Science Fellow on transformations to sustainable urbanisation for the International Social Science Council. Her research focuses upon how everyday experiences and social connections are mediated by digital technologies in the places we live, work, play and stay. As an experienced qualitative researcher, Jenna use methods that are participatory, critical, creative, and digital. Current projects include examining the use of social media by non-profit organisations, particularly within the social housing sector; how location-aware technologies are reworking our social relations; and how digital technologies can be harnessed for urban governance, particularly within urban planning and community safety initiatives.

Dr. Gianluca Demartini is a Senior Lecturer in Data Science at the University of Queensland. His main research interests are Information Retrieval, Semantic Web, and Human Computation. His research has been supported by the UK Engineering and Physical Sciences Research Council (EPSRC) and by the EU H2020 framework program. He received the Best Paper Award at the European Conference on Information Retrieval (ECIR) in 2016 and the Best Demo Award at the International Semantic Web Conference (ISWC) in 2011. He has published more than 70 peer-reviewed scientific publications including papers at major venues such as WWW, ACM SIGIR, VLDBJ, ISWC, and ACM CHI. He has given several invited talks, tutorials, and keynotes at a number of academic conferences (e.g., ISWC, ICWSM, WebScience, and the RuSSIR Summer School), companies (e.g., Facebook), and Dagstuhl seminars. He is an ACM Distinguished Speaker since 2015.

Steven Ginnis is a Research Director at Ipsos MORI, leading both Education, Children and Families research, and innovation in research methods across the UK business. With nine years of experience across central and local government research, Steven is responsible for pioneering the use of new and emerging technologies in public sector research, including mobile research, text analytics, biometrics, neuroscience, and social media research.

He directed the Wisdom of the Crowd project, working with Demos, University of Sussex and Centre for Analysis of Social Media to help embed rigour and ethics at the heart of the social media research process. More widely, he recently led the Dialogue on Data Science Ethics commissioned by the Government Data Science partnership looking at public attitudes towards government use of data science.

Daniel Gray is a PhD student in the Economic and Social Research Council Wales Doctoral Training Partnership in the School of Social Sciences at Cardiff University. His research investigates misogynistic hate speech found on Twitter and other social media, employing big data collection and critical discourse analysis. He has worked with the Social Data Science Lab at Cardiff, using its guidelines for social media research for his projects, including his M.A dissertation on misogynist speech, which is included as a case study in this volume.

Susan Halford is a Professor of Sociology, Director of the Web Science Institute at the University of Southampton and Deputy Director of the EPSRC Centre for Doctoral Training in Web Science Innovation. She was a founding Director of the University's Work Futures Research Centre and has over 25 years' experience of research on organizational change, including digital innovation, employee driven innovation and the voluntary workforce. .

Curtis Jessop is a Research Director in the Longitudinal Surveys team at NatCen Social Research where he manages the NatCen Panel, an open mixed-mode random-probability research panel, and works on large-scale longitudinal surveys such as Understanding Society and the British Birth Cohort Studies. Curtis is the lead for the 'New Social Media, New Social Science' collaborative network which facilitates discussion and knowledge sharing between researchers using social media in their research, including a particular focus on research ethics. He has a particular interest in the ethics and practicalities of linking social media and social survey data to enhance the research potential of both.

Garth Lean is a Lecturer in Geography and Urban Studies in the School of Social Sciences and Psychology at Western Sydney University. His research and writing primarily investigate experiences of travel in a modern, mobile world. He is the lead researcher of the Transformative Travel Research Project (www.transformativetravel.com) and co-lead of the TinDA (Travel in the Digital Age) Project (www.tindaproject.com). He has published a variety of papers on travel, tourism and mobilities, along with the monograph *Transformative Travel in a Mobile World* (CABI Books, 2016), and the edited volumes *Travel and Representation* (Berghahn, 2017), *Travel and Imagination* (Ashgate, 2014) and *Travel and Transformation* (Ashgate, 2014). He is Vice

President of the Geographical Society of New South Wales and a member of the Geographies of Leisure and Tourism Research Group with the Royal Geographical Society.

At the time of contributing to this chapter: Hayley Lepps was a Researcher in the Health Policy team at NatCen Social Research, having previously worked in the Questionnaire Development and Testing Hub at NatCen. Hayley is a mixed-methods researcher with experience in conducting research through depth interviews, focus groups and observations; developing and testing survey questions through cognitive interviews; and managing web and telephone surveys. Hayley is a member of the #NSMNSS (New Social Media, New Social Science) network and is particularly interested in how ethical guidelines for social research apply to research using social media data, following her work on the NatCen project entitled 'Research using Social Media; Users' Views'. Through this work, Hayley was invited to contribute towards 'Social Media Research: A Guide to Ethics', a document intended to provide clear guidelines on the ethical use of social media data in research.

Sarah Quinton is currently the Chair of Research Ethics at Oxford Brookes University where she teaches and researches in the Business School. Her particular area of research interest is how the digital environment is shaping behaviour change across society, business, consumers and citizens. Her recent publications include the *Journal of Industrial Marketing Management*, the *International Journal of Management Reviews*, and the *Journal of Marketing Management*. She believes that digitalisation is impacting on the tools and perspectives within social science research methods and that the new complex research environment that we inhabit requires further consideration.

Nina Reynolds is currently the Professor of Marketing at the University of Wollongong where she teaches and researches in the School of Management, Operations and Marketing. She has a longstanding interest in research methods, originally focusing on design and analysis issues related to international survey research, but now focusing on how technological changes impact on how researchers gain insights into individuals' behaviours. Her other research currently focuses on how we, as consumers, manage and use our personal resources in today's consumption environment, and on the influence of consumption experiences on our wellbeing. Her work has been published in a number of journals including the *Journal of International Business Studies*, the *Journal of Service Research*, the *European Journal of Marketing*, the *Journal of Business Research* and *International Marketing Review*.

Janet Salmons, PhD, is an independent scholar through Vision2Lead. She has authored numerous books and articles about online research approaches and related ethical issues. Her most recent book is *Doing Qualitative Research Online*. Dr. Salmons is based in Boulder, Colorado.

Luke Sloan is Deputy Director of the Social Data Science Lab (http://socialdatalab.net/) and Reader at the School of Social Sciences, Cardiff University. His research is concerned with increasing the utility of Twitter data for the social science community, through the development and evaluation of demographic proxies, to establish who is and who is not represented. He also directs the Cardiff the Q-Step Centre.

Leanne Townsend is a senior researcher based at the University of Aberdeen. Her work explores how technologies can transform rural communities and economies. Her interests include the ethics of social media research; the rural creative economy; rural food producers; marginalised groups; crafting communities; rural economic in-migration and the transformational potential of social media for communities of practice and place. She has led various projects and brought together new networks. She is on the board of directors at the Scottish Sculpture Workshop and on the editorial board at Local Economy. She works collaboratively to co-produce research which seeks positive change and new academic understandings.

Claire Wallace is Professor of Sociology at the University of Aberdeen. She was Leader of the Enterprise and Culture theme of the RCUK dot.rural Digital Economy Hub at the University of Aberdeen. She also worked on the ESRC project on Social Media at the same University on which this report is based. Claire Wallace has published widely on digital communications, quality of life, community and other topics. Her most recent book is *The Decent Society* together with Pamela Abbott and Roger Sapsford and published by Routledge in 2015.

Matthew Williams is Professor of Criminology at the School of Social Sciences, Cardiff University. He was a lead researcher on the Cardiff Online Social Media Observatory (COSMOS) programme (2012–15), and now continues this work as the Director of the Social Data Science Lab (http://socialdatalab.net/), part of the ESRC Big Data Network. He has published extensively on the use of social media data in crime and security research. He was appointed to the ESRC's Big Data Network Phase 3 working group and is Principal Investigator on the ESRC's New and Emerging Forms of Data Policy Demonstrator Grant Centre for Cyberhate Research and Policy.

Brittany Wilcockson is a research assistant and PhD candidate (psychology) within the School of Social Sciences and Psychology at Western Sydney University, Australia. Her research is situated within social and political psychology and explores the cognitive underpinnings of language about 'outsider' groups (groups which are positioned by themselves or government as outside the law, e.g., outlaw motor cycle gangs). Her work also explores the intersection of online research methods and ethics. She is more broadly interested in the use of language data in forensic and investigative settings, and the security and privacy implications of online information storage and use.

ABOUT THE SERIES EDITOR

Dr. Ron Iphofen FAcSS is Executive Editor of the Emerald book series *Advances in Research Ethics and Integrity* and edited Volume 1 in the Series: *Finding Common Ground: Consensus in Research Ethics Across the Social Sciences* (2017). He is an Independent Research Consultant, a Fellow of the UK Academy of Social Sciences, the Higher Education Academy and the Royal Society of Medicine. Since retiring as Director of Postgraduate Studies in the School of Healthcare Sciences, Bangor University, his major activity has been as an adviser to the European Commission (EC) on both the seventh framework programme (FP7) and Horizon 2020. His consultancy work has covered a range of research agencies (in government and independent) across Europe. He was Vice Chair of the UK Social Research Association and now convenes their Research Ethics Forum. He was scientific consultant on the EC RESPECT project (establishing pan-European standards in the social sciences) and chaired the ethics and societal impact advisory board for SECUR-ED (a European Demonstration Project on passenger transport security). He has advised the UK Research Integrity Office; the National Disability Authority (NDA) of the Irish Ministry of Justice; and the UK Parliamentary Office of Science and Technology among many others. Ron was founding Executive Editor of the Emerald gerontology journal *Quality in Ageing and Older Adults*. He published *Ethical Decision Making in Social Research: A Practical Guide*, with Palgrave Macmillan (2009/2011) and coedited with Martin Tolich *The SAGE Handbook of Qualitative Research Ethics* (to appear in 2018).

ABOUT THE VOLUME EDITOR

Kandy Woodfield is a social researcher and learning & development professional. She is Head of Learning and Development at Samaritans and her previous roles include Head of Social Sciences at the Higher Education Academy and Director of Learning & Enterprise at NatCen Social Research. Kandy is a Chartered Fellow of the Chartered Institute of Personnel and Development (CIPD), a Fellow of the Learning & Performance Institue (LPI) and has worked across the academic, public and third sectors. Kandy spent over twenty years in social policy research working across a range of topics including welfare reform and crime & justice before moving into learning & development. She is the founder of the New Social Media New Social Science? (#NSMNSS) community of practice and most recently edited a crowd sourced book of blogs on 'Social Media in Social Research'.*

---

* Woodfield, K. Ed. 2014 *Social Media in Social Research: Blogs on Blurring the Boundaries* (NatCen Social Research; London)

INTRODUCTION TO VOLUME 2: THE ETHICS OF ONLINE RESEARCH

Kandy Woodfield and Ron Iphofen

HOPES AND PROMISES

The Internet, the World Wide Web and social media – indeed all forms of online communications – have been seen as attractive fields of research since their inception for many reasons. Some of the earliest discussion and commentary were eager in terms of the opportunities for methodological initiatives and innovations in research and the 'attractiveness' of easily accessed, massive amounts of primary and secondary data sources.

Using e-mail as a research tool was seen to potentially offer researchers advantages such as easy access to world-wide samples, low administration costs (both financially and temporally), ready-transcribed data and its unobtrusiveness, and 'friendliness' to respondents was also valued (Robson & Selwyn, 1998). Once you became an experienced Web 'surfer,' you could have access to a wealth of valued and authoritative information sources (Peters, 1998). Instant messaging was seen as a cost- and time-effective method for in-depth interviewing (Fontes & O'Mahoney, 2008); online participants might

The Ethics of Online Research
Advances in Research Ethics and Integrity, Volume 2, 1–12
Copyright © 2018 by Emerald Publishing Limited
All rights of reproduction in any form reserved
ISSN: 2398-6018/doi:10.1108/S2398-601820180000002013

be better able to 'tell their story' in a way that suits them and so may even be ethically sounder than conventional methods of narrative data collection. Traditional survey methods have long suffered from increasing costs and declining responses rates – Web surveys offered an attractive alternative and have the advantage of ease in collecting more sensitive data: people have been shown to respond to Web surveys on sex and health more readily and openly than in face-to-face interviews (Burkill et al., 2016). Glaser, Dixit, and Green (2002, pp. 177–193, 189–190) argue the case for better access to 'hard to reach' groups: 'the anonymity of the internet permits research into marginal groups for whom self-disclosure may have costs, and where participants may be suspicious of researchers and outsiders.' And Illingworth (2001) suggests that the Internet affords an efficient way of recruiting specialist participants.

Now we have moved on considerably from the 'simpler' form of the Internet and the World Wide Web. The term 'social media' refers to websites, online platforms, or applications that allow for one-to-one, one-to-many, or many-to-many synchronous or asynchronous interactions/dialogue between users who can create, archive, and retrieve user-generated content. In social media, the user is producer; communication is interactive and networked with fluid roles between those who generate and receive content (see Bechmann & Lomborg, 2013; Salmons, 2014). Online social media cross cultures, communities, populations, and continents. They have the methodological potential of access to large sample sizes and diverse populations for multidisciplinary, multimethod, and multinational purposes. The last decade has seen an explosion in Internet-based social science research and in research which uses social media to attract participants, generate data, disseminate findings, and engage in dialogue with audiences for that research. As indicated above online research has been conducted since the early days of the Internet itself, but the ubiquity of online social platforms in the last decade, such as Twitter or Instagram, has placed the means to deliver social media and internet based research into the hands of all researchers not just those with sophisticated technical skills. It is no longer necessary to be a technical specialist to gather data from online platforms and the computing power required to undertake Internet searches or draw down social media data is now available to the many not the few.

Just as the democratization of the Internet has meant millions of people worldwide now see online interaction as a normal part of their everyday lives, it is increasingly acceptable that social scientists consider the role that Internet data could or should play in their research studies. Of course, to talk of the democratization of the Internet is to underplay the very real power issues that are evident in the use of Internet platforms. Who owns and controls data and who has or does not have access to participate in online discourse and communities is highly contested. As we have seen in Volume 1 in this book series, ethical debates have remained a core element of the social science discourse: what is ethical or 'right' in how we gather and use data from participants remain a continuing thread of lively discussion; the growth in the use of the Internet to recruit participants, gather data, and analyze online experiences, behaviors, and viewpoints is not immune to the same ethical decisions or quandaries. But the most contentious and ongoing debate is about whether 'conventional' research methods and ethical codes/guidelines apply to online research equally well or whether new methods and new codes need to be sought (Eynon, Schroeder, & Fry., 2009). Indeed, some researchers have even suggested online research as a way of evading the bureaucratic 'obstructions' of the formal ethics review process.

CHALLENGES

Most of the ethical issues have considerable overlaps – perhaps even more so than conventional research. It is hard to separate the seeking of informed consent from confidentiality and anonymity, and all have implications for data ownership and the publication of findings. It may be fair to suggest that all of the research ethics issues cohere around the issue of the public and/or private nature of this modern and developing 'research site' and how effective is an 'expectation of privacy' in an essentially public environment?

The concern may be most readily illustrated in research into 'virtual environments' and 'online worlds' that are used for gaming and/or socializing. People experience these spaces as 'other than the ones they are physically in' (Eynon, 2009, p. 189). Within these spaces, researchers can be engaging in experiments in interpersonal behavior, gathering large amounts of data and/ or participant observation. The kinds of ethical issues to be addressed here include how much virtual danger should participants be subjected to? How close to the participants 'real' physical attributes can avatars be permitted to be? Thus, for example, Slater et al. (2006) conducted a *virtual* replication of Stanley Milgram's notorious obedience to authority experiments. Questions arise then about whether it is ethical even to 'abuse' avatars and, though the authors don't mention this, what negative effects such an experiment might still have on the participants – which was the main concern of the after effects of the Milgram studies.

The availability of large amounts of data leads to the temptation to gather them – for social scientific purposes. Such opportunities have been rarely available in the past without a great deal of effort. The question here is 'even if one's behavior is public and can be observed and captured, is it nevertheless always allowable for researchers to use data from these worlds?' (Eynon, 2009, p. 192). Issues involve the possibility of gaining consent, of gathering data without consent/permissions, and the possibilities of linking data to identifiable individuals thereby failing to preserve their anonymity whether they sought it or not. The same position applies to participant observation – just because a researcher engages 'as if' they were a genuine participant, the other interactants may not be aware of that, and may assume the researcher to be a genuine participant unless they are formally informed otherwise. Necessarily, while the latter option is more ethical, the methodological consequence is that participants' behavior might not be quite so authentic.

It might be less challenging simply to avail oneself of the mass of self-evidently publicly available data. But is it ethical to 'harvest' public twitter accounts without users' consent? Looking at the ongoing online debate opinions vary: some say consent is not necessary since the tweets are public, a conscious choice made by the user to allow their activity to be seen by whoever chooses to see it. If you don't restrict access to your account, there cannot be an expectation of privacy. Perhaps one hopes that one's contribution is less public since it might be 'obscured' by the millions of other tweets – 'hidden in plain sight' – but that's an unrealistic, even naive, assumption that, as a consequence, it is *slightly* private! It is public by definition. Some argue that this is not a formal consenting as to how the contributions may be used – collected, stored and analyzed. Obviously, the same could be said of any public text or statement.

The UK research carried out by NatCen (National Centre for Social Research; Beninger, Fry, Jago, Lepps, Nass, & Silvester, 2014) suggests that a first principle of online usage of any kind is that the user must bear the responsibility for choosing where to post and how privately to post. Of course, they can't do that alone since the site owner shares a mutual responsibility – site owners must make clear just how public the data are and who is able to access them. Given all of that then there are still times when informed consent should be sought. There seems to be a great deal of consensus around the moral requirement to seek consent for data access and analysis even if it is not legally required. In such a way, at least some measure of trust is promoted between researchers and online participants.

Such trust is all too easily breached if the implications of a promise of, say, confidentiality are not fully considered – by both researcher and researched. Eynon et al. (2009), for example, advocate an enhanced sensitivity to context on the grounds that the distance between researcher and research is greater than in conventional research and people have a range of different expectations about the nature of online interactions, and one cannot always know directly what those understandings are. Moreover, once you describe a computer-mediated community it is relatively easy to find out which one it is and who is on it. Complete anonymity is impossible since it is almost impossible to remove the trace of computer-transmitted messages. The 'personal' is not necessarily 'private' (Robson & Robson, 1999; Robson & Selwyn, 1998; Zimmer, 2010).

MEETING THE CHALLENGES

During 2017, there was widespread discussion about social media and Internet-mediated research, this was not the case 5 or 10 years ago. These debates have become part of mainstream methodological debate, and researchers are developing new tools and approaches for exploring social media data and understanding the social media dimension of contemporary life. It is hard to find any sector of life where the promise and potential of 'big data' have not been touted as the next 'big thing.' However, this new frontier of social science research has posed an increasingly knotty set of challenges for researchers.

We have faced, and continue to face, methodological challenges around the quality, quantity, and representativeness of social media datasets. Conducting research in this new domain has forced us to consider questions of representation, power, and authenticity in our research. In fact, most social media data is *not quantitative data, rather qualitative data on a quantitative scale* (Francesco D'Orazio on https://www.pulsarplatform.com), and we have yet to fully address the high proportion of social media traffic that consists of pictures, not text. The social science of images and visual data are not well served by current social science approaches and tools that focus on text and numerical data. We continue to have much to learn from colleagues in the digital humanities, computer science, and artificial intelligence (AI) disciplines.

There is also a collaborative challenge. As a new, developing field, it is clear that the most powerful insights from social media and Internet-mediated research will come from transdisciplinary efforts drawing on the varied insights and skills of, for example, statisticians, qualitative researchers, digital curators, information scientists, machine learning experts, and human geographers. We have a window of opportunity to forge a new shape and rhythm for our research methods and epistemologies. We are progressing but not yet fulfilling the potential transformative nature of this moment.

In a world where technology moves fast, we are also faced with a capability challenge. Are we conversant with the social worlds we research, are we sufficiently confident and competent to understand the complex algorithms and processes that increasingly define our interactions? Which brings us to the connective or contextual challenge how can we research what we do not understand or use? Discussions at #NSMNSS network meetings, online discussions, and conferences have revealed that many research methods lecturers, research supervisors, research commissioners, and research ethics review committee members do not feel adequately equipped to make rounded, informed decisions about the quality, ethics or value of social media research projects and proposals.

We also face a synthesis challenge, how if at all can new forms of research and findings map onto, elaborate or further inform conventional social research data?

This volume focuses on perhaps the knottiest of the challenges facing researchers – the ethical dimensions of Internet-mediated and social media research. It largely concentrates on the use of social media data and platforms for social science research although chapters also look more broadly at the ethical challenges of 'big data.'

BACKGROUND TO THIS VOLUME

The origin of this volume was the formation of an online community of practice called 'New social media, New Social Science?' (or #NSMNSS for short) in 2011. #NSMNSS was established with a 12-month grant from the National Centre for Research Methods in the UK (NCRM) to provide a year of facilitated dialogue and knowledge exchange for researchers using social media and Internet forums or platforms in their social science research projects. It aimed to provide a safe, collaborative place to explore the challenges and issues that researchers were facing in trying to explore these new online spaces for research purposes. Membership was not limited to those using certain methods or approaches and we actively sought to encourage participation from all sectors in the research community including those working in the academic sphere, not-for-profit sector, in government and public services, and those working in market research. The only limits placed on membership were that participants needed to be investigating social science questions and making use of the Internet and social media in their work. Throughout the life of the network, the dominant issue has persistently been an uncertainty over the ethical boundaries of Internet mediated research, a sense of a lack of guidance over what is and is not acceptable ethically and a growing sense of the need to debate these issues. At the time the network began, there was limited guidance for researchers in existing ethical codes of practice relating to Internet-mediated research.

We might feel that our social science research is a benign endeavor contrasted to the commercial *harvesting* of customer insight data, but we all face similar ethical and legal challenges, as we always have done: Whose data? Whose consent? Whose ownership? All are complex issues about how researchers collect and use the data of people using social media and other Internet platforms. We have only just begun to scrape the surface of these discussions, and meanwhile, data is being mined, harvested, analyzed, and reported in increasing volume. The critical moments that will shape and define the ethical and legal frameworks for the use of social media data may not come from social science research but from the use of social media data in the commercial world or media realm, these industries practices may shape our future access to research data. Are we engaging enough with these sectors and issues? Have the voices of researchers in the social sciences been loud enough in ongoing legislative debates around the use of personal data?

These challenges are hard things to tackle, but they also give us great opportunities to push the boundaries of our practice as social scientists. Social media research needs social science as much as it does data science, it needs anthropology and ethnography as well as big data analytics, it needs to reflect, explore, and understand the context and communities that anchor and shape social media data.

This volume presents nine chapters each of which addresses the ethical challenges of particular research issues, social media platforms, or approaches. The authors describe the research they have conducted and provide an insight into the ethical state of play for Internet-mediated research.

Many interesting questions are raised including just how different should ethical guidance be for internet-mediated research? Are the issues new or is it merely a matter of change in context – in the research site? Familiar issues are addressed such as informed consent, anonymity, confidentiality, privacy, protection from harm, social benefits; but there are no easy answers. Do we really need a new ethical code of research practice, or do we just need to be agile in applying our existing social science ethics to this new area of operations?

OUTLINING THE VOLUME

Susan Halford's opening chapter addresses the inadequacy of the current ethics review process at meeting many of the challenges referred to above.

Methodological innovation is a necessary feature of responding to the rapid development of digital technology and online communications. The process of research ethics review could obstruct progress in this field since 'it' does not know how to handle the 'disruptions' caused by researchers keen to enter these new and attractive research sites. Halford's account draws on her experiences of teaching doctoral students how to engage in Web science and their collective attempts to seek ethical approval for innovative online research. The five 'disruptive' concerns that Halford addresses are: the data are in essence necessarily secondary – existing already and not 'created' by the research engagement; that means the data are beyond the control of the researcher – already public and so not so easily 'protected' by the researcher; datasets are potentially infinite, not 'bounded' for targeted care and attention, and only limited by the time the researcher has available to collect and study them; the scale of the data alters the nature of relationships between researcher and researched; and, the attractiveness of access to such data blurs boundaries between professional research domains, almost 'requiring' interdisciplinary cooperation in order to more fully understand what their analysis entails. Halford suggests further consideration of the 'situational' ethics approach that has grown in recent years and which is returned to in subsequent chapters in this Volume. Unless both ethics codes and guidelines are updated and ethics review committee topic 'checklists' are amended to take account of such disruptions, valuable innovative research opportunities into rich and meaningful modern data sources will be lost. Worse, unless responsible social science researchers manage the means of online data access and use there are others with different political and commercial aims who could contaminate the field for all future research attempts.

In the second chapter, Matthew Williams and colleagues directly address users' expectations about how their online activities should be exploited for research purposes. Whether realistic or not, there is an expectation of privacy, anonymity, and confidentiality. Such expectations place perhaps an even greater ethical burden on online researchers to respect participants' wishes and a sustained ethical reflexivity as a consequence of the 'blurred' relationship between researcher and researched in online environments. Williams and colleagues rehearse the legal, professional, and moral guidelines that researchers should follow in ensuring research integrity and ethical practice and show the relevance of these principles in a study of their own. Readers will find many useful, practical suggestions for handling online research ethics in the lessons learned from this particular engagement.

Sarah Quinton and Nina Reynolds focus more particularly on the changed relationship between researcher and researched in online environments.

Qualitative researchers have long held concerns for the nature of this relationship – how it is developed and managed. Issues of sensitivity and vulnerability are linked to refining questions of consenting and anonymity, and all are connected to research impact. There has been an assumption that the necessary physical distance between the 'actors' in digital research engagements removes the more delicate aspects of their relationship. This is far from the truth and, if anything, the relationship is more complex and requires more understanding of consequences than has previously been assumed – or, rather, presumed by those not regularly engaged in online research.

Wasim Ahmed and colleagues form a research postgraduate supervisory team and so have a particular interest in assuring their Ph.D. students get the ethics of online research right. Their interest is even further specific in targeting social media use, in this case Twitter, during infectious disease outbreaks. It may be particularly important to understand how people make use of social media during times of crisis and emergency – so in the focused study what they report can help understand how people manage their online social networking during other times of crisis and incident. Any researcher wishing to target Twitter as a research site will do well to start here and learn the legal and ethical issues this team has benefitted from understanding and is able to share in preparation for a research project and ethics review. The case studies drawn upon are especially illustrative of the issues that arise and the care that needs to be taken to both review and conduct studies of this nature.

Janet Salmons is well known for her writing and training for some years in this field so her contribution here will be particularly instructive for newcomers to online social media research. She points to the nuanced understandings necessary for gaining consent in and from online communities in terms of the meaning of being 'fully informed' and having the 'capacity to consent.' The detailed coverage of processes and procedures offered here through cases and exemplars almost amounts to a technical manual for conducting qualitative online social research. Finally, Salmons offers some practical templates that will assist researchers presenting their protocol for ethics approval.

In their chapter, Jenna Condie and colleagues raise another set of issues not fully understood by research ethics committees – location-aware social discovery applications for smartphones. The temptations offered for data mining and data extraction are hard to resist for the curious and diligent researcher. Their 'application of interest' is Tinder, a social relationship-building app that uses geolocation to enable people to make connections wherever they may be – geographically. What is particularly insightful from this study is how researchers-as-users drew on their own personal experiences of using Tinder to reflect upon its implications for social research in the move from a 'social space' to a 'research context.' These insights are enhanced in the ways in which the authors show how conventional formal research ethics approval applications cannot easily make sense of the required transformations of consenting, confidentiality, secondary data access, and so on. Once again, there is much to be done in ensuring the ethics approval process keeps pace with such rapidly developing social media technologies.

Libby Bishop and Daniel Gray address issues that some commentators regard as more related to research integrity than ethics per se – dissemination and data sharing. Clearly, there are overlaps between ethics and integrity. An inevitable consequence of the seeking of open access publishing is a push toward open data access – the opportunity to share data in order to conduct further analyses. Data archiving has long addressed such concerns for secondary access to data and has mainly relied on gaining permissions for durable use. Once again, online social networking research raises additional difficulties connected with how the data were originally derived and the public/private domain debate. While the sharing of data is often seen as 'good in itself' and related to principles of public benefit, transparency, and equitable access to knowledge, there remain concerns with online data that, due to the sophistication of digital technologies, it may be much harder to prevent the revelation of personal data and its associated sensitivities via shared data. With case studies of Twitter and Facebook, Bishop and Gray illustrate directly how these issues play out in specific contexts. They show how the conventional ethical principles can be more severely challenged by the extended linkages made possible with digital technologies. Importantly, they argue that the responsibility for ethical behavior cannot only reside with the researcher 'on the ground' – or rather, in cyberspace – in addition, the institutional structures that both permit and enhance data sharing opportunities must bear some responsibility for how shared data can be used and abused.

The chapter from Leanne Townsend and Claire Wallace offers a practical ethical framework as guidance for online researchers. The framework was developed in collaboration with key experts who have been working in the online research environment in the UK and was 'tested' in application to fictionalized case studies that represent exactly the kinds of contexts in which such research is likely to be conducted. This chapter serves as practical guidance and the cases studies reflect exactly the kinds of ethical dilemmas researchers will face and which they must make judgments on. Solutions to the dilemmas presented by the case studies are offered by Townsend and Wallace and their collaborators, and these, once again, illustrate the enduring problem of research ethics and integrity – solutions may be refined by other commentators and, even, other solutions might be suggested. What is vital here is how the proposed framework is applied and the research engagement thought through in an ethically robust manner.

The final contributed chapter in this collection is from Steven Ginnis and, as in the previous chapter, draws on collaborative work that seeks to offer practical guidance to best practice in ethical online social media research. In essence, this chapter reports what can best be described as a 'standard-setting' project – ensuring that those who are conducting online social media research have the technical skills and ethical awareness to do it well. When new research opportunities arise, keen researchers are eager to innovate, access the new data, and make contributions while the field is still fresh and fertile. The problem is that such eagerness may not be equally matched by the cautions required to ensure that both data producers and data users are protected from both anticipated and unpredictable consequences. The research drew on a large population sample to assess users' views of the reasons for research on social media, its value, and how it is conducted. A particular valuable insight is taken from including the views of younger social media participants. As a result, the series of recommendations for best practice offered here can be seen as assuredly resting upon public perceptions of and wishes for how research is conducted.

In fact, we are confident that this Volume in the Advances in Research Ethics and Integrity Series will make a much-needed contribution to the quality of online social media research and help ensure the public trust in how researchers are likely to engage them in the future. The contributors are all expert in their field and have conducted research and training with new entrants to online research. Most importantly, in addition to covering the range of ethical issues that need to be borne in mind, they have offered practical suggestions about how to address them. These can only count as recommendations since it is certain that this fertile field is likely to continue to change just as rapidly in the future as it has up to now. And just as the technology evolves, so too will users' use of it – and researchers' eagerness to understand them.

REFERENCES

Bechmann, A., & Lomborg, S. (2013). Mapping actor roles in social media: Different perspectives on value creation in theories of user participation. *New Media & Society*, *15*(5), 765–781. doi:10.1177/1461444812462853

Beninger, K., Fry, A., Jago, N., Lepps, H., Nass, L., & Silvester, H. (2014). *Research using social media: Users' views*. London: National Centre for Social Research.

Burkill, S., Copas, A., Couper, M. P., Clifton, S., Prah, P., Datta, J., ..., Erens, B. (2016). Using the web to collect data on sensitive behaviours: A study looking at mode effects on the British National Survey of Sexual Attitudes and Lifestyles. *PLoS ONE, 11*(2), e0147983. doi:10.1371/journal.pone.0147983

Eynon, R., Schroeder, R., & Fry, J. (2009). New techniques in online research: Challenges for research ethics *Twenty-First Century Society: Journal of the Academy of Social Sciences, 4*(2), 187–199. Methodological innovation and developing understandings of 21st century society. Published online: 15 Jun 2009.

Fontes, T. O., & O'Mahony, M. (2008). In-depth interviewing by instant messaging. *Social Research Update*, Volume 53. Guildford, UK: University of Surrey.

Glaser, J., Dixit, J., & Green, D.P. (2002). Studying hate crime with the internet: What makes racists advocate racial violence? *Journal of Social Issues, 58*, 1.

Grinyer, A. (2007). The ethics of Internet usage in health and personal narratives research. *Social Research Update*, Volume 49. Guildford, UK: University of Surrey.

Illingworth, N. (2001). The internet matters: Exploring the use of the internet as a research tool *Sociological Research Online, 6*(2). Retrieved from http://www.socresonline.org.uk/6/2/illingworth.html

Peters, S. (1998). Finding information on the World Wide Web. *Social Research Update*, Volume 20. Guildford, UK: University of Surrey.

Robson, K., & Robson, M. (1999). Your place or mine? Ethics, the researcher and the internet. In T. Welland & L. Pugsley (Eds.), *Ethical dilemmas in qualitative research* (pp. 94–107). Aldershot: Ashgate.

Robson, K., & Selwyn, N. (1998). Using e-mail as a research tool. *Social Research Update*, Volume 21. Guildford, UK: University of Surrey.

Salmons, J. (2014). *New social media, new social science … and new ethical issues!* Retrieved from https://drive.google.com/file/d/0B1-gmLw9jo6fLTQ5X0oyeE1aRjQ/edit

Slater, M., Antley, A., Davison, A., Swapp, D., Guger, C., Barker, C., Pistrang, N., and Sanchez-Vives, M.V. (2006). A virtual reprise of the Stanley Milgram obedience experiments. *PLoS ONE, 1*(1): e39. Retrieved from https://doi.org/10.1371/journal.pone.0000039

Zimmer, M. (2010). 'But the data is already public': On the ethics of research in Facebook. *Ethics and Information Technology, 12*(4), 313–325.

CHAPTER 1

THE ETHICAL DISRUPTIONS OF SOCIAL MEDIA DATA: TALES FROM THE FIELD

Susan Halford

ABSTRACT

This chapter explores the perfect storm brewing at the interface of an increasingly organized ethics review process, grounded in principles of anonymity and informed consent, and the formation of a new digital data landscape in which vast quantities of unregulated and often personal infor-mation are readily available as research data. This new form of data not only offers huge potential for insight into everyday activities, values, and networks but it also poses some profound challenges, not least as it disrupts the established principles and structures of the ethics review process. The chapter outlines four key disruptions posed by social media data and con-siders the value of situational ethics as a response. Drawing on the experi-ences and contributions of Ph.D. students in interdisciplinary Web Science, the chapter concludes that there is a need for more sharing of the ethical challenges faced in the field by those at the 'cutting edge' of social media research and the development of shared resources. This might inform and speed-up the adaptation of ethics review processes to the challenges posed by new forms of digital data, to ensure that academic research with these

The Ethics of Online Research
Advances in Research Ethics and Integrity, Volume 2, 13–25
ISSN: 2398-6018/doi:10.1108/S2398-601820180000002001

data can keep pace with the methods and analyses being developed else-where, especially in commercial and journalistic contexts.

Keywords: Social media data; ethical disruptions; data ownership; social life of data; scale and granularity; interdisciplinarity; web science

INTRODUCTION

Over the past 30 years, the ethics landscape for social research has undergone some fundamental changes. Even as recently as the late 1980s – when I started my Ph.D. – there were no formal ethics procedures for social scientists, at least where I was working. This is certainly not to say that, as researchers, we did not consider the ethics of our research but rather that we relied on our own judgment and on the norms of practice in our field, among our peers and on the advice of our supervisors to guide our practice. Mostly very sensible decisions were made but so too some extraordinary things were done, and some ill-considered risks were taken, at least by today's standards. Overall, in my experience, research practice appeared to be broadly ethical – but by individual disposition, cultural environment and (sometimes) by luck, rather than by design.

Over the intervening years, there has been a progressive organization and bureaucratization of the UK university research ethics: the establishment of standardized rules and procedures, using specified forms and checklists, within institutionalized workflows and hierarchies of decision-making. The roots for this lie at least as far back as the 1960s, with calls for the introduction of an ethics review process in biomedical research (Kerrison & Pollock, 2005) and with attention to the issue filtering slowly into individual universities, including into the social sciences (Tinker & Coomber, 2005). By 2003, the Economic and Social Research Council began the process of establishing a Research Ethics Framework,[1] which was introduced in 2006 and rapidly became established as the benchmark across social science research and – in particular – prescribed a governance framework for institutions wishing to receive ESRC funding (strengthened by updates in 2010). Alongside this, the UK Universities Research Ethics Forum was established in 2005 as a sectorwide group for sharing experience and practice and the UK Research Integrity Office was launched in 2006. The UK ethics governance structure continues to develop, with the publication in 2012 of the Concordat to Share

Research Integrity by a consortium of University and Government research agencies, followed by the Economic and Social Research Council's own more specific and updated Framework for Research Ethics in 2015.

Within this infrastructure, appropriate standards of practice are defined, within a professional framework that provides layers of protection for the researchers and institutions involved. In the interests of our participants, contemporary ethic processes seek to ensure rights, protection from harm, and an active voice in the research process. These processes also protect the researcher from potentially risky situations, and the harms that might result, and from legal liability so long as research is conducted as proposed. In turn, this protects the status, corporate reputation, and financial interests of the universities and research institutions. In Weberian terms these standardized rules offer a progressive means toward efficiency and fairness (Weber, 1964; Clegg, 1990). In more Foucauldian terms, we might also see these changes as part of a shift in the wider organizational discourse, as a new assemblage of values and practices are institutionalized as the 'right and proper' values, standards, and practices, where the possible ways of ethical social science research have been narrowed to the 'best' way of ensuring ethical research and, it can seem, presented as the 'only' way of achieving this. We might think here of informed consent, anonymization and individual protection from harm – the gold standards of the social science ethics regime, echoing the original concerns from biomedicine (Neuhaus & Webmoor, 2012; Kernagham, 2014; Zwitter, 2014).

Meanwhile, as these processes were underway, so too was a remarkable set of changes in the nature of the data that social researchers have available to them. As public applications for the Internet began to take-off in the 1980s, e-mails, bulletin boards, and UseNet groups became a rich new source of 'found' data for researchers (Dery, 1994; Rafaeli & Rose, 1993; Rheingold, 1993; Sproull & Kiesler, 1986). But this was nothing compared to what came next. In 1989, Tim Berners-Lee wrote a memorandum proposing a new global information-sharing system that would come to be known as the World Wide Web. Berners-Lee's original motivation was to find a means through which researchers working in remote teams could share data more easily, using standardized protocols on top of the Internet (Berners-Lee, 2000). This was a rather successful idea, of course, with the number of web pages rising from 0 in 1990 to almost a billion today.[2] A significant source of information for researchers across the academy, as well as for governmental and independent research institutes. However, by the mid-2000s, it became clear that this too was just the beginning. What had started as a means of *sharing* data was becoming a means of *generating* data – 'big data' – of a variety, scale, and velocity unimaginable in 1989. We might think, for example, of the all the browser searches and link-clicks that can be captured as the digital traces of our preoccupations and preferences as we surf the Web and which are fuelling a new data economy (Mayer-Schönberger & Cukier, 2013). Unfortunately, few of these data are accessible to researchers (outside of the corporate giants that own them). However, the evolution of the Web from 'read only' to a 'read-write' Web that was both driven by and fuelled the take-off of social media has generated another remarkable new source of data for social research, some of which is readily available to researchers, online, and at no cost (e.g., from Twitter, Instagram, and You Tube). These data provide digital traces of the everyday, at an individual and often a remarkably inti-mate level of detail. As Latour (2007, p. 2) has remarked '[…] it is as if the inner workings of private worlds have been pried open.'

So we have a perfect storm. On the one side, we have the cumulative bureaucratization of research ethics review processes, shaped by a particu-lar set of discourses that define appropriate research practice. On the other a radical transformation in our data landscape through processes that fall outside of the remit of our formalized ethics processes and which disrupt the bureaucracy of ethical practice in its current form and the discursive for-mation that supports this. These are disruptions have become increasingly apparent for those of us working with social media data across the academic field and – more locally – for us in the Web Science Institute, at the University of Southampton, UK, where we undertake a wide range of research with social media across the disciplines, in particular thorough the Centre for Doctoral Training in Web Science. The following discussion is grounded in this practical experience, organized into three sections. Section 1 outlines in principle five of the key ethical disruptions posed by the use of social media data in social research. Section 2 considers some of the consequences of these as they appear in the practice of research, including the turn to situational ethics. Building on this, Section 3 suggests how the practice of situational eth-ics might be supported. These observations draw on my own experience, on discussion with colleagues over the years, and, in particular, on the contribu-tions of Ph.D. researchers working at the cutting edge of research with social media data under the interdisciplinary umbrella of Web Science.

DISRUPTIONS

In what follows, I outline five ethical disruptions that have arisen in the con-text described above. These are grounded in our experience. It is, no doubt, an idiosyncratic list and is intended as a starting point, rather than a finished description. In order to develop our understanding of the ethical issues involved in using social media data, researchers will need to share experiences and explore the points of overlap and difference. Important points of difference to consider will include sensitivity to both the different types of data that we use, and the questions that we ask of these data.

These Data are Already Created

Our current ethics regime, and its associated bureaucracy, assumes (very largely) that we are seeking approval to generate *new* data. The existing assumption is that we design the methodology, we negotiate the terms of access, and we deploy the methods that turn our research into 'generated' data. We control the means of production, so we can ensure that this is ethically done. We know who the participants will be, will avoid unnecessary exclusions/appropriate inclusions or protect vulnerable groups, won't ask about certain things, will seek informed consent, ensuring that our participants understand their right to withdraw, and we won't conduct covert research (or almost never unless safe, secure, and absolutely necessary). In contrast, social media data are already produced and can be deeply personal. We don't always know for sure who has produced them or their age or status in terms of the categories of vulnerability we are used to (under 18, unable to give consent, and so on) or, from a more formal, legal perspective, the jurisdictions in which they are produced. And whatever the data were produced for, however much the intention may have been to make a public expression of creativity or to 'be seen' (at least at the time) users' knowledge and understanding of whether their social media posts are 'data' are uneven and their views on the re-use of this material are complex (Beninger et al., 2014; Evans, Ginnis, & Bartlett, 2015).

These Data are Beyond Our Control

In completing research ethics review applications, we promise to care for our data, keeping them in a locked filing cabinet and on servers behind a university firewall and password-protected computers. This is underpinned by the assumption that what happens to the data is in our power and that we can use that power to behave ethically. So, we are assumed to be able to guarantee confidentiality and anonymity to our participants, ensuring that no personal details are made public, because no one else has access to the data to interrogate it. An exception to this is the (increasing) expectation or even requirement from funders that data be made available through archives for secondary analysis but even then, it is possible to make the argument that the sensitive nature of particular data sets makes them unsuitable for deposit. If we do deposit our data, we can redact sections to exercise control over anonymization, and the full individual level data sets – qualitative data sets especially – are rarely (as yet) published in their entirety online. In short, the current ethics regime assumes that we can and should make effective assurances to participants about what happens to their data. In contrast, social media data are already published, available to anyone, and computational methods can compare incomplete data to similar data sets published elsewhere, and/or cross reference with other related data sets, at scale and speed, making irreversible anonymization nigh on impossible, especially if we consider the possibilities of as yet uninvented methods for reverse engineering.

These Data are Not Finite

The current ethical regime presumes a bounded data set, with rules that apply internally to that data set and what we do with it. But the digital nature of these data and distributed access to them changes what can be done with them and by whom. Social media data have a social life of their own, beyond their repurposing as research data, circulating in timelines, retweets, and online conversation, for example, and may change status over time, for example, as a user deletes content, radically extending the principle of the 'right to withdraw' from research beyond the lifetime of a project to potentially in perpetuity. This raises new ethical questions and challenges in terms of implementing ethical commitments, not least as the provenance of data – past and present – may be difficult to track, or even to discover. There is also the linked issue of the potential for linkage of digital data. The capacity to combine large data sets can reveal intimate details of individuals' lives – things they may not even have told their friends of families – and can be used to generate new social categories that may contain biases or, at least, have consequences for individuals' life chances (Jernigan & Mistree, 2009; Pasquale, 2015). This raises questions not only about the ethical boundaries of our own actions, as researchers, but also the opportunities for others to combine our data with other sources, potentially with the intent to de-anonymize (as above) or (perhaps more likely) with the intent to pursue new research questions that might inadvertently de-anonymize (Crawford & Schultz, 2013).

There are Some Implicit Assumptions about Scale and Granularity

There are some implicit assumptions about scale and granularity that shape how the ethical relationships with research participants is conceptualized within the existing ethics review regime. We are used to relatively small sample sizes – maybe in the tens for qualitative research, the hundreds or low thousands for quantitative research. This means that we can have (close) relationship with our research participants: they know who we are and we know who they are. Often we can speak to our participants, discuss the research with them, and offer feedback on our findings. For larger-scale research, we are still able to inform, offer information on our lines of accountability, and offer feedback. The scale of social media data reduces the possibility of a direct relationship between researchers and these 'participants' (even the term seems inappropriate – are they 'authors,' 'text creators' or 'data subjects'?). At least, we do not currently have established methods to support this. Furthermore, in the existing ethics regime, the level of granularity is protection of the individual (see Zwitter, 2014 for a good discussion of this). Yet the social nature of social media data means that one of its most attractive elements is the trace of social interaction that these data provide and, of course, their digital nature makes it possible to trace this at scale in ways that have never been possible before. Similarly, the digital nature of these data also makes it possible to interrogate and combine in order to explore and delineate social groups. This is well established in the field of marketing (Webber et al., 2015), also in surveillance (Lyon, 2014) and raises questions about the ethical boundaries for social researchers.

These Data are Attracting Interest in Social Research from across the Entire Research Field

These data are attracting interest in social research from across the entire research field where once social research required the specialist expertise of social scientists, who honed particular techniques to collect data (Savage, 2010), the emergence of these new forms of data require expertise more commonly found in the mathematical and computational sciences who can engage with these data in ways that most social scientists cannot (Savage, 2010; Tinati, Halford, Carr, & Pope, 2014). This disciplinary disruption means that social research is moving into new disciplinary jurisdictions and meeting new ethical regimes that look different to those we are familiar with. Here we see profound differences between how the computational sciences regard social media data – as published, in the public realm and therefore not in need of ethical regulation – and how we as social scientists see this, coming as we do from principles of informed consent, anonymization, and individual protection from harm.

CONSEQUENCES

So here the problem is that our established ethics regime reveals itself to be constructed on the basis of particular types of data, and disciplinary settlements, but we are faced with new forms of data that do not fit neatly into established practice, and an associated unsettling of the disciplinary boundaries. This has some profound practical consequences for researchers using social media data. Indeed, consultation with our Ph.D. researchers identified the single biggest challenge of working with social media data as *the ethics process itself*, which demands advance precision on the ethical contours of research, where these may be hard to determine:

> With social media research, one of the things I have observed is that institutional processes for establishing formal ethics for research projects tend to focus on static statements which do not allow for the incorporation of flexibility that is necessary when studying group activities online. (Nicole Beale)[3]

There was concern that, on occasion, the process itself may become a tokenistic hurdle, rather than a constructive way of supporting research in the field:

> There is procedural over-emphasis on trying to cover all corners which tends to encourage (well-meant) guess-work just to get a green light; worse it can encourage non-disclosure to avoid edge cases. Less well imbued in the current process is the importance of considering what you do when encountering the unforeseen. A paternalistic 'no colouring outside the lines' approach lets the legal department sleep at night but may not aid research. (Mark Anderson)

And, worse, that the current process did not fully understand the technical issues

> Researching forums on Tor focusing on the sale of illicit goods has been my biggest ethical challenge [...] In my opinion the lack of understanding of underground forums/marketplaces of the ethics committee slowed my research down a bit. (Geert Jan van Hardeveld)

Or the changing nature of the data landscape:

> I think for me the biggest ethical challenge is [...] the gulf between the practice of ethics as exemplified by the [formal] process and the reality. In completing [the ethics process]

I promise to do things I know I am technically unable to do – I cannot truly delete all the personal data held at the end of the project [...] it would not take much effort to re-identify anonymised data [...] the process [of ethics review] is possibly the most ethically compromising part of my research. That's not right. (Jo Walker)

These experiences are echoed in a recent survey of researchers using social media data commissioned by the ESRC in 2015, which found that fewer than 10% of respondents felt that the current ethics guidelines were adequate for their research.[4]

It is in this context, that a turn to *situational ethics*[5] has emerged. With roots in virtue ethics and a feminist ethics of care, situational ethics emphasizes the dialogical and relational process of ethical responsibility (Cupurro & Pingel, 2002) and the emergent nature of both ethical challenges and ethical responses in social research. In contrast to the deontological and consequentialist emphasis that underpins current research ethics approval regimes, situational ethics recognizes the importance of moral deliberation throughout the ethics process (Edwards & Mauthner, 2012, p. 20). This approach is gaining attention, most recently in the UK in the *Concordat to Support Research Integrity* (2012), and may be of particular use to social media researchers. This potential has been most beautifully articulated in the Association of Internet Researchers' revised guidelines (2012) which offer a worked through set of principles – human dignity, autonomy, protection, maximization of benefit, and minimization of harm, respect, and justice – in place of bureaucratic prescriptions for ethical research practice.

Exactly how situational ethics are implemented in practice is an open question. An ESRC survey in 2015 found that 90% of researchers using social media data assembled their own combination of discipline specific guidelines with institutional requirements, peer support, and personal ethics. To some extent, of course, this has continued to be the case for many researchers – and especially those doing qualitative research. Even where sophisticated ethics review processes are in operation, I suggest that the advent of new forms of digital data and the disruptions that these pose to established processes make this situation more common and extensive for researchers using these sources. However, we must not take this to mean that we can, or should, return to the practices of the 1980s and leave the question of ethical practice solely to the individual. While the concept of situational ethics provides us with a sound philosophical base on which to build, the ESRC survey also showed that researchers want to engage in and learn from (more or less formally) organized communities of practice that transcend the serendipities of everyday experience.

The Way Forward?

We urgently need self-reflexive examples of the challenges faced and the practices that are developed to deal with them in order to provide a shared context for the development of situational ethics when working with social media data. Anecdotal evidence suggests that as researchers we are wary of openly discussing our practices in a field where the norms of situational ethics are emergent. Furthermore, even among social media researchers, it is clear that the norms are dynamic. We are all learning as we go and decisions made in good faith five years ago might seem less appropriate in the light of ongoing debate and emergent awareness of the consequences of particular decisions. We must also take into account the way that the field is shaped by external actors, outside the usual research field. For example, the social media companies that own these data impose terms and conditions on use, such that what may seem ethical (e.g., anonymization of data) may be trumped by what is legal (where, for instance, the terms and conditions of data use state that changing content in the data harvested is not permitted). Similarly, when working with data sets that cross national boundaries and/or in collaboration with multiple stakeholders – different owners and users of data – complex questions arise about the boundaries of ethics processes and the potential for conflict, or at least contradictions, between different practices. For example, where data are shared by stakeholders from different sectors – across commerce and academia for instance (something that is increasingly common in the collaborative projects favored by many funding councils these days) – there may be very different interpretations of how the data should be treated and used. Similarly, different legal jurisdictions pose challenges for international teams, international data archives, and research ethics governance (Wilson et al., 2016).

Beyond this, it is also clear that we need to promote more interdisciplinary dialogue. Whatever the intention of bureaucratized ethics review processes, there may be a degree of local interpretation:

> Just recently my PhD cohort were discussing ethics issues on Facebook and I asked at what point the observation of publicly available data became an ethics-bounded issue. Suffice it to say there was no clear [...] consensus – between doing nothing without first seeking approval or that it didn't matter at all [...] I suspect the range of opinion divided along disciplinary background. (Mark Anderson)

> Having observed differences between Faculties at Southampton, and conversations with others at different institutions, there is no concurrence on what constitutes ethical online research. I feel this is one of the main factors that could be slowing progress of qualitative online research in particular. (Becki Nash)

Currently there seems to be very little interdisciplinary thinking when it comes to the formal ethical processes. I suspect future challenges and opportunities include developing a greater appreciation of why different disciplines tend to prioritize different ethical issues e.g. personal data, anonymity, safety, and so on. (Ian Brown)

Our Ph.D. researchers' experience suggests that these differences undermine the credibility of research ethics review processes, and the practicality of interdisciplinary research. Assuming that we are going to continue with some kind of systematic ethics reviewing process, it is essential that this is seen to operate with consistency and fairness. This will need to step back from formulaic questions that assume particular norms toward more philosophical questions that recognize the unknown nature of the exercise and require reflection and recognize the contingency of solutions. Without this, we may be encouraging poor practice and risk reducing the quality of research.

Notwithstanding the frustrations described earlier in the chapter, we should look to ethics committees as sources of informed guidance: a much-needed resource in this changing landscape. There is certainly evidence to suggest that there is commitment to this:

To be honest [the experience of applying for ethical approval was] not as bad I had been led to expect. The ethics board have in recent years become more aware and comfortable with online research methods, thanks in large part to the doctoral students and Web Science researchers who have proven the breadth and usefulness of these methods. The board were not only understanding but supportive and enthusiastic in their responses to my proposed methods. (Elzabi Rimmington)

Changing cultural, social, and economic processes are changing the ethics regime and, I am sure, will change the artifacts, workflows, and hierarchies of decision-making in bureaucratized ethics processes. This support will be particularly important as we move from a position where ethical practice is determined in advance where we know what is ethical upfront (or we think we do) to a situation where the ethics are more emergent, and just as importantly where an increasing focus for ethical practice is in data stewardship, that is, how we ensure ethical practice with data that does not have consent and is not anonymized, rather than making these prerequisites for data collection.

Finally, a point about the wider politics of data: looking at our own internal practices as social science researchers is important, but we need to situate this on a wider landscape. For all that we agonize about how we should practice, others beyond the academy – in government, journalism, or commercial organizations, for instance – may be less hesitant about using social media data, not least because they are not subject to the same ethics review processes. It is important that we pay attention to this for at least two reasons. First, it may be these uses of social media that provoke the highest levels of public concern with the potential to start a backlash that will affect all of us who see value in these data. Think, for instance, of the public outcry at the infamous Facebook emotion experiment[6] or the Cupid 'bad' dating experiment.[7] Second, if academic social media research falls (even further) behind its counterparts elsewhere in terms of methodological and analytical expertise in working with social media data, we will be less well placed to interrogate the claims made by others from these data or to counter these with alternatives. This is absolutely not to say that we should join the 'gold rush' without appropriate ethical governance, and I recognize that this takes time, but it is to say that we need to push forward and think creatively beyond the established ethics review bureaucracies and discourses that, after all, were shaped on a different data landscape. Not least, what can be known and by whom will be shaped by data practices and the ethical regimes that shape them. In a climate where public concern about privacy and data ownership is rising, the importance and, indeed, credibility of ethical practice may also be rising and our attention to these details may put academic researchers in a position to make powerful contributions to public policy and debate and that is a responsibility, perhaps an ethical responsibility, that we should take very seriously.

NOTES

1. https://www.york.ac.uk/res/ref/documents.htm. Accessed on 04/04/17.
2. http://www.internetlivestats.com/total-number-of-websites/. Accessed on 17/10/16.
3. With huge thanks to the Ph.D. researchers who shared their experiences so generously and openly. With permission of all the researchers, their names are included here alongside their contributions. For more information on individual projects please see http://dtc.webscience.ecs.soton.ac.uk/people-and-partners/list-of-students/
4. Social Media Data for Social Research (SMD4SR), commissioned as part of ESRC Big Data Research Programme, Phase 3. Unpublished.
5. Sometimes also referred to as 'agile ethics' (Neuhaus & Webmoor, 2011) or 'open source ethics' (Berry, 2004).
6. https://www.theguardian.com/technology/2014/jun/30/facebook-emotion-study-breached-ethical-guidelines-researchers-say. Accessed on 16/12/16.
7. http://www.bbc.co.uk/news/technology-28542642. Accessed on 16/12/16.

REFERENCES

Berners-Lee, T., & Fichetti, M. (2000). *Weaving the Web: The original design and ultimate destiny of the world wide web.* New York, NY: HarperCollins.

Berry, D. M. (2004). Internet research: Privacy, ethics and alienation: An open source approach. *Internet Research, 14*(4), 323–332.

Capurro, R., & Pingel, C. Ethical issues of online communication research. *Ethics and Information Technology, 4,* 189–194.

Clegg, S. (1990). *Modern organizations.* London, Sage.

Dery, M. (Ed.). (1994). *Flame wars: The discourse of cyberculture.* Durham, NC: Duke University Press.

Evans, H., Ginnis, S., & Bartlett, J. (2015). *Social ethics: A guide to embedding ethics in social media research.* London: Ipsos MORI.

Jernigan & Mistree. (2009).[1] http://firstmonday.org/article/view/2611/2302. Accessed 17/10/16

Kernagham, K. (2014). Digital dilemmas: Values, ethics and information technology. *Canadian Public Administration, 57*(2), 295–317.

Kerrison, S., & Pollock, A. (2005). The reform of UK research ethics committees: Throwing the baby out with the bath water?' *Journal of Medical Ethics, 31,* 487–489.

Latour, B. (2007). Beware, your imagination leaves digital traces. *Times Higher Literary Supplement.*

Lyon, D. (2014). Surveillance, snowden, and big data: Capacities, consequences, critique. *Big Data & Society, 1*(2), 1–13.

Mayer-Schönberger, V., & Cukier, K. (2013). *Big data: A revolution that will transform how we live, work and think.* London: John Murray.

Neuhaus, F., & Webmoor, T. (2012). Agile ethics for massified research and visualization. *Information, Communication & Society, 15*(1), 43–65.

Rafaeli, S., & La Rose, R. (1993). Electronic bulletin boards and 'public goods' explanations of collaborative mass media. *Communications Research, 20,* 277–297.

Rheingold, H. (1993). *The virtual community: Homesteading on the electronic frontier reading.* MA: Addison-Wesley.

Savage, M. (2010). *Identities and social change in Britain since 1940: The politics of method.* Oxford: Oxford University Press.

Sproull, L., & Kiesler, S. (1986). Reducing social context cues: Electronic mail in organizational communication. *Journal of Management Science, 32*(11), 1492–1512.

Tinati, R., Halford, S., Carr, L., & Pope, C. (2014). Big Data: Methodological challenges and approaches for sociological analysis. *Sociology, 48*(4), pp. 663–681.

Tinker, A. & Coomber, V. (2005). *University Research Ethics Committees: Their role, remit and conduct.* London: Nuffield Foundation.

Universities UK. (2012). *Concordat to support research integrity.* London: Universities UK.

Weber, M. (1964). *Theory of social and economic organization.* New York, NY: Free Press.

Zwitter, A. (2014). Big data ethics. *Big Data and Society, 1*(2), 1–6.

CHAPTER 2

USERS' VIEWS OF ETHICS IN SOCIAL MEDIA RESEARCH: INFORMED CONSENT, ANONYMITY, AND HARM

Matthew L. Williams, Pete Burnap, Luke Sloan, Curtis Jessop and Hayley Lepps

ABSTRACT

Some researchers consider most social media communications as public, and posts from networks such as Twitter are routinely harvested and published without anonymization and without direct consent from users. In this chapter, we argue that researchers must move beyond the permissions granted by 'legal' accounts of the use of these new forms of data (e.g., Terms and Conditions) to a more nuanced and reflexive ethical approach that puts user expectations, safety, and privacy rights center stage. Through two projects, we present qualitative and quantitative data that illustrate social media users' views on the use of their data by researchers. Over four in five report expecting to be asked for their consent and nine in ten expect anonymity ahead of publication of their Twitter posts. Given the unique nature of this online public environment and what we know about users'

The Ethics of Online Research
Advances in Research Ethics and Integrity, Volume 2, 27–52
Copyright © 2018 by Emerald Publishing Limited
All rights of reproduction in any form reserved
ISSN: 2398-6018/doi:10.1108/S2398-601820180000002002

views pertaining to informed consent, anonymity, and harm, we conclude researchers seeking to embark on social media research should conduct a risk assessment to determine likely privacy infringement and potential user harm from publishing user content.

Keywords: social media; digital data; Twitter; safety; privacy law; privacy rights; privacy infringement

INTRODUCTION

Social media platforms offer social scientists previously unrealized access to real-time naturally occurring[1] data, and researchers are using sites such as Twitter, Flickr, Tumblr, and Facebook to collect open source online communications and publish content without anonymization or informed consent. In this chapter, we argue research conducted using social media platforms must be subject to the same ethical scrutiny as offline research, and in some cases, an additional level of scrutiny may be needed. Indeed, 'online research presents new ethical problems and recasts old ones in new guises' (Jones, 2011). Researchers have struggled to adapt existing frameworks to a mode of inquiry that takes place in a rapidly changing medium that is characterized by a blurring of the public and private, where data are created at scale outside of a 'for research' context. This blurring has resulted in a schism in the perceptions held by researchers and the users of social media with respect to what is reasonable use of these open data for social science research. This chapter provides qualitative and quantitative insights into these user views and argues for a reflexive ethical approach to using social media data in social research.

Context to the Research

The New Social Media, New Social Science (NSMNSS) network[2] was set up in 2012 as a community of practice to help foster links between social media research practitioners and across disciplines; to catalyze discussions, address challenges, and to share best-practice, approaches, tools, and experiences. The Economic and Social Research Council (ESRC) funded Social Data Science Lab[3] was established in 2015 and continues the successful Cardiff Online Social Media Observatory (COSMOS) program of research that ran between 2011 and 2015. The Lab brings together social and computer scientists to study the methodological, theoretical, empirical, and technical dimensions of 'New and Emerging Forms of Data' in social and policy contexts. This empirical social data science program is complemented by a focus on ethics and the development of new methodological tools and technical/data solutions for the UK academic and public sectors. One of the key issues that came out of NSMNSS network discussions and Lab research was the ethics of social media research, and what was felt to be a lack of guidance in this area. A literature review from Salmons (2014) identified some initial ethics sources, and as social media research has developed as a field within the social science community, ethical guidelines too have been developed (e.g., British Psychological Society, British Educational Research Association, and British Sociological Association guidelines).

However, often what are missing from the conversation are the views of users. How do they curate their digital lives? What do they understand about how their information is used and shared on the Internet? What do users think about their information being used by researchers in online and social media research? Further, one of the particular characteristics of social media that presents challenges to social researchers is how the various platforms mediate and alter the relationship between the researcher and research participant. Within this context, in 2013, the National Centre for Social Research (NatCen) and, in 2015, the Social Data Science Lab conducted exploratory qualitative and quantitative research with social media users into how they feel about their online posts being used in research and their understanding of this type of research. The goal of these research projects was to reveal insights that researchers and practitioners could apply in their research design, recruitment, collecting or generating of data, and reporting of results.

EXISTING LITERATURE ON ETHICS IN SOCIAL MEDIA RESEARCH

Legislation on Data Collection and Use in the UK

Data extracted from Social Media Application Programming Interfaces[4] (APIs) contain personal data[5] meaning they are subject to the UK Data Protection Act (DPA), and as such it must be processed fairly and lawfully. In cases where informed consent cannot be sought from users (likely to be the majority of cases if thousands of posts are being subject to analysis), a social researcher should establish the fair and lawful basis for collecting personal information. A researcher can accept that social media network terms of service provide adequate provision to cover this aspect of the DPA. However, if the data have been collected using a service that provides additional derived data on users, such as sensitive personal characteristics (e.g., ethnicity and sexual orientation) based on algorithms that make estimations, the legal issue of privacy may be compounded as it is not information that the user has chosen to make 'public.' Under the DPA, sensitive personal information can only be collected if the user has a legitimate need for processing. Deriving sensitive information and making conclusions about a person or persons' views or philosophy and publicly releasing this information without anonymization could lead to stigmatization or actual bodily harm (in this case of extremist views for example), should the location of the social media persona be established. Furthermore, it is possible that legal proceedings could follow. The DPA allows cases to be brought on a personal basis, so it is possible that the researcher and not the institution could be liable. Within the EU, the General Data Protection Regulation will replace the DPA in 2018. It includes provisions for the erasure of personal data and restrictions on data dissemination to third parties. However, it also imposes limitations on the right to be forgotten, including cases in which data are processed for historical, statistical, and scientific purposes. To what extent these proposals will impact upon social media research is unclear.

Learned Society Guidelines on Social Media and Internet-Based Research

Several learned societies have recognized the need for and introduced ethical principles for research in digital settings, including the British Psychological Society (BPS), the British Society of Criminology (BSC), the British Educational Research Association (BERA), the European Society for Opinion and Market Research (ESOMAR), and the Association and the Association of Internet Researchers (AoIR). Broadly, most guidelines adopt the 'situational ethics' principle: that each research situation is unique and it is not possible simply to apply a standard template in order to guarantee ethical practice. Maybe the most thorough set of guidelines are those developed by AoIR. AoIR was one of the first learned societies to introduce a set of guidelines, which are now in their second iteration. These guidelines highlight three key areas of tension: the question of human subjects online; data/text and personhood; and the public/private divide (AoIR, 2012).

The guidelines advance the idea that the notion of the 'human subject' is complicated when applied to research within online environments. For example, can we say 'avatars' are human subjects? Does digital representation and automation of some online 'behaviors' call into question the definition of human subjects in Internet-based research? If so, then it may be more appropriate and relevant to talk of harms, vulnerabilities, personal identifiable information, and so on. In addition, the Internet complicates the conventional construction of 'personhood' and the 'self,' questioning the presence of the human subject in online interactions. Again, can we say an avatar is a person with a self? Is digital information an extension of a person? In some cases, this may be clear-cut: emails, instant message chat, newsgroup posts are easily attributable to the persons that produced them. However, when dealing with aggregate information in social media repositories, such as collective sentiment scores for subgroups of Twitter users, the connection between the object of research and the person who produced it is more indistinct. Attribute data on very large groups of anonymized Twitter users could be said to constitute non-personalized information, more removed from the human subjects that produced the interactions as compared to, say, an online interview. In these cases, the AoIR (2012, p. 7) guidelines state 'it is possible to forget that there was ever a person somewhere in the process that could be directly or indirectly impacted by the research.'

In relation to informed consent, BERA specifically state that social networking and other on-line activities present challenges and the participants must be clearly informed that their participation, and their interactions are being monitored and analyzed for research. On anonymity the guidelines state one way to protect participants is through narrative and creative means, which might require the fictionalizing of aspects of the research or the creation of composite accounts, such as in vignettes, providing generalized features based on a number of specific accounts. In relation to consent, ESOMAR states that if it has not been obtained researchers must ensure that they report only depersonalized data from social media sources. If researchers are using automated data collection services, they are recommended to use filters and controls to remove personal identifiers such as user names, photos and links to the user's profile. In relation to anonymity the guidelines state where consent is not possible their analysis must only be conducted upon depersonalized data, and if researchers wish to quote publicly made comments, they must first check if the user's identity can be easily discoverable using online search services. If it can, they must make reasonable efforts to either seek permission from the user to quote them or mask the comment.

Academic Literature

There is some consensus about what ethical research involves, at least at the level of abstract principles (Webster, Lewis, & Brown, 2013), concerning obtaining informed consent, maintaining confidentiality and anonymity, and minimizing risk of harm to participants and researchers. Yet we do acknowledge some of the robust opposition to 'principlism' in social science research ethics, a perspective 'imported' from biomedical ethics models.

Informed Consent

Gaining informed consent is a vital part of the early stages of research and must be negotiated and secured as early as is practically possible in the process. Ethical guidelines state that participants should understand the purpose of the research, what taking part will involve and how the data will be used. Participants require this information to make an informed decision about participation (ESRC, 2015; GSR, 2006; MRS, 2012). Questions have been raised about the process of consenting and how it needs to be done differently for different forms of research (Iphofen, 2011), or whether consent is required for all types of online research, or whether there are exceptions.

There are two schools of thought on informed consent. One position is that data posted in open spaces without password or membership restrictions would usually be considered to be in the public domain. This means they can be used for research purposes without the need for informed consent from individuals (see e.g., ESOMAR, 2009; Thelwall, 2010). The need to gain informed consent becomes relevant when data are obtained from closed websites requiring login details. This is challenged by the Market Research Society (MRS) discussion paper on online data collection and privacy (2012). Researchers should take into account the unique nature of online public environments. Internet interactions are shaped by ephemerality, anonymity, and a reduction in social cues, leading individuals to reveal more about themselves within online environments than would be done in offline settings, blurring the public and the private (Joinson, 1998; Lash, 2001; Williams, 2006). Research has highlighted the disinhibiting effect of computer-mediated communication, meaning Internet users, while acknowledging the environment as a (semi-) public space, often use it to engage in what would be considered private talk (Williams, 2006). Online information is often intended only for a specific networked public made up of peers, a support network, or specific community, not necessarily the Internet public at large, and certainly not for publics beyond the Internet (boyd, 2014). When it is viewed by unintended audiences, it has the potential to cause harm, as the information is flowing out of the context it was intended for (Barocas & Nissenbaum, 2014; Nissenbaum, 2008). Accepting this view, the AoIR (2012, p. 7) guidelines state that social, academic, and regulatory delineations of the public–private divide may not hold in online contexts and as such 'privacy is a concept that must include a consideration of expectations and consensus' within context. In the final analysis, the subject of informed consent for social media research remains contentious among social scientists and views change depending on the topic, website, and sample population being worked with.

Regardless of the stance an individual takes on informed consent, obtaining it from individuals can in practice be very difficult. Social media research does not typically offer the opportunity to verbally reiterate what participants are consenting to; researchers can be less confident that the key pieces of information have been relayed and understood. Further, researchers cannot verify a participant's identity to assess their capacity to consent. Where researchers cannot be certain the participant is of age, for example (Bull et al., 2011), it may be necessary to contact the guardians of children if possible (British Psychological Society, 2013).

Confidentiality and Anonymity
Conducting online and social media research presents three key challenges related to confidentiality and anonymity: safe data collection and storage may depend on platform security; that participants may want to be credited for their information and therefore not want to remain anonymous; and the possibility of breaking confidentiality when reporting findings.

Existing ethical guidelines state that researchers should ensure no one knows who has said what in a report (i.e., anonymity) and that participant information should be securely stored and shared (i.e., confidentiality; ESRC, 2015; GSR, 2006; MRS, 2012). However, in research using social media data, the risks of not upholding confidentially are greater as a researcher has less control over data protection than in offline research (British Psychological Society, 2013). There is a permanent record of any information that is posted (Roberts, 2012), and direct quotations from participants can be traced back to the original source (BPS, 2007) through search engines like Google. In this case, anonymity cannot be protected. Anonymity is also related to the issue of copyright. For example, in the attempt of anonymizing participant data researchers may exclude the participant's name; however, some users may feel that they should be given credit for their information being used (Barrett & Lenton, 2010; Lui, 2010; Roberts, 2012).

In cases where consent is not provided to directly quote without anonymization, Markham (2012) suggests some innovative methods for protecting privacy in qualitative social media research. Acknowledging that traditional methods for protecting privacy by hiding or anonymizing data no longer suffice in digital settings that are archived and searchable, Markham advocates bricolage-style reconfiguration of original data that represents the intended meaning of interactions. However, given Twitter rules on not changing the content of tweets in publication or broadcast, researchers are required to generate synthetic data that retains the meaning and sentiment of the original post. While this may be suitable for general thematic analysis, it may not satisfy the needs of more fine-grained approaches, such as conversation and discourse analysis.

Harm and Risk to Participants and Researchers
Researchers have an obligation to avoid causing physical, emotional, or psychological harm to participants. Research should also be conducted in a way to minimize undue harm to the research team. Appropriate support for participants needs to be in place following a research interaction, just as it would in face-to-face settings. Discussions of sensitive or emotional topics (e.g., posts about criminal activity, financial problems, mental health issues and feelings of suicide, extramarital sexual activity, controversial political opinions, and activism) have the potential to put participants at risk of emotional or psychological harm (Townsend & Wallace, 2016). Furthermore, the use of algorithms in social media research can expose users to harm. Taking the example of cyberhate on social media, Williams and Burnap (2016) employed machine-learning algorithms to classify hateful content and users (see also Burnap & Williams, 2015). They report that automated text classification algorithms perform well on social media datasets around specific events. However, their accuracy decreases beyond the events around which they were developed due to changes in language use. Therefore, an ethical challenge arises about how researchers should develop, use, and reuse algorithms that have the consequence of classifying content and users with sensitive labels often without their knowledge. Where text classification techniques are necessitated by the scale and speed of the data (e.g., classification can be performed as the data are collected in real-time), researchers should ensure the algorithm performs well (i.e., minimizing the number of false positives via continual testing) for the event under study in terms of established text classification standards. Furthermore, researchers have a responsibility to ensure the continuing effectiveness of the classification algorithm if there is an intention to use it beyond the event that led to its design.

High-profile failures of big data, such as the inability to predict the US housing bubble in 2008 and the spread of influenza across the United States using Google search terms, have resulted in many questioning the power and longevity of algorithms (Lazer, King, & Vespignani, 2014). Algorithms therefore need to be openly published and transparent for reproducibility (including classifier configuration and threshold settings), such that they can be routinely tested for effectiveness and may need to be 'refreshed' with new human input and training data if false positives are to be minimized, avoiding the mislabeling of content and users. Where such information is published, every effort must be made to maintain anonymity, including efforts to reduce the likelihood of deductive disclosure (e.g., the linking of different social media for a single user can reveal their identity; Stewart & Williams, 2005).

Public Attitudes

The Eurobarometer Survey 359 Attitudes on Data Protection and Electronic Identity in the EU (2011; $N = 26,081$) found that 58 percent of European Internet users read online privacy policies.[6] Over 70 percent were aware of the purposes for which social media networks can and may collect, use, and share personal data of users. Around 70 percent of European citizens were concerned about how companies use their data. More recently, Evans, Ginnis, & Bartlett (2015) conducted a survey of users' attitudes toward social media research in government and commercial settings. While 60 percent of respondents reported knowing that their social media data could be shared with third parties under the terms of service they sign up to, the same proportion felt that social media data should not be shared with third parties for research purposes. These views softened when users were offered anonymity and where only public data were to be used in the research. In the report, the majority of users rejected the position that accepting the terms of service was enough to establish consent, preferring instead opt-in consent for each individual research project. To date no research has attempted to model the predictors of the views of the public toward the use of their social media data in various settings. An overview of the methodologies of the two projects outlined in this chapter follows.

METHODOLOGY

Both the NatCen (Beninger, et al., 2014) and Social Data Science Lab projects sought to address the issues raised in the preceding section by putting a series of open and closed questions to users on the use of their social media data for research.

NatCen Qualitative Research

The research used two qualitative methods for collecting data on users' perceptions of their use of social media data in research:

- Four focus groups
- Two paired and two depth interviews

The sample for the fieldwork was partly recruited from the British Social Attitudes 29 survey and partly from an external recruitment agency. It was purposively selected to ensure the views of low, medium, and high users of social media were included,[7] and to ensure diversity in relation to a number of characteristics including age, gender, ethnicity, and use of a variety of social media platforms for different purposes. Individuals who did not use the Internet were excluded from the study. In total 34 participants took part in an interview, paired interview, or focus group.

Focus groups and interviews were conducted by NatCen researchers using a topic guide covering themes such as general use of social media; views on research using social media; and key messages to researchers using social media in their research. The topics explored were acknowledged to be difficult to explain to participants who may not be familiar with social media or the terminology used. Many of the topics covered also required participants to think hypothetically so vignettes were used to illustrate key points and stimulate discussion.

Social Data Science Lab Survey

The Bristol Online Survey tool[8] was used to design and distribute the ethics survey via social networks. The use of online media in social research is now well established and can yield reliable and valid results in a short period of time (Williams et al., 2017). Nonprobability sampling was employed to derive the sample of respondents. While sample bias is a fundamental shortcoming of nonprobability sampling, Meyer & Wilson (2009) note that this is often the only option available to researchers embarking on exploratory research. Furthermore, as the hypotheses tested in this analysis are concerned more with the existence of inter-variable relations and strengths of association than estimating population prevalence, the use of nonprobability sampling does not fundamentally weaken the design of the study (Dorofeev & Grant, 2006). Moreover, our study is principally concerned with 'soft' measures (attitudes, perceptions, and opinions), which have no absolute validity (they cannot be compared with any authoritative external measure). However, Meyer and Wilson (2009) caution that sampling bias can still affect analysis if a sample is significantly uncharacteristic of the target population. The sample does not deviate significantly from what we know about the population of Twitter users. As our sample reflects, Twitter users are more likely to be younger, low- to middle-income earners, and are less likely to have children as compared to the general population (Sloan, 2017; Sloan & Morgan, 2015; Sloan, Morgan, Burnap, & Williams, 2015; Sloan et al., 2013;). However, given the size of the sample and the violation of the normality assumption for ordered linear regression analysis, the bias was corrected and accelerated bootstrapping technique was utilized[9] (Efron & Tibshirani, 1993). Given the nature of the research topic, the authors made efforts to establish informed consent via the introduction page to the online survey. The research aims and objectives were clearly expressed, and all the respondents were informed that the data produced would be anonymized and would remain confidential. Those under 18 were not permitted to complete the survey.

Qualitative Findings

Behaviors on, and Awareness and Understanding of Social Media

To better understand the context within which social media users' views on social media research were formed, the interviews and focus groups explored participants' behaviors on, and awareness and understanding of, social media.

Online behaviors varied widely between participants depending on the platform type and the intention of its use (e.g., social, leisure or business purposes, or a combination of them). Within these contexts, participants demonstrated three distinct (but overlapping) behaviors:

- 'Creators' post original content on platforms including text, videos, and images.
- 'Sharers' re-tweet, share, or forward content posted by others.
- 'Observers' read and view content on social media and other sites but tend not to pass on this information.

The extent to which participants were aware of and understood social media varied, and depended on their sources of information. These included terms and conditions of the platforms, friends, and family, and online sources such as search engines. Participants reported not reading terms and conditions, accepting them only to progress to using the websites, due to the density of the content. They also conveyed difficulty in staying up-to-date with the terms and conditions of platforms as they are 'constantly changing.' As a result, participants were not always aware of their privacy settings, and whether they were still sufficient for their needs after terms and conditions had changed.

Social media websites were described as 'boundless' as they cross international boundaries and, therefore, may be regulated by a country's laws that differ from the laws of the user's country of residence. This linked in to a lack of confidence about the regulation of the use of content shared on social media and what social media sites can store on users from different countries.

The sources of information accessed by participants helped them to understand and be aware of issues inherent in social media, including its public nature (which raised issues of data ownership) and the difficulty of permanently deleting information. These two characteristics then related to three key concerns participants had about using social media:

- Maintaining privacy
- Protecting the reputation and identity of themselves, friends, and family
- Ensuring safety

Participants employed a number of strategies to mitigate the potential risks they identified. Participants discussed restricting the type of content shared (e.g., personal details or content that may 'shed you in a bad light') to address risks of undue intrusion, reputational concerns, and safety. Participants also mentioned adjusting privacy settings so that only their family and friends could access their content. Parents discussed monitoring what their children access and post on social media websites, for safety purposes and to protect them from possible reputational damage. However, participants' views on what was 'sensitive,' and the extent to which it should be shared varied by user. Also, not all participants were aware of how to adjust privacy settings, and there was a view that platforms change quickly and one cannot stay up to date with what their settings now mean.

Awareness and Views of Research Using Social Media
Participants' awareness of research using social media varied. Some participants struggled to understand how social media could be used for research, or found it difficult to distinguish between social and market research, while others (typically more frequent users) had a better understanding of the term. This awareness of using social media for research, as well as their knowledge

of social media more generally was closely related to their views on the subject. Participants' feelings about research using social media fell into three categories: acceptance, skepticism, and ambiguity.

Participants who accepted research using social media discussed the value of this methodological approach and the benefits it may have to society. These participants recognized that social media data collection methods could be beneficial when trying to understand broad social trends as the volume of data could mitigate extreme views, and that people may be more open or honest online than in, for example, a face-to-face survey. Accepting views were also expressed by those users who 'self-regulated' online. These participants only posted online what they were happy for others to access and, therefore, accepted that researchers may use their information and were comfortable with this.

Skepticism about social media research was expressed by participants and found to be related to uncertainty about the validity or value of data from social media, compared to traditional research methods. Participants also had concerns about the lack of transparency online, particularly in relation to who was conducting the research and its purpose. Participants were concerned that their data may be taken out of context to support something they did not agree with and that they were not able to confirm the legitimacy of 'who they're dealing with.'

Ambivalent participants, who expressed neither concern nor acceptance of social media research, felt that whatever their view it would not be listened to and that there was little they could do to stop it from happening. Participants worried about 'Big Brother' culture and saw the use of social media data as inevitable; it was accepted that having your information used was part what happens when you put it online.

Informed Consent
Participants identified four key factors that influenced the importance of researchers gaining consent:

- Mode and content of the posts;
- Social media website being used;
- The expectations the user had when posting, and;
- The nature of the research

Participants who 'self-regulated' did not think researchers needed to gain consent and this held true whatever the type and content of the post. However, others felt it was important. Some users suggested that researchers should ask to use any written content, in particular if it were to be published alongside the username. A different view was that the researcher did not need to ask for consent as long as they were sure the Tweet was an accurate representation of the users' views. Images were identified as particularly problematic, and it was questioned what rights individuals had when they were included in photos posted by other social media users. Finally, participants suggested that researchers should go to greater lengths to gain consent and/or protect anonymity when using posts with more 'sensitive' content.

The type of social media website was another factor in the qualitative study that influenced whether or not participants thought consent definitely needed to be gained by a researcher. Social media websites with a 'social' purpose were viewed differently from websites with a professional aim. Websites with a 'social' purpose were thought to contain more 'personal' content, whereas content posted to 'professional' sites was less so. In light of this, participants thought that it would be acceptable for researchers to access the latter without gaining consent because the risks associated with being identifiable through personal information are lower.

Participants' views were also influenced by user expectations. If a user intended for their post to be widely accessible, then it was felt that a researcher would not necessarily need to gain consent to use it, though this assumed users understood the openness and accessibility of the platform, which may not be the case. In contrast, if a user had not meant it to be public in the first place, or it was posted for a different purpose, then it should not be used. This was felt to be more important than the site from which a researcher took it. For researchers, this means that no matter how open or public a site is considered to be, the user's expectation about how the post should be used is what should be considered.

Finally, the nature of the research and the nature of the organization also affected participants' views on research ethics. Use of social media data was affected by the affiliation of the researcher and the purpose of the research. The type of organization that the research was affiliated with (e.g., charitable or commercial) influenced whether or not participants viewed research to be of 'good quality.' Research being conducted by a not-for-profit organization (typically a university), rather than for 'commercial' reasons, was preferred because the former were felt to be more 'productive,' more 'ethical' and 'not exploitative.' Further, participants did not like to think of their social media posts being used to generate a profit for others although it was acknowledged that this was already happening. As elsewhere, participants of the opinion that once one posts to a social media platform you waive your right to ownership were not concerned about the affiliation of the researcher. Other users were unaware of the differences between not-for-profit and commercial researchers or did not care about the distinction, and therefore had little to say about how researcher affiliation might influence their desire to agree to informed consent. Although concern about the affiliation of the researcher was not widespread, concern about the 'purpose' of the research was. Participants expressed worry about their posts being used to 'drive an agenda' they would not have agreed to if the researcher had asked them. Using social media content to 'drive an agenda' was seen differently from research offering a social benefit such as research aimed at providing more knowledge about a particular social issue or improving public services. In these instances, the potential benefit to society was seen to outweigh the risks to the user.

Quantitative Findings

The Social Data Science Lab ethics survey ($N = 564$) revealed that 94 percent of respondents were aware that Twitter had terms of service, and just below two-thirds had read them in whole or in part. Seventy-six percent knew that when accepting terms of service, they were providing consent for some of their information to be accessed by third parties (see Table 1). Least concern was expressed in relation to Twitter posts being used for research in university settings (84 percent of respondents were not at all or only slightly concerned, compared to 16 percent who were quite or very concerned). Concern in relation to Twitter being used for research rose significantly in government (49 percent were quite or very concerned) and commercial settings (51 percent were quite or very concerned). Respondents expressed high levels of agreement in relation to the statements on consent and anonymity in Twitter research. Just under 80 percent of respondents agreed that they would expect to be asked for their consent before their Twitter posts were published in academic outputs. Over 90 percent of respondents agreed that they would want to remain anonymous in publications stemming from Twitter research based in university settings.

Four factors emerged as statistically significant in relation to concern in university settings (see Table 2). Unsurprisingly, those with no knowledge of Twitter's terms of service consent clause were more likely (odds increase of 1.59) to express concern in this setting. Those who use the Internet for more hours in the day were also more likely (odds increase of 1.10) to express concern, but the effect was marginal. Of the demographic variables, parents of children under 16 were more likely (odds increase of 2.33) to be concerned compared to nonparents. Female respondents were more likely (odds increase of 1.92) to be concerned compared to male respondents. Several predictors

Table 1.   Sample Descriptives.

	Coding	%/Mª	Nᵇ/SD
Dependent Variables			
Concern – University	Not at all concerned	37.2	136
Research	Slightly concerned	46.4	170
	Quite concerned	11.2	41
	Very concerned	5.2	19
Concern – Government	Not at all concerned	23.3	85
Research	Slightly concerned	27.7	101
	Quite concerned	25.5	93
	Very concerned	23.6	86
Concern – Commercial	Not at all concerned	16.8	61
Research	Slightly concerned	32.1	117
	Quite concerned	29.4	107
	Very concerned	21.7	79
Expect to be asked for	Disagree	7.2	26
Consent	Tend to disagree	13.1	47
	Tend to Agree	24.7	89
	Agree	55.0	198
Expect to be anonymized	Disagree	5.1	18
	Tend to disagree	4.8	17
	Tend to Agree	13.7	48
	Agree	76.4	268
Independent variables			
Frequency of posts daily	Scale (range: 1 'Less than once' to 7 'over 10')	1.75	1.23
Postpersonal activity	Yes=1	37.7	161
Postpersonal photos	Yes=1	19.0	81
Knowledge of ToS consent	Yes=1	75.5	317
Net use (years)	Scale (range: 1 'Less than year' to 9 '15+ years')	6.59	1.76
Net use (hours per day)	Scale (range: 1 'Less than hour' to 10 '10+ hours')	6.03	2.52
Net skill	Scale (range: 1 'Novice' to 10 'Expert')	7.69	1.60
Sex	Male = 1	48.93	276
Age	Scale (range: 18–83)	25.38	10.17
Sexual orientation	Heterosexual = 1	83.6	357
Ethnicity	White = 1	91.1	389
Relationship status	Partnered = 1	45.4	194
Income	Scale (range: 1 'below 10K' to 11 '100K+')	3.72	3.07
Has child under 16	Yes = 1	7.3	31

*Notes:*ªMean and standard deviation given for scale variables.
ᵇReduction in sample size due to missing data; bootstrapped (BCa) results reported.

Table 2. Ordered Regression Predicting Concern about Using Social Media Data in Three.

	University				Government				Commercial			
	B	SE[a]	Wald	Exp(B)	B	SE[a]	Wald	Exp(B)	B	SE[a]	Wald	Exp(B)
Frequency of posts	0.048	0.093	0.266	1.05	-0.067	0.089	0.564	0.94	-0.227*	0.09	6.304	0.80
Postpersonal activity	0.216	0.246	0.771	1.24	0.101	0.235	0.184	1.11	0.470	0.237	3.926	1.60
Postpersonal photos	0.132	0.27	0.237	1.14	0.119	0.259	0.209	1.13	0.133	0.261	0.259	1.14
Knowledge of ToS consent	-0.465*	0.244	3.626	0.63	-0.246	0.234	1.104	0.78	-0.289	0.235	1.505	0.75
Net use (years)	-0.041	0.071	0.335	0.96	-0.059	0.068	0.746	0.94	0.059	0.068	0.731	1.06
Net use (hours per day)	0.092*	0.043	4.478	1.10	0.089*	0.042	4.598	1.09	0.062	0.042	2.255	1.06
Net skill	0.078	0.071	1.202	1.08	0.149*	0.068	4.783	1.16	0.135*	0.068	3.91	1.14
Sex	-0.659**	0.246	7.193	0.52	-0.291	0.232	1.569	0.75	-0.353	0.233	2.304	0.70
Age	0.003	0.014	0.038	1.00	0.072**	0.015	21.995	1.07	0.066**	0.015	19.497	1.07
Sexual orientation	-0.27	0.29	0.866	0.76	-0.752**	0.281	7.143	0.47	-0.653*	0.282	5.373	0.52
Ethnicity	0.055	0.383	0.021	1.06	-0.311	0.377	0.679	0.73	-0.422	0.378	1.247	0.66
Relationship status	-0.414	0.216	3.677	0.66	-0.206	0.206	1.006	0.81	-0.363	0.207	3.072	0.70
Income	-0.045	0.034	1.774	0.96	-0.045	0.032	1.921	0.96	-0.053	0.033	2.66	0.95
Has child under 16	0.846*	0.416	4.137	2.33	0.27	0.408	0.437	1.31	0.498	0.409	1.481	1.65
Model Fit												
-2 Log Likelihood	790.730				944.497				920.106			
Model Chi-square	31.182				65.712				66.789			
df	15				15				15			
sig.	0.00				0.00				0.00			
Cox and Snell Pseudo R²	0.08				0.17				0.17			
Nagelkerke Pseudo R²	0.09				0.18				0.18			

Note: [a]Bootstrapped (BCa) standard errors reported; Reduction in sample size due to listwise deletion of cases necessary for regression.
* = p < .05; ** = p < .01

emerged as significant for concern in government and commercial settings that were not significant for concern in university settings. Lesbian, gay, and bisexual (LGB) respondents were more likely to express concern over their Twitter posts being used in government (odds increase of 2.12) and commercial settings (odds increase of 1.92), compared to heterosexual respondents. Older respondents were also more likely to report higher degrees of concern in both these settings, as were those who had a higher level of Internet expertise. Those who posted information most often on Twitter were less likely to be concerned with their information being used in commercial settings.

Those respondents who reported familiarity with Twitter's terms of service consent clause were significantly less likely to expect to be asked for their informed consent by university researchers to publish content (odds decrease of 0.62; see Table 3). Early adopters of the Internet were likely to hold the same view, but to a lesser degree. Female Twitter users and those who post personal photos were more likely to expect anonymity in publishing (odds increase of 1.47 and 1.61, respectively). By far, the most striking result was that of BME tweeters who were much more likely (odds increase of 3.90) to want anonymity compared to white tweeters. These findings lend support to the position that for Twitter-based research to be conducted in an ethical manner it is possible to rely on terms of service to harvest data, but personal information (e.g., extreme opinion, photo, demographic information, location) should not be directly quoted in publication without some form of informed consent.

DISCUSSION

The NatCen qualitative study and the Social Data Science Lab survey provided a first look at users' concern over being included in social media research in various settings and their expectations regarding consent and anonymity. While both the qualitative and quantitative data showed a general lack of concern from social media users over their information being used for research purposes (with university research attracting least concern), the majority of respondents stated that they would want to be asked for consent and to remain anonymous in publications reporting social media research. These patterns reflect those found in the Eurobarometer Survey (2011) that showed three-quarters of Europeans accepted that disclosing personal information was now a part of modern life, but only a quarter of respondents felt that they had complete control over their social media information and 70 percent were concerned that their personal data may be used for a purpose other than for which they were archived. A clear majority of Europeans

Table 3. Ordered Regression Predicting Expectation of Request for Informed Consent and Anonymity in Social Media Research in University Settings.

	Informed Consent				Anonymity			
	B	SE[a]	Wald	Exp(B)	B	SE[a]	Wald	Exp(B)
Frequency of posts	−0.05	0.095	0.275	0.95	−0.097	0.11	0.771	0.91
Post personal activity	0.034	0.253	0.018	1.03	0.311	0.314	0.979	1.36
Post personal photos	−0.272	0.277	0.961	0.76	0.471*	0.33	2.037	1.61
Knowledge of ToS consent	−0.478*	0.262	3.315	0.62	0.115	0.318	0.131	1.12
Net use (years)	−0.155*	0.074	4.388	0.86	−0.105	0.091	1.321	0.9
Net use (hours per day)	0.055	0.045	1.480	1.06	0.049	0.056	0.758	1.05
Net skill	−0.063	0.075	0.710	0.94	−0.109	0.093	1.363	0.9
Sex	−0.241	0.244	0.974	0.79	−0.385*	0.299	1.656	0.68
Age	−0.020	0.014	2.004	0.98	0.017	0.02	0.735	1.02
Sexual orientation	−0.167	0.298	0.316	0.85	0.004	0.356	0.001	1.00
Ethnicity	0.160	0.394	0.165	1.17	−1.369*	0.318	10.13	3.90
Relationship status	−0.019	0.222	0.008	0.98	−0.129	0.275	0.222	0.88
Income	−0.021	0.034	0.380	0.98	−0.004	0.044	0.009	1.00
Has child under 16	0.243	0.431	0.318	1.27	0.052	0.298	0.030	1.05
Model fit								
−2 log likelihood	788.767				526.805			
Model chi-square	24.762				18.68			
df	15				15			
sig.	0.00				0.00			
Cox and Snell pseudo R^2	0.09				0.09			
Nagelkerke pseudo R^2	0.09				0.09			

(75 percent) want be able to delete personal information on a website whenever they decide to do so, supporting the 'right to be forgotten' principle. Taken together, these findings show that there may be a disjuncture between the current practices of researchers in universities, government departments, and commercial organizations in relation to the harvesting and representation of social media data, and users' views of the appropriate use of their online information and their rights as research subjects.

Informed Consent

The Social Data Science Lab survey showed that nearly 80 percent of respondents agreed to some extent that they should be contacted for their informed

consent before their posts are published in academic outputs. Participants
in the qualitative study expressed a range of views about the extent to which
researchers should seek informed consent when observing or collecting data
from social media platforms. Some participants did not think consent needed
to be gained because 'there is no such thing as privacy online,' and by posting content you automatically consent to its wider use – if you did not wish
your data to be used you should adjust your privacy settings. However, others
believed consent should always be sought due to common courtesy and to
protect the 'intellectual property' rights of users, to the extent that some felt
that using content without permission may be illegal. It was recognized that
gaining consent may be impractical, but for those that felt consent should be
gained this was not viewed as a justification not to ask permission.

Anonymity

The survey showed that over 90 percent of respondents agreed to some extent
that they would want to remain anonymous in publications stemming from
social media research (in particular female and BME tweeters and those
posting personal photographs). Anonymity for participants in the qualitative
study meant not having their name, or username, used in any research outputs alongside any content they posted online. It was felt anonymity should
be upheld for two reasons: to avoid judgment from others and to prevent
reputational risk. Of course, this goal of anonymity does not balance well
with ideas of intellectual property and the importance of proper referencing,
also discussed by participants. For participants who disagreed with the need
for anonymity, the reason was similar to those who did not think informed
consent was needed, that is, it is up to the user to manage their identity when
online. There was also a view that some responsibility should fall on platform
owners to educate users about the potential risks of sharing content online.
Regardless of these various viewpoints, anonymity is not possible in the case
of Twitter given their Developer Agreement (see Appendix). Furthermore,
even if the user name was removed, this is not enough to preserve anonymity
as tweet text is searchable.

Avoiding Undue Harm

Participants in the qualitative study were wary about how they could be
sure of what researchers were saying, and how difficult it would be online

to decide if they were 'legitimate' researchers. Closely related to anonymity, participants felt that being identifiable in research could lead to unsolicited attention online and, more seriously, 'abuse.' This might be from people they knew, or from organizations that could 'exploit' them. For others it meant use by the police or courts, for purposes of prosecution. These concerns relate to the abundance of sensitive information about users available on social media and generated by algorithms based on account meta data and communication patterns. The survey found associations between sexual orientation, ethnicity, and gender and feelings of concern and expectations of anonymity. Such characteristics may be considered sensitive under the UK Data Protection Act. A principle ethical consideration in most learned society guidelines on digital social research is to ensure the maximum benefit from findings while minimizing the risk of actual or potential harm during data collection, analysis, and publication (interpreted as physical or psychological harm, including discomfort, stress, and reputational risk). Potential for harm in social media research increases when sensitive data are estimated and harvested. These data can include personal demographic information (such as ethnicity and sexual orientation), information on associations (such as memberships to particular groups or links to other individuals known to belong to such groups), and communications of an overly personal or harmful nature (such as details on morally ambiguous or illegal activity and expressions of extreme opinion). In some cases, such information is knowingly placed online, whether or not the user is fully aware of who has access to this information and how it might be repurposed (Dicks et al., 2006). In other cases sensitive information is not knowingly created by users, but it can often come to light in analysis where associations are identified between users (not everything can be known about another user before connecting nor can changes in affiliation be monitored on a routine basis) and personal characteristics are estimated by algorithms (van Dijck, 2013; Sloan et al., 2015).

CONCLUSION AND RECOMMENDATIONS

This chapter outlines users' views on the use of their social media data in social research. Over four in five reported expecting to be asked for their consent and nine in ten reported expecting anonymity ahead of publication of their qualitative social media posts. However, some researchers consider most social media communications as public, and data from networks such as Twitter are routinely harvested and published without anonymization and without direct consent from users. Contrary to this practice, we argue that while it may be reasonable for researchers to rely on the T&Cs of social media companies as an indication of informed consent with respect to data collection, a more reflexive approach to research ethics is needed in the later stages of the research process. Researchers should consider users' views and expectations, in addition to legal data protection requirements, when setting out to analyze (including the use of algorithms), publish, and store social media data.

With respect to publishing social media data, given the unique nature of this online public environment and what we know about users' views pertaining to informed consent, anonymity, and harm, we recommend that researchers seeking to embark on social media research should conduct the following risk assessment process to determine likely privacy infringement and potential user harm from publishing nonanonymized data (a necessity given Twitter's Developer Agreement and the ability to search content):

- Are social media posts from individual private users, with no public profile (i.e., not celebrities or public figures[10])? If so, in almost every case researchers should seek opt-out consent[11] to publish content without anonymization.
- Are social media posts from organizational accounts (such as government departments, businesses, charities) where users are tweeting on behalf of the organization (and not personally) or public figures/celebrities? If so, consider as truly 'public data,' and in almost every case publish without informed consent.
- Are posts identified as sensitive (e.g., posts about criminal activity, financial problems, mental health issues and feelings of suicide, extramarital sexual activity, controversial political opinions and activism; Townsend & Wallace, 2016)? If so, researchers should seek opt-in consent.
- Are private users identifiable as vulnerable (e.g., children, learning disabled, and those suffering from an illness)? If so, opt-in consent should be sought from the user and/or guardian or proxy.
- Have tweets been deleted (either individually or via a deleted account) at the time of writing? If so, consider content removed from the public domain, and do not publish (unless they are from an organizational or public figure account – see above).
- Are tweets from identifiable bots? If so, consider user as non-human subject and publish without consent.

Codes of ethical conduct that were first written over half a century ago are being relied upon to guide the representation of digital data. This risk assessment process updates these frameworks allowing researchers to move beyond the permissions granted by 'legal' accounts of the use of these new forms of data (e.g., T&Cs) to a more nuanced and reflexive ethical approach that puts user expectations, safety, and privacy rights central stage.

NOTES

1. Although we acknowledge communications are mediated by technology in ways that are sometimes obfuscated to the user and analyst.

2. Nsmnss.blogspot.com

3. socialdatalab.net

4. APIs are Internet interfaces that facilitate programmatic access to online data feeds.

5. The DPA states personal data means data which relate to a living individual who can be identified – (a) from those data, or (b) from those data and other information which is in the possession of, or is likely to come into the possession of, the data controller, and includes any expression of opinion about the individual and any indication of the intentions of the data controller or any other person in respect of the individual.

6. We assume read in whole or in part.

7. Low users were defined as people who did not use social media websites, or used them once a week or less, medium users as those who used websites from twice a week up to once a day, and high users as those who used social media websites several times a day.

8. See http://www.survey.bris.ac.uk/

9. A nonparametric resampling procedure used to empirically estimate the sampling distribution of the indirect effect, thus reducing problems with type I errors and low statistical power endemic to analyses that rely on assumptions of sampling distribution normality.

10. Researchers should consult existing ethical guidelines that provide definitions of public figures (e.g., politicians and celebrities who aim to communicate to a wide audience).

11. In the case of opt-out consent, researchers may wish to set a reasonable time window for a reply (e.g., 2 weeks to 1 month), and repeat consent requests several times should a timely response not be forthcoming. If the tweeter is no longer active (i.e., has not tweeted in last 3-6 months), consider the account as inactive and do not publish (as we can reasonably assume the tweeter has not seen the request and therefore cannot take up the option of opting-out).

REFERENCES

AoIR (Association of Internet Researchers). (2012). Ethical decision-marking and internet research. Retrieved from http://www.aoir.org/reports/ethics2.pdf. Accessed on 15 January 2016.

Barocas, S., & Nissenbaum, H. (2014). Big data's end run around procedural privacy protections. *Communications of the ACM, 57*(11), 3–33.

Barrat, M. J. and Lenton, S (2010). Beyond recruitment? Participatory online research with people who use drugs. *International Journal of Internet Research Ethics, 3*(12), 69–86.

boyd, d (2014). It's complicated: Social lives of networked Teens. New Haven, CT: Yale University Press

British Psychological Society. (2013). *Ethics Guidelines for Internet-mediated Research*. British Psychological Society: London.

Bull S. S., Breslin L. T., Wright E. E., Black S. R., Levine D., Santelli J. S. (2011). Case Study: An Ethics Case Study of HIV Prevention Research on Facebook: The Just/Us Study. *Journal of Pediatric Psychology.* doi: 10.1093/jpepsy/jsq126.

Burnap, P., Gibson, R., Sloan, L., Southern, R., & Williams, M. L. (2016). 140 characters to victory?: Using Twitter to predict the UK 2015 General Election. *Electoral Studies, 41*(2), 230–233.

Burnap, P., & Williams, M. L. (2015). Cyber hate speech on Twitter: An application of machine classification and statistical modeling for policy and decision making. *Policy & Internet, 7*(2), 223–242.

Burnap, P., & Williams, M. L. (2016). Us and them: Identifying cyber hate on Twitter across multiple protected characteristics. *EPJ Data Science, 5*, article number: 11. doi:10.1140/epjds/s13688-016-0072-6

Burnap, P., Williams, M. L., Rana, O., Edwards, A., Avis, N., Morgan, J., et al. (2014). COSMOS: Towards an integrated and scalable service for analysing social media on demand. *International Journal of Parallel, Emergent and Distributed Systems*.

Dicks, B., Mason, B., Williams, M., & Coffey, A. (2006). Ethnography and data reuse: Issues of context and hypertext. *Methodological Innovations, 1*(2), 33–46.

Dorofeev, S. & Grant, P. (2006). Statistics for real-life sample surveys: Non-simple random samples and weighted data. Cambridge: Cambridge University Press.

Efron, B., & Tibshirani, R. (1993). *An Introduction to the Bootstrap*. London: Chapman and Hall.

ESOMAR (2011). ESOMAR guideline on social media research. ESOMAR: Amsterdam.

ESRC (Economic and Social Research Council) (2015). ESRC Framework for Research Ethics. Swindon: Economic and Social Research Council.

Eurobarometer Survey 359. (2011). *Attitudes on data protection and electronic identity in the European Union*. EU: Brussels.

Evans, H., Ginnis, S., & Bartlett, J. (2015). SocialEthics: A guide to embedding ethics in social media research. London: Ipsos MORI.

GSR (Government Social Research Unit) (2006). *GSR Professional Guidance: Ethical Assurance for Social Research in Government*. London: HM Treasury.

Joinson, A. N. (1998). Causes and effects of disinhibition on the Internet. In J. Gackenbach (Ed.), *The psychology of the Internet* (pp. 43–60). New York, NY: Academic Press.

Jones, C. (2011). *Ethical issues in online research*. British Educations Research Association.

Lash, S. (2001). Technological Forms of Life. *Theory, Culture and Society, 18*(1), 105–120.

Lazer, D., King, G., & Vespignani, A. (2014). The parable of Google Flu: Traps in big data analysis. *Science, 343*(6176), 1203–1205

Liu, S. B. (2010). The Emerging Ethics of Studying Social Media use with a Heritage Twist: Revisiting Research Ethics in the Facebook Era: Challenges in Emerging CSCW Research. Workshop at ACM Conference on Computer-Supported Cooperative Work (CSCW 2010), Savannah, GA.

Markham, A. (2012). Fabrication as ethical practice: Qualitative inquiry in ambiguous Internet contexts. *Information, Communication and Society*, *15*(3), 334–353.

Meyer, I. H., and Wilson, P.A. (2009). Sampling Lesbian, Gay, and Bisexual Populations. *Journal of Counseling Psychology*, *56*(1), 23–31.

MRC (Market Research Society) (2012). *MRS Guidelines for Online Research*. London: MRS Evidence Matters.

NatCen. (2014). *Research using social media: Users' views*. London: NatCen.

Nissenbaum, H. (2009). Privacy in context: Technology, policy, and the integrity of social life. Stanford, CA: Stanford University Press.

Roberts, L. (2012). Ethical Issues in Conducting Qualitative Research in Online Communities. *NSMNSS Blog*.

Salmons, J. (2014). New social media, new social science… and new ethical issues! Retrieved from http://nsmnss.blogspot.co.uk/2014/02/new-social-media-new-social-science-and.html

Sloan, L. (2017). Who tweets in the United Kingdom? Profiling the Twitter population using the British social attitudes survey 2015. *Social Media and Society*, *3*(1). doi: https://doi.org/10.1177/2056305117698981.

Sloan, L. & Morgan, J. (2015). Who Tweets with their location? Understanding the Relationship Between Demographic Characteristics and the Use of Geoservices and Geotagging on Twitter. *PLoS ONE*, *10*(11), 1–15.

Sloan, L., Morgan, J., Burnap, P., & Williams, M. L. (2015). Who Tweets? Deriving the demographic characteristics of age, occupation and social class from Twitter User Meta-Data. *PLOS ONE*, *10*(3):e0115545. doi: 10.1371/journal.pone.0115545.

Sloan, L., Morgan, J., Williams, M. L., Housley, W., Edwards, A., Burnap, P., Rana, A. (2013). Knowing the Tweeters: Deriving sociologically relevant demographics from Twitter', *Sociological Research Online*, *18*(7). Retrieved from http://journals.sagepub.com/doi/10.5153/sro.3001

Stewart, K. F., & Williams, M. L. (2005). Researching online populations: The use of online focus groups for social research. *Qualitative Research*, *5*(4), 395–416.

Thelwall, M. (2010). Researching the public web. eResearch Ethics. Retrieved from http://www.ehumanities.nl/researching-the-public-web/

Townsend, L., & Wallance, C. (2016). Social media research: A guide to ethics. Scotland: University of Aberdeen.

Twitter. (2015). Developer agreement, San Francisco: Twitter. Retrieved from https://dev.twitter.com/overview/terms/agreement-and-policy

Twitter. (2016). Broadcast guidelines, San Francisco: Twitter. Retrieved from https://about.twitter.com/en-gb/company/broadcast

van Dijck, J. (2013). *The Culture of Connectivity*. Oxford: Oxford University Press.

Williams, M. L., & Burnap, P. (2016). Cyberhate on social media in the aftermath of Woolwich: A case study in computational criminology and big data. *British Journal of Criminology*, *56*(2), 211–238.

Webster, S., Lewis, J., and Brown. A. (2013). Ethical Considerations in Qualitative Research. In *Qualitative Research Practice: A Guide for Social Science Students and Researchers* (pp. 77–107). London: Sage.

Williams, M. L. (2006). *Virtually Criminal: Crime, Deviance and Regulation Online*. London: Routledge.

Williams, M. L., & Burnap, P. and Sloan L. (2017). Crime sensing with big data: The affordances and limitations of using open source communications to estimate crime patterns. *British Journal of Criminology*, *57*(2), 320–340.

APPENDIX

Twitter Terms of Service
The Twitter Developer Agreement (Twitter 2015) terms of service states that
all users of its API must:

Maintain the integrity of Twitter's products by ensuring:

i)   Usernames are always displayed (and name if possible) with tweet text;
ii) Users of the API respond to content changes such as deletions or public/
     private status of tweets; and
iii) Content of tweets is not modified, translated or deleted (in part or in whole).

Respect Users' Privacy and get the user's express consent before they do
any of the following:

i)   Take any actions on a user's behalf, including posting content and modi-
     fying profile information;
ii) Store nonpublic content such as direct messages or other private or confi-
     dential information;
iii) Share or publish protected content, private or confidential information.

In the case of the reproduction of tweets (exhibition, distribution, transmission, reproduction, public performance, or public display of Tweets by any
and all means of media) the Twitter guidelines state broadcasters & publish-
ers should:

i)   Include the user's name and Twitter handle (@username) with each Tweet;
ii) Use the full text of the Tweet. Editing Tweet text is only permitted for
     technical or medium limitations (e.g., removing hyperlinks);
iii) Not delete, obscure, or alter the identification of the user. Tweets can be
     shown in anonymous form in exceptional cases such as concerns over user
     privacy;
iv) In some cases, seek permission from the content creator, as Twitter users
     retain rights to the content they post.

CHAPTER 3

THE CHANGING ROLES OF RESEARCHERS AND PARTICIPANTS IN DIGITAL AND SOCIAL MEDIA RESEARCH: ETHICS CHALLENGES AND FORWARD DIRECTIONS

Sarah Quinton and Nina Reynolds

ABSTRACT

The purpose of this chapter is to situate how the digitalized research environment is changing the roles of researchers and participants, and how these changes lead to more complex and less discrete ethics challenges. Incorporating contemporary examples from the social sciences, we outline the core challenges of the changing research landscape that embrace both research actors (researcher, participant, and research users) and data issues. The ethical implications related to research actors' roles are discussed by considering how data is accessed, how people can now participate in research, and issues related to accessing participants. Digital data and associated ethical issues are explored through examining authorship and

The Ethics of Online Research
Advances in Research Ethics and Integrity, Volume 2, 53–78
Copyright © 2018 by Emerald Publishing Limited
All rights of reproduction in any form reserved
ISSN: 2398-6018/doi:10.1108/S2398-601820180000002003

ownership, how digital data is produced, and how research transparency can be achieved. Following on from this consideration of research actors and data issues, we suggest which challenges have been re-contextualized by the digital environment, and which are novel to the digital research context, outlining six practical yet reflective questions for researchers to ask as a way to navigate ethics in the digital research territory.

Keywords: Digital research ethics; roles; social media research; co-creation of data

INTRODUCTION

Digital technology has infiltrated society such that it is embedded in multiple aspects of modern life. It impacts on the lives of citizens, means communities are no longer defined by place, is entangled with all elements of business, has altered how governments communicate with and serve their citizens, and has changed not only how the third sector operates but also some of the issues that it focuses on. The digital landscape that we, in the modern world, inhabit has both extended existing human behaviors (e.g., methods of communication) and introduced new ones (e.g., blogging/microblogging); the digital landscape makes some things easier (e.g., tracking down old friends), but makes others harder to achieve (e.g., avoiding distractions). Advances and contributions to scholarship across all disciplines have and continue to be facilitated by the Internet and digital technologies (Meyer & Schroeder, 2015). This evolving digital landscape challenges the norms and boundaries of research practice established prior to the embedding of digital activities and behaviors into our everyday lives. For example, the removal of distance as a barrier to individuals, businesses and researchers changes the meaning and consequences of nondigital actions (e.g., long-distance relationships), and the compression of time and the increase in volume of available data in the digital landscape impacts on how we assess the immediacy and currency of information (e.g., what we view as up-to-date news). These, and other, socio-technological changes impact on what we, as researchers, research, our roles in research, the type of data we collect, and how we ensure we are responsible researchers.

As researchers, the digital landscape presents manifold opportunities as it provides us with new ways of accessing information about human behaviors, attitudes, and emotions, and presents us with new phenomena to investigate. Alongside these new opportunities, the digital landscape presents us with new challenges. For researchers, these challenges are embedded in the technologies' ability to both process and store data, and they emerge as a need to understand the boundaries and limitations of newly emerging research techniques; unpick the role of the participant (and the researcher) in the interactive fast-paced digital environment; integrate the knowledge produced from, or through, the digital environment with existing knowledge; and, maintain the integrity of research, both in terms of the veracity of our results and in terms of the ethical standards applied to the research.

Research ethics, at its core, revolves around the principle of 'do no harm.' This is an ambiguous and complex principle that arouses differing opinions within social science researchers, some of whom view minimizing harm as the foundation for their research while others may view research as being potentially positive for participants and thus 'minimizing harm' is an inappropriate starting point. These perspectives may have developed as a result of the subject norms in which the researchers sit. Nevertheless, as researchers, we take on an active role in our impact on research participants through the choices we make concerning the research topics we investigate, and how we access (research design) and interpret (analyze and report) data. We take on ethics responsibility toward the others involved in the research, be they fellow researchers, research participants, or research users. Our role as researchers places us at the interface between participants and research users. Our overall aim as researchers is to produce a fair and accurate representation of a research topic, without exposing those who were involved in the research to physical, psychological, sociological, economic, or any other type of, harm. Our ethics responsibility to research users is to ensure that they can be confident of the accuracy and fairness of the data representation we produce. With topics, research designs, and/or interpretations, which might expose research actors (generally researchers and/or research participants) to harm, our ethics obligations require us to consider how (indeed whether) we will be able to produce a fair and accurate representation without harm occurring. The digital research environment has brought to the fore how we, as researchers, enact our ethics responsibilities. Using methods we do not understand could be considered unethical as we might be inadvertently exposing research participants to harm, and we would be unable to provide an accurate assessment to research users of the representation's accuracy/fairness. For example, the use of algorithms in sampling or analysis where we cannot access the parameters of their design. Consequently, the digital research environment requires us, as researchers, to reappraise how we enact our ethics responsibilities.

The pervasive impact of the ever-changing digital milieu on the sociocultural and technological contexts in which we live and research provides an opening for us to re-examine current ethics guidelines, norms, and research practices. Some research ethics questions raised by researchers are the same questions asked previously, but within the new digital contexts, they raise new concerns (e.g., understanding participant vulnerability). Here, the underlying ethical issues remain the same but are exacerbated by the digital context. Other issues have not previously presented ethics concerns, but the data storage and/or data processing capabilities of digital technologies means that ethical questions now need to be addressed (e.g., the ability to combine data from multiple anonymized databases may enable individuals to be identified). Two underlying questions need to be addressed in the digital environment: (1) What are the ethics practices that need to be repurposed? and (2) Are there new ethics issues that need to be understood? Addressing these questions may help to identify the underlying principles, and individual elements, that make up digital research ethics 'good-practice.' Exploring questions around how underlying ethics principles are enacted in the digital landscape, and whether we need to reconsider the roles of researchers and participants in digital and social media research, may also reflect on nondigital research practices in the changing social environment. While the underlying ethics principle of 'do no harm or minimizing harm' remains, retaining predigital ethics practices may no longer be effective in achieving this goal. The digital landscape requires ethics norms and practices that accurately address the environmental challenges of the digital, and the sociocultural, context in which we live.

Alongside other authors (Mckee & Porter, 2009), august bodies such as the Economic and Social Research Council (ESRC), the British Academy of Management, and the Academy of Social Sciences, as well as universities' research ethics committees, we consider the first principle of research ethics is to either do no harm, or minimize any harm perceived or actual, and to encourage research which has benefit to society. In digitalized societies, this can become more complex than previously considered, often due to unforeseen consequences of research activity in or through the digital medium. The importance of themes of ethics and privacy are reflected in the recent increase in debates and concerns expressed in the broader sociocultural environment and reproduced on university ethics panels, and in legislation. There have, for example, been court cases requesting the removal of a deceased loved-one's digital footprint from Facebook, and questions raised by universities over the use of third-party social media images in doctoral research.

Research within the digital environment surfaces contexts that require careful thinking about ethics questions that have an established understanding of what is, and is not, ethical research. These include questions surrounding the level of informed consent achievable, or even desirable, for participants, and in addition to the possibility of extending the established notion of protecting individuals in research to incorporating the protection of groups or online communities. Privacy issues also need revisiting in the digital context. What is considered 'public' in the digital environment and how to deal with issues such as consent when such 'public' data are collected from the digital archive, as well as how researchers contemplate the possible unintended privacy consequences of combining different data sources, require consideration. The possibilities of research in digitalized society come with complex ethics responsibilities for those attempting to chart this new digital landscape. The digital landscape has impacted ethics issues associated with both the people involved in research (research actors) and the data used in research. These are considered in the next two sections.

RESEARCH ACTORS: RESEARCHER, PARTICIPANT AND RESEARCH USER

Research is gathered by someone (or something), from someone (or something), and consumed by someone. Understanding how the researcher, the researched, and research users can and do use digital technology, and how individual and social perspectives have been impacted by that technology, is essential to ethical research. Current research practices, and their associated ethics considerations, usually contain the underlying assumption that the researcher, the researched, and the research user are separate entities that can be clearly distinguished.[1] However, these assumptions do not always hold within digital environment. Consequently, ethics guidelines concerning the rights of participants, such as consent, confidentiality, anonymity, and the right to withdraw, all need to be reconsidered in a digital context. Research designers need to consider how the characteristics of the digital environment impact the boundaries between the researcher, the researched, and research users. What is the impact of the dissolution of temporal and/or spatial boundaries on ethical issues? How does the ability of digital users to create a boundary between their digital and nondigital identities impact on the practice of research ethics? The impact of behaviors that the digital environment enables, particularly those around connectivity (i.e., always on, 24/7 access) and interactivity (i.e., engagement between people on and through digital and social media platforms), on research ethics also need to be understood. Do behaviors in the digital environment impact on research roles? How do connectivity and interactivity impact on research ethics? How does the removal of place barriers impact on digital research?

Accessing Data in the Digital Environment

In some cases, the temporal/spatial boundaries of the digital archive that existed in the nondigital environment have been removed by key technological advances such as digital technology's ability to search and the capability to store vast amounts of data at a low cost. The production of data (e.g., interviews) and the protection of those data from unauthorized access by research users even when it was digitalized (e.g., requirements to store transcripts under password protection), created spatial boundaries between the researched and the research user. These boundaries can no longer be assumed to exist in the digital environment as much of the data used by digital researchers is drawn from publically available sources. This leads to a need to consider how research evidence is reported to research users. For example, if Tweets are used as a source of digital data, the research user would be able to match 'anonymous' quotes reported in a research report to their (potential) source through a straightforward Internet search. The role of the researcher in anonymizing the data, and as such protecting participants' identities, is as such changed by the digital environment. The storage capacity and processing capability of digital technologies effectively open up access to the raw data for the research user. This requires the researcher to rethink how they report their research results if they are to ensure their participants' anonymity.

On the one hand, the lack of temporal boundaries of data due to technology's ability to store vast volumes of data indefinitely also impacts on how the past views and behaviors of participants are accessed. Time as a barrier to accessing raw data has diminished to the extent that if data ever existed digitally, the main barrier to accessing historic data is technological expertise. In contrast, nondigital research that attempts to recreate the past views and actions of the researched rely on participants' reconstructions of those views and events. Psychological research on topics such as eyewitness testimony and false memories has shown that our memories of the past are not necessarily accurate as they can be modified by information and experiences that occur after the event (Loftus, 2005). In contrast, the reconstruction of views and events from digital archives provides an accurate reflection of what happened in the past as long as those archives are complete. While being exposed to an accurate account of past views and behaviors is unlikely to be problematic for many participants, some participants may find the blurring of their past and present selves uncomfortable. This possibility could lead to questions concerning whether participants could potentially be exposed to harm, and as such, needs to be considered from an ethics standpoint. The removal of boundaries between the researched and the research users, and between the research participant's present and past selves, represent a breakdown of access barriers to data about ourselves and others.

On the other hand, more boundaries in the digital environment are present than in the nondigital environment. Not being able to independently verify the identity of research participants and control who contributes raw data to a research project are examples of issues resulting from the removal of boundaries in the digital environment related to an individual being able to have multiple and often unverifiable identities. The former includes the ethical challenges associated with protecting a vulnerable[2] participant. How, for instance, can digital researchers be certain that they are not including participants who are vulnerable if they cannot identify exactly who the participants are? The lack of boundaries associated with verifying online identities may also impact on the assessment of whether a research participant is part of the population of interest in the research, especially if the digital environment is being used as a research tool and the population of interest is defined in non-digital terms. How, if participants are anonymous, can researchers assess whether they have a representative sample (in quantitative research) or suitable range of participants (in qualitative research), if the only information they have of their participants is what they choose to say about themselves and what they do? While these are more normally classed as general methodological issues rather than specifically as ethics issues, they become an ethics issue for researchers if they are aware of weaknesses in their research design, but do not report those weaknesses to the research user.

The challenges associated with the dissolution of temporal/spatial boundaries in the digital environment include ensuring that all those contributing to the research are not only aware that they are taking part in research (i.e., consent) but also include issues associated with understanding what is being researched and who/what needs to be consulted in order to gain consent (e.g., individual, group, and entity). The lack of temporal boundaries of data leads to challenges with gaining 'informed consent.' Accessing archived digital data may mean that it is not be possible to gain consent from any participant, nor is it possible to retrospectively inform participants that they are in a 'public-space' where data are being collected for research. Common digital practices across multiple platforms such as posting comments and/or liking (e.g., Facebook, YouTube) presents similar issues concerning the maintenance of participants' rights. Additionally, as the identity of individuals contributing to a discussion may be hidden, consent cannot be obtained, which poses problems for researchers trying to apply previously established ethical norms developed in the nondigital environment. The challenge of gaining appropriate consent is compounded by questions of data authorship and ownership (discussed later). To conduct ethical research, should the researcher have the consent of the author of the data, should the legal owner of the data be consulted (which may for example be a social media platform not an individual), or, if the data are in a 'public' space, is no permission required?

Digital Enabling Participation in Research

Connectivity and interactivity in the digital research environment have facilitated opportunities for coproduction and/or cocreation[3] of research at a scale that has previously not been accessible or possible; for example, participative research with citizens using mobile phone devices to document events or accessing images to assist in Big Data analysis. This connectivity and interactivity that make sharing between people possible is a core characteristic of the digital environment and has enabled the unprecedented scale of involvement of people in research projects. This section focuses on the involvement of people in the design, data collection, and analysis of research. Certain research institutions and authors have termed this the 'crowdsourcing' of research (Brawley & Pury, 2016; Pew Internet Organization, 2016).

The notion of consumers/citizens/employees being actively involved in producing a research output is being transferred to the digital research arena on a scale not previously imaginable. In nondigital research, the roles of the researcher and researched are generally distinct, and in digital research they are often blurred. Those who have been researched are now themselves becoming part-time researchers. Some authors (Halfpenny & Proctor, 2015) suggest that digitalization has, in part, democratized research by enhancing opportunities for citizens to participate in a wide variety of research. For example, cocreated citizen science projects such as marine mammal identification projects and star counting develop collaborative knowledge through a rigorous and transparent research approach. Consequently, digital research value can now be cocreated by both the researcher and the more active copartner who was formerly 'just' a participant. This blurring of boundaries and subtle change in the role of the participants has ethical implications for the researcher, especially as the participant coproducer/cocreator is unlikely to be fully aware of ethics norms, guidelines, or frameworks that impact on many of their research partner's decisions and actions.

Digital's Reach and Research Participants

Researchers acknowledge that it is increasingly difficult to obtain research participants, and the need to identify and access research participants have contributed to the growing popularity of both paid and unpaid online research participant platforms (e.g., Amazon's MTurk and Callforparticpants. com, respectively). The use of these online platforms can be effective as an approach to obtain a sample/collect a data set. However, the type of participant platform and whether participants are paid or not, as well as the underpinning premise of the platform including any compliance with ethics policies, needs careful scrutiny. Critics might suggest this quasicommercial model of accessing and utilizing people in research is similar to current Market Research firm recruitment. However, Market Research firms are governed by industry-based ethics guidelines (e.g., Market Research Society code of ethics), whereas crowdsourcing research platforms are not.

A characteristic of digital access to potential participants is that there is less restriction by place, so participants can be drawn from a broader geographic area. This geographic derestriction means digital platforms have the ability to pay local market rates for labor reducing research costs. However, geographic derestriction can also mean a lack of control and/or inequity concerning workers labor conditions. For instance, the incentive structure can differ according to where in the world the worker registered creating the potential for research 'sweatshops.' In developing economies, there is frequently organized third-party group involvement whereby payment goes to an intermediary company, which then uses its workers to complete the tasks as a requirement of their employment for a very small financial gain. These people are not necessarily 'willing' or able to give 'informed consent' to participate in the research, but their participation represents their main source of income. Putting aside for a moment the question this raises concerning research data quality, authors such as Brawley and Pury (2016) and Barger et al. (2011) suggest that 'standard ethical procedures' should be employed regarding informed consent, confidentiality, and pay. However, no details are provided concerning how to implement these procedures, signaling that these standard ethical procedures are unrealistic and difficulty, if not impossible to implement. Without the ability to identify participants (as discussed in the previous section), the individual researcher (or even a research group) cannot confidently assess, never mind police, the conditions experienced by those participating through these online marketplaces. Consequently, the suggested 'standard ethical procedures' cannot be applied. Thus the use of participant platforms has implications related to 'doing no harm.'

Looking more closely at the researcher's responsibility to the research user to produce a fair/accurate representation, there are several methodological issues that relate to participants sourced in this way. While these issues include the identification of research participants (where identification is required) common to most digital research, several additional issues are specific to research that uses participant platforms. First, workers on these platforms are frequently not one-time participants in a single academic study. This may be problematic if a researcher assumes a naive participant, particularly if the research uses a single participant platform for a multipart study (e.g., a series of independent experiments). Second, the real profile of the worker may not be reflected in their responses to sample selection criteria as online message boards exist where information is shared between workers regarding what a study requires. This lack of participant authenticity has obvious implications for research quality. Third, routine answering can and does occur without consideration of the questions as the workers seek to complete any tasks in the quickest possible manner. This leads to impact on the data quality and the resulting data may be less authentic and reliable for the data user.

An illustrative example of the importance of understanding the nuances of digital research and in particular, sampling and ethics can be highlighted through examining the use of Mechanical Turk (Mturk). Mturk is an Amazon-owned 'distributed workforce service' or crowdsourced data gathering platform that has been frequently used for research studies across many subject areas such as social sciences, psychology, consumer studies, economics, and medicine. It functions on the basis that it connects those who wish to work (or their employers) anywhere in the world with tasks that can be completed on line including online surveys and online experiments involving identifying visual images. Small payments are made to the 'Turkers' or workers who complete the tasks. The average payment is approximately $3 per hour (as of Spring 2015), but there is a lack of transparency in this owing to the piece payment system. While participant platforms superficially appear to be an efficient way of connecting potential participants to research tasks, multiple methodological and ethics issues are prevalent. Interestingly, Professor Dholakia, a noteworthy Marketing academic, who has published multiple studies using Mturk changed his opinion of the mechanism after experiencing life as a Turker as a self-experiment. The new perspective he gained included the decision to use Mturk only for pretesting studies and for exploratory research (Dholakia, 2015). The illustration above and Dholakia's reflections provides insight into the overlap between ethics and methodological issues that increasingly face researchers involved in internet mediated research.

Many of the ethical and quality issues associated with the digital environment's ability to allow researchers to reach new participants are being recognized in the research community, and an increasing level of scrutiny is now applied to research using online marketplace data (e.g., MTurk data). Several university research ethics boards in countries such as the USA, Australia, and Canada no longer approve its use, although more than 500 academic research articles that used Mturk were published in 2015 according to a Google Scholar search. The example of Mturk is given to encourage researchers to question our decision-making about the use and consequences of engaging in particular types of paid-for participant platforms. Just as we would scrutinize both the efficacy and the ethics of nondigital participant pools, we need to ensure that the need for participants does not short circuit our responsibility to act ethically toward those apparently distant participants, nor our considerations about the impact of the participants on the quality of the resulting data.

While the use of unregulated paid-for online marketplaces can be ethically problematic, using the digital environment's reach to access participants can be an effective use of the limited resources that are often a factor with academic research. Online panels that are regulated by Market Research industry's ethical practices, or community-based platforms where no payment occurs, also exist and may present possible options for participant recruitment. For example, a noncommercially founded platform that originates from a recognized university purely designed to facilitate research and endorsed by external research bodies may be preferable over the plethora of commercial platforms offering to solve your research recruitment challenges for a fee. These institutional-based platforms are likely to have been through an internal vetting procedure, and their underpinning ethos will be based on the encouragement of rigorous academic research.

Nevertheless, online platforms present a valuable resource for researchers, making previously exorbitant studies financially feasible. For instance, researchers interested in geographically dispersed participants, or cross-cultural researchers, can exploit the cost–benefits associated with digital data collection to increase the feasibility of their studies. As such, we suggest that the following questions are considered prior to engaging with participant and data collection platforms: What are your research institution's or university's policies with regard to the use of participant platforms for sample recruitment? If there is approval for their use, what are the criteria used to select suitable platforms? What are the platform's stated criteria for participant recruitment (if any), and how do they enforce them? Are participants actively recruited and is their participation in research projects monitored, or do participants self-select for the platform and/or research projects? What can be determined about the sampling frame on the platforms, are they distorted from the population of interest or a fair reflection? While we recognize that commercial Market Research organizations have mechanisms to validate recruitment of research participants for sample integrity, the digitalized research environment's enabling of online platforms has created the need for heightened awareness of the responsibility of the researcher toward the research participant and the research user.

Beyond platforms restricted to participant recruitment, there are also platforms that host data collection instruments such as questionnaires, technologies that allow direct access to participants (e.g., Skype), and the possibility that the researcher can entirely outsource the data collection. However, the ethics issues associated with these are closely aligned with those of the familiar nondigital research environment, and as such, not considered in detail here.

Ethics Associated with Research Actors

The digital research environment has the potential to expose raw data to research actors in different ways, has changed how individuals participate in research, and has the potential to extend the reach of researchers to new participants. As such, maintaining the principle of 'do no harm' or at least minimizing the potential for harm means that the researcher has to consider potential ethics challenges when designing research in the digital environment. While the ethics issues considered cover topics addressed by all researchers (e.g., participant vulnerability), the digital context adds complexity due to technology's processing ability, storage capacity, and facility to provide anonymity. The list below provides examples of additional questions that might be more problematic in the digital environment.

- Participant vulnerability – How can the participant's identity be protected when reporting research? Does exposing participants to particular data have the potential to 'do harm' to them? Is there potential for the data collection method (coproduction/cocreation, recruitment) to exploit research participants? Are participants paid or offered other incentives? If so, when, what for (e.g., participation and completion), and at what level?

- Participant researcher/research relationship – How is data shared with or between participant researchers? Is it necessary to maintain the participant researcher's anonymity? If so, how is this achieved? How does the research organizer ensure that they are not exploiting (the labor of) participant researchers?
- Digital host/supplier's credentials – Is it clear who owns the digital host/ supplier, and what the core purpose of the organization is? Are there any external indicators that the digital host/supplier (e.g., online panels) complies with particular research standards (e.g., codes of ethics)?
- Data handling issues – Does the digital host/supplier disclose how data is stored, and for how long? Is data storage secure? Are relevant legal standards for data protection followed at national, or regional level (e.g., EU data regulations)? Is it clear who will own and/or be able to use any data collected? Is it clear whether the data collected via the digital host/supplier can be sold on, or used by others?
- Participant management – Who is able to access the participant pool? What are the rules with respect to the type of research that can/cannot be undertaken using the participant pool? How is unforeseen participant distress identified and managed? How are participants' demographic details obtained/checked? How does the platform ensure that 'professional' participants do not contaminate the participant pool? What measures are in place to ensure that participants do not misrepresent themselves with respect to fitting the sample?

Having considered participants and their more active role in digitally enabled research, we now turn to the new data that are now available and reflect on the research implications and the ethics challenges they present.

DIGITAL DATA

The data that are generated though digital technologies present methodological and ethics challenges that can be related to data authorship and ownership, how the data is produced, and research transparency.

Data Authorship and Ownership

One approach to categorizing digital data is by whether those data were authored by an individual, an institution/organization, or a group. Data authorship can be critical when considering ethics issues as it is the starting point to unpicking ownership – who (or what) should be asked for consent (permission) to use the data? What also needs to be considered is how authorship might be associated with the provision of data versus the production of data. For example, an individual navigating a website is providing the input, but the data is produced through tracking their activities. Considering who provides the data is, nevertheless, worthy of reflection. An individual may actively produce digital data in the form of their comments, perceptions, or expressed attitudes toward an event, or through created images such as photographs. In marketing and business research, this might be viewed as consumer-generated content. This type of data is perceived to be of value as it generally comes directly from a consumer experience. Social science researchers might be interested in this type of data as comparator data, comparing individuals' experiences of education, or local government services. Alternatively, an individual might passively provide data through, for example, enabling geo-location on an app. This data might contribute to understanding human behavior across multiple fields including business, criminology, and geography. However, depending on the location of the online data, the owner of the data might not be the author. The terms and conditions of many social networking platforms and apps, for instance, mean that the host owns the data not the individual who authored it. Ethics issues here include the need to untangle the legal ownership of data from the authorship. Should the owner or the author be asked for consent? Is, for example, acquiescence to the terms and conditions of a social networking site equivalent to 'informed consent'? If yes, why; if no, why not?

Organizational and/or business-related digital data might also be provided by individuals and can be of interest to those investigating a specific industry, for example, website data concerning human resource training resources within the school teaching sector or hotel responses to poor online reviews. This type of individual data has parallels in nondigital attitudinal research. From a research ethics standpoint, research has generally collected these data via some form of direct communication with the participant (e.g., survey, focus group, and interview), and this has occurred with the participant's knowledge and consent. While individual digital data of this type may be collected in similar ways in the digital environment, often this type of data is collected passively from participants without their explicit knowledge such as, scraping[4] comments from social networking, or microblogging hosts (e.g., comments made by individuals on Twitter regarding the recent American presidential election). Ethically, collecting data without the individual's knowledge presents problems with respect to informed consent. Additional issues arise if automated processes such as algorithms are used to access the data, as these processes are not always transparent. The ethical issues arise here as the researcher is unable to be sure of the quality or completeness of their data set. Consequently, the researcher's ability to verify that they are accurately reflecting the attitudes and behaviors of their population of interest is compromised.

Data generated by groups, such as shared interest groups, all of whose participants have a common reason for interacting and participating can be extremely useful sources of data. Homophilic groups are common across social media and digital online communities, and are often drawn from individuals who are geographically dispersed. Having identified the shared interest or purpose that is the focus of the research, the locating of these groups can be completed via search engine searches. For example, localized groups such as choirs or patient and carer groups can be found via these searches. Collecting data from these groups leads to the question of whether the group needs to consent – in which case, how is an appropriate representative of the group identified – or whether all individuals in the group need to consent for data to be collected. Organizational groups may have more formalized structures and membership criteria. For example, within online communities, professional membership bodies such as chartered engineers can be found as LinkedIn groups. Although platforms such as LinkedIn tend to contain more data that are expressions of the individual rather than the organization or the group, there is much content found online and in social media that are organizationally authored and for which a researcher may well require a different level or type of permission to use in research. Individual, group, and organizationally authored content can contain highly focused and relevant data for research but careful consideration of which permissions are required or advisable, versus nondisclosed data scrapping should be made.

Pursuant to the question of data authorship and its categorization into singular or group may be that this dichotomy in itself is a false distinction. Data authorship in coproduced and cocreated research can be extremely complex. Much research data of this type is interactional in nature, owing in part to the nature of the digital communication mechanisms, and thus limiting the data collected to an individual's contribution may limit the ability to produce a holistic view by only utilizing one side of an interaction. An individual's view or perception may also not be representative of the sample you are interested in. In addition, the criticism afforded to social media and online communities and in particular that these groups are narrowly constituted, and reflect only the more vocal members of the shared interest community who have access to, and expertise in communicating via, digital technologies (Preece & Maloney-Krichmar, 2005). As a counter to such criticism some social science researchers have research evidence to suggest that 'peripheral' groups have been given a voice through social media and online communities, for example, survivors of domestic abuse, refugee seekers, and those involved in the sex industry have had their voices heard through research projects where anonymized sharing of experiences as data has proved valuable to all involved (Andrade & Doolin, 2016; Clarke, Wright, Balaam, & McCarthy, 2013). The confusion concerning data authorship/ownership in online communities leads to ethical questions concerning what is appropriate consent.

Looking more closely at the question of data ownership uncovers further issues, especially if research is becoming more of a collaborative effort between participants/coproducers, then we need to reflect on the ownership of the data involved in any research. There are questions to be asked around the ownership of the original data. For example, was the photograph posted on social media taken and 'owned' by the person posting it or was it taken by someone else and correctly attributed, 'tagged' or not attributed? The ownership of data that are shared, passed on, augmented, and passed on again may be multilayered and challenging to determine for a researcher. Similarly, edited or 'mashed-up' video material of music festivals, advertisements, film trailers, etc., creates headaches for researchers in terms of attribution, informed consent, and ownership. Further levels of complexity are then created by the inclusion of third-party content that may be in comments or identifying images, as well as the rights granted to platform owners when Terms and Conditions (T&Cs) are agreed to.

Another research ethics question concerning ownership arises with the eventual outputs of research activity. This question predates the digitalized environment. However, it is heightened as research outputs are now more widely distributed owing to the connectivity and extended reach of computer mediated technologies. Although some publications do make explicit their acknowledgments and appreciation of those who participated in digital research, as most data are to some extent anonymized, researchers may feel that that is sufficient. However, if research is coproduced and the resulting insight cocreated, then there may be an argument for giving greater appreciation of the contribution made, through a more explicit, shared ownership of the research output. The established notion of the data being 'owned' by the university or institution or commercial firm in which the staff or researchers were situated when the research was conducted may now be questioned as research becomes more distributed through digital technologies (Marres, 2012).

Data Production: Reporting and Tracking

Paralleling nondigital data production, digital data can be gained through observation or communication. Data from observation might reveal information about the individual that they are unaware they are sharing, or that they do not know themselves, while communication data consists of information that the individual choses to share online. Observation can be self-tracking data (e.g., observation of self through technological devices such as fitness wearables) or the traces a person leaves in the digital sphere (e.g., navigation data). The collection of observation-based digital data creates a set of diverse ethics challenges around the responsibility of reporting. Self-tracking data might reveal harmful things about the participant to the researcher that the participant is unaware of. For example, if self-tracking fitness wearable data indicated a participant might have dangerously high blood pressure, should the researcher report this and if so to whom? To what extent might the reporting of the data overstep the role of the researcher, and the confidentiality of the participant whom we may not be able to identify. Where does the moral duty lie? Observation of the digital traces people leave behind might also present ethical dilemmas to the researcher. For example, if dark web data are being collected and illegal activity is captured as part of a data set, should this activity be reported and to which authorities? Although these are not new dilemmas, our ability as researchers to capture and be party to these data creates more complex ethics challenges related to how we should respond.

Communication can be direct with the researcher (e.g., online questionnaire), or can consist of the individual's communications with others (e.g., social media network posts). Unlike the nondigital environment, many individuals have multiple digital identities such that each digital identity is only a partial representation of themselves and the ethics difficulties that might be associated with gaining consent when the researcher cannot connect a nondigital individual to a digital identity complexity. This lack of a direct connection between a single individual and a particular digital identity can have methodological implications for researchers. As the researcher has an ethics responsibility to the research user for the veracity of their research findings, researchers need to be aware of the disconnection that might exist between the digital and nondigital entity and reflect this potential disconnection in their research reporting.

Research Transparency

Digitalization has led to some aspects of research being hidden from the researchers, consequently elements of digital research methods can take on a 'black box' quality. Research transparency issues include the shrinking of access to digital data (Wessels et al., 2014), and digital sampling algorithms such as those used by Twitter or YouTube. While there is an almost boundless quantity of digital data being generated, accessing these data is becoming more difficult for academic researchers. An ethics question arising from the lack of access to data, though beyond the remit of individual researchers, is the extent to which these data should be closed off from independent investigation, and further to this, if the data sets are not open to independent interrogation how can the research community be reassured of the outputs? Overall, the access to these data potentially shifts the power away from individuals or small research groups to a selected group working with data controlled by countries or a few commercial firms, which could create ethics issues for the right to access data that we as citizens and researchers have generated. The 'black box' elements of research methodology mean that the output of a process such as sampling is visible, but the algorithms by which that output was achieved is hidden. Mechanisms such as Twitter's sampling algorithm can distance both the participant and the researcher from elements of the research process and lead to fewer opportunities for coproduction and cocreation of research, as well as removing participant choice essential to/associated with research ethics, and reducing the researcher's ability to assess the quality of their research methodology. Despite this distancing, some researchers seem unaware of the potential pitfalls related to these hidden mechanisms.

A similar issue is faced with the analysis of digital and social media data. Owing to the potential commercial value to be made from digital data analysis, increasingly large commercial firms are creating proprietorial tools for the analysis of digital data (e.g., IBM, Microsoft, and Google). There has also been limited attention paid to more widely available and affordable tools for analysis such as ATLAS.ti or NVivo or the development and support of open source analytical software, e.g., NodeXL. Thus researchers are often faced with expensive licensing fees in order to maximize the potential insight to be gained through analysis of these data. This is a further, broad ranging ethics question, beyond the scope of this chapter or text, but the choking of data to researchers who do not have extensive funds or commercial affiliations should be of concern. In this instance, the role of the individual researcher is significantly diminished. In line with this logic, the recently announced partnership between a small number of very large corporations (Amazon, Facebook,

Google, IBM, and Microsoft) for the purposes of conducting and disseminating research relating to Artificial Intelligence and the production of research standards for the future is worth noting. The launch statement made explicit that information would be provided under open license and invitations to join the partnership would be made to selected academics (Hern, 2016). How the selection of academics will be made and what data they might be able to access remains to be communicated. Having outlined the changing roles of researchers and participants within the digital and social media research context and highlighted some of the pertinent challenges we will now move forward to suggest key questions to assist in resolving some of these ethics dilemmas.

REASSESSING ETHICS IN DIGITAL RESEARCH

The existing ethics questions asked of and by researchers, and the institutions in which we work and study, become increasingly complex when we enter the domain of undertaking digital research. Not only do some of the established ethical questions get more complicated, but the advent and adoption of novel data formats raises new ethics questions. The new types of data that are now easily collected, such as video material or covert scraping of social media data, have modified existing ethics questions and created new ones that require a more contextual approach. New data types will continue to emerge as digital technologies morph and advance, thus understandably there is no fixed set of ethics codes, although useful baselines such as AoIR exist, and the idea of 'rules' might no longer be realistic. However, there is a need for a contextually based, flexible but fair approach to ethics decisions for digital researchers in relation to the protection from harm principle and this requires specific, careful appraisal concerning the collection and use of digital data.

The blurring of roles discussed earlier, coupled with the importance of context creates a complicated set of responsibilities for the digital researcher. If looking for advice and a way to navigate these blurred roles the existing digital research community may offer useful guidance based on previously encountered (and we hope resolved) ethics challenges, see, for example, the #NSMNSS Twitter community. In addition, research ethics officers within an institution you may work, or research, in should be able to offer institutional good practice advice. Although in the nascent area of digital and social media research it is often more helpful in the first instance to speak to someone who has or is using digital or social media data in their own work. An assumption that all the ethics questions remain the same as with the old offline research context is not sufficient. We suggest asking the following key questions that will help in resolving complex ethics dilemmas in digital and social media research. Although the first four questions are also relevant to nondigital research, the added complexity of the digitalized environment requires heightened consideration of them as they are recontextualized for the digital environment. The final two questions have been brought about owing to the characteristics of the digital environment and as such are novel to digital research.

How Sensitive is the Research and Who Will it Impact?

Some social science researchers will be involved in socially sensitive research – for example, the use of legal highs by adults in the UK, or subjects such as identity conflict in transgender communities. Alternatively, research may focus on understanding activism within extreme political parties or research that requires data collection of illegal activity, such as organized crime behavior. Additionally, researchers need to consider not just how sensitive the research is in relation to their participants but also who might be impacted more broadly. For example, with politically sensitive topics, it is possible that family/friends of the participant will need to be considered as well as the participant themselves? While this question has been relevant for established offline research, it is recontextualized within the digital environment as the digital footprint, reach and spread of research necessitates that this question is reflected on in light of the borderless digital research landscape. The role of the researcher here is to think broadly about the potential impact of the research and what processes might be employed to mitigate any potential harm to the research participants and the communities in which they have a presence. Greater attention may need to be paid not only to anonymizing the data but also potentially to clouding the data content to prevent potential harm.

What is the Level of Research Participant Vulnerability?

The level of vulnerability, as discussed earlier in this chapter, may overlap with the level of sensitivity of the phenomenon to be researched. Vulnerability needs to be assessed psychologically, physically, economically, and socially when considering what might 'harm' the participant. Nondigital research has long considered the potential for psychological harm – that is, asked questions concerned with whether participants' identity or well-being would be detrimentally impacted by undertaking the research. Physical safety has also been considered in a nondigital sphere – such as whether exposing participants to particular situations was appropriate. The physical safety of research actors might become more sensitive with, for example, research examining, running and cycling activity through apps such as Strava via which community members can identify routes, dates, and times of activities, possibly opening up those who share that data to physical harm. Economic harm might also result if researchers are not aware of how data might be de-anonymized when combining multiple databases. Social harm (e.g., harm to relationships or social standing) has generally been mitigated by ensuring that data are collected 'privately' – for example, using individual interviews rather than focus groups – and reported in such a way as to ensure the anonymity of participants. In some contexts, 'private' collection of digital data is not feasible, adding to the potential to cause social harm to research participants. Overall, the context within which the participant is engaging with the research becomes more sensitive in digital research. For example, online transgender communities would be considered as potentially more vulnerable to harm – psychologically, physically, economically, and socially – than wine industry professionals on LinkedIn. The complexity of the digital environment makes the researcher's role more difficult with respect to executing their ethical responsibilities to participants and research users.

How Can Third-Party Data be Evaluated?

As digital researchers, we are much more likely to become involved with and either deliberately or randomly collect a wide variety of data including third-party data and the ethical implications of this need to be dealt with explicitly. By third-party data, we mean participants who might join in an online community conversation without being aware that the data is being collected. This does not happen in established off-line research such as interviews or focus groups where the number of participants is finite, predetermined and screened. Third-party data capture can also come in the form of images, someone can forward, repost, or retweet someone's else images of a holiday or party. If you are a researcher investigating the use of images to denote self-identity or consumption practices, then you might wish to include such data. It is unrealistic to suggest that you attempt to contact each person individually (you may not have their contact details). Nevertheless, as researchers, we need to consider how data (whether images or comments) will be reported such that neither the original participant, nor the third-party 'participant' can be identified. How, that is, can we maintain confidentiality and anonymity for participants – whether their contribution to the research is knowing or not? Clarification has been provided earlier in this chapter as to the changed role of participant as coproducer or cocreator in digital research, as well as authorship of data; however, a more difficult question is raised here. How these third-party data are evaluated in terms of data quality and against what criteria is not always clear-cut and distinct, thus third-party data capture should be reviewed on a case-by-case basis, also bearing in mind the questions of sensitivity and vulnerability.

Does the Research Require Informed Consent?

As digital and social media research may involve multilayered data collection processes and outputs (e.g., the production and analysis of digital images) the contents of which are not known at the outset, establishing trust and obtaining consent, where practical, are important. The layering of data and the increased variety of possible data types creates a need for greater sensitivity over the issue of informed consent. In cases of research data layering, or evolutionary cocreated research, a process of ongoing consent can be introduced at different stages of the research rather than relying on one-off consent at the beginning of a research project. We have transferred this idea from certain arts-based subjects such as Social Sculpture, where research is often a series of progressing interventions, with unknown outputs at each stage. As a result of requesting consent at different stages of the research, trust may be enhanced between researchers and participants. Increasingly, as image-based data grows in volume, acknowledgment of participants' attachment to artifacts could also assist in developing trust between the researcher and the participants. Participants, particularly in social media and visual-based research may have strong attachment to the content that has been either self-generated or has strong connective associations for those participants (Gubrium, Hill, & Flicker, 2014). Insufficient consideration has been given in research to how people feel about visual content and it relation to a sense of self (Belk, 2013). An explicit statement conceding the value attached by participants to visual artifacts could be included within any research design.

How Critical are New Data Formats to the Research?

Although apparently counterintuitive to this text, we suggest you ask yourself if it would be appropriate and possible to use other data sources to answer your research question. Can nondigital material be collected and if so how? More basically, are the digital data being collected because they are 'novel' or is there an underlying theoretical basis for thinking that a contribution to knowledge (whether academic or practical) can be made by using digital data. In the nondigital environment, this question often arises in relation to cross-cultural/cross-national research. Here naive research may propose that insights into a phenomenon will occur by looking at that phenomenon in an unexamined culture or country; the argument that because 'the question has never been asked there before' it must make a contribution to knowledge, is unsophisticated. The more sophisticated researcher would counter with 'maybe that's because there is no (theoretical or practical) reason to believe that the results will be different there,' and instead asks for reasons, why the phenomenon will differ in that new context. Returning to the digital environment, we need to take care to avoid naive digital research (it has never been considered in the digital context before) and evaluate how and why digital data will add to the knowledge base we want to contribute to. However, if your research concerns a digital phenomenon (Salmons, 2015), for example, analyzing social media network influence in the take up of alternative treatments by cancer sufferers, then it is probable and we suggest, desirable, that you will be accessing digital data in order to fully answer your research question. The role of the researcher here is to ensure relevancy and appropriateness of the data formats used for their research projects.

Does Participant Anonymity Require Additional Consideration?

While the ubiquity and versatility of digital data present great opportunities for social science researchers, they also present complexities in the levels of anonymity required. For example, it is not sufficient to remove a Twitter handle and the unique referencing number of the Twitter interface API from a Tweet to make it anonymous, as the tweet itself can be traced backwards to identify the individual posting. This creates a potential issue for the researcher. A question to ask here is how important is it to report or quote verbatim the Twitter message? If content analysis is not your aim, and thus exact content is not the core focus of your research, then the substitution of words with synonyms without changing the central meaning will significantly improve anonymity. Even if there is a need to use exact data for the analysis, this does not necessarily require that the reporting requires the identification of individual data points (i.e., exact quotes). Recently published work in sociology and criminology takes this approach (see e.g., the work of Davies, 2017, and also Sugiura, Pope, & Webber, 2012). A further case is the use of geolocation data where the identification of precise streets or exact neighborhoods may cause issues for those inhabitants, in terms of further targeting those places or by impacting house prices, etc. Studies involving urban crime data statistics or poor school performance need to consider carefully how accurately they may wish to 'pinpoint' the location of particular findings, particularly in presenting results using visualization tools and maps, and when the data are not already publically available. The protection of the local residents from the psychological or social harm of having their neighborhood 'shamed' should be considered. Again, some published research chooses to broaden a location so that specific streets or exact locations cannot be identified, thus preserving the anonymity of those communities. The researcher here has an enhanced role in taking responsibility for understanding the data format and the implications of their use. For example, participants and physical communities in geolocational research should be given the right to request blurring of precise locations.

In this chapter, we have delineated the digital research landscape that many researchers now inhabit, including the novel research possibilities afforded by digital and social media technologies. We have discussed the shifting roles of research actors and the changing nature of data, and the ethics challenges these present. The enhanced complexity of the responsibilities of the researcher to the research user have also been highlighted in this chapter as data collected by and through digital means and on digital phenomena may lack transparency. How we, as researchers, approach the ethics challenges presented by the changing sociotechnological context is a key factor in the maintenance of research integrity in the digital environment. How we interpret and enact research in an ethical way in the digital environment is critical to developing the opportunities afforded by digital technologies. A set of six overarching questions related to these ethics challenges have been identified to assist researchers navigate a way forward in this complex new territory. These questions will help researchers in both reaching appropriate ethics decisions in their own work and also when appraising the work of others within the digital/social media research landscape.

NOTES

1. Some forms of research such as action research, or community-based PAR, already blur the role of the researcher – as the researcher is part of the community

being researched – and the researched – as participants have a say in the research direction. However, these are less mainstream than in digital research, and as such, the lack of distinction between the researcher and researched have not been at the forefront of research ethics in nondigital research.

2. It should be noted that vulnerability takes many forms and vulnerabilities may not be known until research probes a particular phenomenon (Iphofen, 2011). For example, the labelling of a research participant as vulnerable as opposed to them self-identifying as such may have consequences for the participant and should be reflected on by both digital and non-digital researchers as a potential ethical issue.

3. See Humphreys and Grayson (2008) and Zwass (2010) for a detailed discussion of coproduction and cocreation.

4. Scraping refers to the collection of quantities of social media content such as comments, likes, shared images direct from the platform.

REFERENCES

Andrade, A. D., & Doolin, B. (2016). Information and communication technology and the social inclusion of refugees. *MIS Quarterly, 40*(2), 405–416.

Barger, P., Behrend, T. S., Sharek, D. J., & Sinar, E. F. (2011). IO and the crowd: Frequently asked questions about using Mechanical Turk for research. *The Industrial-Organizational Psychologist, 49*(2), 11–17.

Belk, R. W. (2013). Extended self in a digital world. *Journal of Consumer Research, 40*(3), 477–500.

Brawley, A. M., & Pury, C. L. (2016). Work experiences on MTurk: Job satisfaction, turnover, and information sharing. *Computers in Human Behavior, 54*, 531–546.

Clarke, R., Wright, P., Balaam, M., & McCarthy, J. (2013). Digital portraits: Photo-sharing after domestic violence. *Proceedings of the SIGCHI conference on Human factors in computing systems*, April, ACM (pp. 2517–2526).

Davies, H. C. (2017). Learning to Google: Understanding classed and gendered practices when young people use the Internet for research, *New Media and Society*, (forthcoming).

Dholakia, U. (2015). *My experience as an Amazon Mechanical Turk (MTurk) Worker*. Retrieved from http://ww.linkedin.com/pulse/my-experience-amazon-mechanical-turk-mturk-worker-utpal-dholakia

Gubrium, A., Hill, H., & Flicker, S. (2014). A situated practice of ethics for visual and digital methods in public health research and practice: A focus on digital storytelling. *American Journal of Public Health, 104*(9), 1606–1614.

Halfpenny, P., & Procter, R. (Eds.). (2015). *Innovations in digital research methods*. London: Sage.

Hern, A. (2016). Partnership on AI formed by Google, Facebook, Amazon, IBM and Microsoft. Retrieved from http://www.theguardian.com/technology/2016/sep/28/google-facebook-amazon-ibm-microsoft-partnership-on-ai-tech-firms

Humphreys, A., & Grayson, K. (2008). The intersecting roles of consumer and producer: A critical perspective on co-production, co-creation and prosumption. *Sociology Compass, 2*(3), 963–980.

Iphofen, R. (2011). *Ethical decision making in social research*, New York, NY: Palgrave.

Loftus, E. (2005). Planting misinformation in the human mind: A 30-year investigation of the malleability of memory. *Learning & Memory, 12*(4), 361–366.

Marres, N. (2012). The redistribution of methods: On intervention in digital social research, broadly conceived. *The Sociological Review*, *60*(1), 139–165.

Mckee, H. A., & Porter, J. E. (2009). *The ethics of internet research: A rhetorical case based process*, 59. New York, NY: Peter Lang Publishing Inc.

Meyer, E. T., & Schroeder, R. (2015). *Knowledge machines, digital transformations of the sciences and humanities*. Cambridge, MASS: MIT Press.

Pew Internet Report (2016), Research in the crowdsourcing age: A case study. Available from http://www.pewinternet.org/2016/07/11/research-in-the-crowdsourcing-age-a-case-study/

Preece, J., & Maloney-Krichmar, D. (2005). Online communities: Design, theory, and practice. *Journal of Computer-Mediated Communication*, *10*(4), 00–00.

Salmons, J. E. (2015). *Doing qualitative research online*. Thousand Oaks, CA: Sage.

Sugiura, L., Pope, C., & Webber, C. (2012). Buying unlicensed slimming drugs from the Web: A virtual ethnography. *Proceedings of the 4th Annual ACM Web Science Conference*, June, ACM (pp. 284–287).

Wessels, B., Finn, R. L., Linde, P., Mazzetti, P., Nativi, S., Riley, S., & Wyatt, S. (2014). Issues in the development of open access to research data. *Prometheus*, *32*(1), 49–66.

Zwass, V. (2010). Co-creation: Toward a taxonomy and an integrated research perspective. *International Journal of Electronic Commerce*, *15*(1), 11–48.

CHAPTER 4

USING TWITTER AS A DATA SOURCE: AN OVERVIEW OF ETHICAL, LEGAL, AND METHODOLOGICAL CHALLENGES

Wasim Ahmed, Peter A. Bath and Gianluca Demartini

ABSTRACT

This chapter provides an overview of the specific legal, ethical, and privacy issues that can arise when conducting research using Twitter data. Existing literature is reviewed to inform those who may be undertaking social media research. We also present a number of industry and academic case studies in order to highlight the challenges that may arise in research projects using social media data. Finally, the chapter provides an overview of the process that was followed to gain ethics approval for a Ph.D. project using Twitter as a primary source of data. By outlining a number of Twitter-specific research case studies, the chapter will be a valuable resource to those considering the ethical implications of their own research projects utilizing

The Ethics of Online Research
Advances in Research Ethics and Integrity, Volume 2, 79–107
Copyright © 2018 by Emerald Publishing Limited
All rights of reproduction in any form reserved
ISSN: 2398-6018/doi:10.1108/S2398-601820180000002004

social media data. Moreover, the chapter outlines existing work looking at the ethical practicalities of social media data and relates their applicability to researching Twitter.

Keywords: Ethics; privacy; Twitter; Social Media; research integrity

BACKGROUND

The use of social media and social networking websites has increased rapidly in recent years with more households, organizations, and individuals having access to the Internet (OECD, 2016). There are more social media platforms and more members of the public, businesses, charitable, and other organizations that are using these platforms (Chaffey, 2016). Online interaction, therefore, is now a regular part of daily life for a demographically diverse population of billons of people worldwide (Golder & Macy, 2014). Those who use social media may post their thoughts, feelings, and/or opinions on almost every aspect of life (Chew & Eysenbach, 2010). Social media content, therefore, presents academic researchers with important new opportunities to study a range of topics in a naturally occurring setting. There are a number of ethical issues associated with undertaking this research, which will be discussed in this chapter; however, there are enormous benefits that can be derived from this research, in understanding what and how people communicate in particular situations.

We have a special interest in how Twitter is used by citizens during extreme circumstances, and the authors of this chapter form part of a Ph.D. supervisory team that looks at the use of Twitter during infectious disease outbreaks. The overall aim of the Ph.D. project is to gain a better understanding of the types of information that was shared on Twitter during the 2009 Swine Flu outbreak and the 2014 outbreak. This comparison will allow for the two outbreaks to be compared in regards to any similarities, differences, and trends in how Twitter users respond to infectious disease outbreaks. As the Ph.D. project makes use of Twitter data, we are able to report on the ethical challenges and wider methodological issues that were faced across the conception and design of the study.

Social media are changing the way people communicate, both in their day-to-day lives, but also during extreme circumstances, for example, disasters that may threaten individuals, groups of people, and overall public health in local and regional areas (Merchant, Elmer, & Lurie, 2011). Merchant et al. (2011)

suggested that engaging with, and using, social media platforms such as Twitter may place the emergency-management community in a better position to be able to respond to emerging disasters. As the use of social media has changed the way in which people communicate (Cameron, Power, Robinson, & Yin, 2012), for example, during emergencies, information is now available from the public, and it can be used to inform the situational awareness of emergencies and to help crises coordinators respond appropriately.

Research on Twitter ranges from analyzing tweets related to riots (Procter, Vis, & Voss, 2013), natural disasters (Lachlan, Spence, Lin, Najarian, & Greco, 2015; Mendoza, Poblete, & Castillo, 2010), and crisis events (Gupta, Joshi, & Kumaraguru, 2012; Simon, Goldberg, Aharonson-Daniel, Leykin, & Adini, 2014). The studies in relation to natural disasters have found that Twitter offers a decisive channel of communication between government, emergency responders, and the public during crises (Cameron et al., 2012; Simon et al., 2014).

Although these new information sources will not replace existing sources of information, they can provide a new source of data that potentially could have many applications within emergency management and crisis coordination. Social media can play a role in the pre-incident activity, near real-time notification of an incident occurring, first-hand reports of the impact of an incident occurring, and gauging the community responses to emergency warnings (Merchant et al., 2011).

Twitter has become a data source that can be utilized by emergency services during disasters (Tomer, Avishay, & Bruria, 2015). Twitter data, in comparison with other social media platforms such as Facebook, are more openly accessible and, for a proportion of tweets, can contain valuable meta-data, including geospatial data, such as the precise latitude and longitude coordinates from which a Tweet was posted. These data can be used to provide important aid to those in need during a natural disaster. Moreover, it is now also possible to use these data to monitor political events, disasters, health problems in real time and provide support to people in the location and at the time it is most needed. However, the immediacy of social media research can potentially place participants at risk of greater harm after an event has occurred because of the potential to link Tweets to specific geolocations and individuals. Not all Twitter users are aware that all their posts are public, or that they are available for analysis and scrutiny. Tweets and posts may be quoted by newspapers and other news organizations soon after the occurrence of an event and potentially linked back to individuals. In addition, data from Twitter, and other platforms, are being used by academic researchers to develop a better understanding of how people are using social media in specific circumstances. The issue around whether tweets are public is open to debate and will be further discussed in this chapter.

There are legal and ethical implications to using social media data posted by people who may have been sending tweets while in a vulnerable state of mind, e.g., during a disaster, or health outbreak. For instance, someone tweeting during an emergency may not necessarily realize that their tweet may be being collected and analyzed, either to help coordinate relief activities, or to be reported in a research article. Therefore, it is important for those undertaking social media research to critically reflect on the possible implications of a research project involving social media data to the persons involved in creating or being mentioned in such content.

Instagram, Facebook, and Twitter are among some the most popular places online interactions take place (Chaffey, 2016; Macy, Mejova, & Weber, 2015), though Twitter is one of the most researched platforms in regards to academic research (Weller & Kinder-Kurlanda, 2015)

In terms of the overall structure of this chapter, we first look at the popularity for using Twitter within a research context and some of the key issues that can arise in social media research. Previous work by NatCen and Ipsos Mori will be outlined and related specifically to Twitter. The chapter then outlines a number of academic and industry case studies and highlights issues that can arise in research that uses Twitter data. Finally, the steps and arguments that were made in order to obtain research ethics approval for a Ph.D. project that is using Twitter as a primary source of data are outlined as well as some of the issues that have arisen, as the project is underway.

TWITTER

Twitter reports having 316 million monthly active users, there being 500 million tweets posted per day, and 80% of active Twitter users use a mobile device (About Twitter, n.d.). Tweets contain a wealth of data, and mining these data can provide insight into public opinion and behavior responses in particular situations (Chew & Eysenbach, 2010). Twitter was described by Purohit et al. (2013) as a microblogging platform that acts as a medium for the flow of information where users can post updates and subscribe to other users, known as 'following,' in order to receive updates or microblogs from other users.

It is important to understand the features of a social media platform fully before a research project commences, or is even considered, as these features may have ethical implications that should be considered. For example, although as we indicated in the previous section, people may not be fully aware that their Tweets are publicly viewable, some researchers (Townsend & Wallace, 2016) argue that if a tweet contains a hashtag, then the user tweeting this has intended for their tweet to be visible to a broader audience, and therefore, informed consent is not necessary when reproducing the tweet in an academic article. Purohit et al. (2013) described the key features of Twitter:

- A tweet is a short message also known as a post, status, or microblog from a user on Twitter and which consists of a <140 characters, these tweets may contain updates about user activities, or share useful information.
- Tweets can contain links to web-pages, blogs, etc., and, to avoid lengthy URLs, Twitter users will use condensed versions of URLs which are shortened by external services such as http://bit.ly/
- A hashtag, is denoted by a word preceding with the '#' symbol, (e.g., #EbolaOutbreakAlert). The hashtag is a platform convention for user-defined topics, and which was intended to identify a topic of communication, for example, #Brexit
- The reply feature is platform provided to communicate with the author of a tweet by clicking on Twitter's 'Reply' button in response to a tweet.
- The retweet function forwards a tweet from a user to their followers and this is similar to forwarding an email to one's email contacts, for example. The 'mention' feature acknowledges a user with the symbolic '@' sign, but this does not use the reply platform feature, for example, 'Thanks @userhandle.'
- A new feature implemented after the paper by Purohit et al. (2013) was published is that Twitter allows users to retweet with a comment. Users can now quote a tweet and attach a comment to it, for example, users tweet '[Original tweet]' as @userhandle I agree [@userhandle1 today is a good day]
- A trend also known as 'trending' on Twitter refers to when a topic (a keyword or hashtag) is popular at a specific time. Twitter provides a list of topics that are currently trending for users, based on the frequency of particular hashtag.

There are a number of existing software applications that researchers can use to retrieve data from Twitter such as NodeXL (Smith, Milic-Frayling, Shneiderman, & Mendes Rodrigues, 2010) or Discover Text (n.d.). There are also a number of software applications that are available at no cost such as Mozdeh (n.d.), Chorus (n.d.), or TAGs (n.d.). Data from Twitter can be retrieved at either no cost via the Search *Application Programming Interface*

(API), or at a fee via the Firehose API. The Search API is where the majority of Twitter research has focused, and for those undertaking social media research, it is important to have some understanding of APIs. In simple terms, APIs are '[…] sets of requirements that govern how one application can talk to another,' and they govern how applications can talk to one another by '"exposing" a program's internal functions to the outside world in a limited fashion. This makes it possible for applications to share data and take actions on one another's behalf without requiring developers to share all of their software's code' (*What APIs Are and Why They're Important*, 2013). So for Twitter, this means that it will allow members of the public to create tools that can be used to download data. This effectively enables anyone with an Internet connection the ability to obtain Twitter data. The difference between using a software application that retrieves data for free via the Search API is that the data will not be a complete record of tweets, whereas via a paid API such as the Firehose API, researchers will have a complete record of tweets. The differences, therefore, relate to the amount of data that is retrieved as the Firehose API retrieves almost a complete record of tweets, whereas the Search API provides a sample of tweets.

Twitter is known to attract more research in comparison to other social media platforms such as Facebook. The next section explores some possible reasons for the popularity of Twitter and compares these to that of Facebook.

Popularity of Twitter for Research

Researchers among the New Social Media New Social Science (NSMNSS), an online peer led community, have hypothesized the reasons for why Twitter has attracted more academic research compared with other social media platforms. The NSMNSS network is an online peer led community that was established in 2011 with a small grant from National Center for Research Ethics (NCRM) in order to provide a space for reflective discussions about how working with new forms of data, including social media data, was likely to challenge conventional approaches to social science research (Woodfield et al., 2013).

There are at least five possible reasons for the popularity of Twitter in academic research (Ahmed, 2015a):

1. The Twitter API is more open and accessible compared with other social media platforms. This makes Twitter more favorable to developers creating tools to access data. This consequently increases the availability of

software and online tools to researchers. Facebook data, in comparison, are very difficult to obtain and are only available on an aggregate level for marketing purposes.

2. Twitter makes it easier to find and follow conversations as Twitter has a search feature that allows users to look up tweets, and tweets also appear within Google search results, which makes it easier to locate tweets. Facebook can be considered more of a private platform and not all public posts appear in Google Search results. Facebook also provides users with more privacy controls.

3. Twitter has a strong hashtag culture that makes it easier gathering, sorting, and expanding searches when collecting data. Therefore, Twitter data is easier to retrieve as major incidents, news stories, and events on Twitter tend to be centered on a hashtag. Facebook does have hashtag capability, however, the use of hashtags does not appear to be as widespread as on Twitter.

4. Twitter may be a popular platform due to the attention it can receive from the mainstream media and can attract more research due to its cultural status. Twitter is also widely used by journalists, both to identify newsworthy events as well as to distribute breaking news. In comparison with Facebook, it could be argued that Twitter receives much more media attention because celebrities, politicians, and sports starts often tweet about current events, and some tweets may be controversial and are therefore reported in the news.

5. Many researchers use Twitter themselves and, due to their favorable personal experiences, they may feel more comfortable when they research a more familiar platform. Facebook may be used by academics, however, it is rarely used during conferences in comparison with Twitter.

This list is not intended to be exhaustive but to offer a suggestion of some of the reasons Twitter has surged in popularity.

Key Ethical Issues for Social Media

In this section, we explore some of the key issues within social media research, such as whether social media spaces are private or public spaces, and will explore some of the challenges of obtaining informed consent on Twitter. For example, questions may arise such as: How much weight should assign to the views of social media users as they may not fully comprehend the Terms and Conditions of a social media platform? Is ignorance really a justification for a researcher to override the privacy rights of a user?

Public Versus Private Spaces

The British Psychological Society (2013) in their ethics guidelines for Internet-mediated Research have written that

> In an IMR context, the distinction between public and private space becomes increasingly blurred, however. For one thing, much internet communication is conducted in both a private (e.g., the home) and public (e.g., open discussion forum) location simultaneously. Secondly, in this new medium it is not always easy to determine which online spaces people perceive as 'private' or 'public'; where they might be happy to be observed, or otherwise. To complicate things further, a communication perceived as private at the time (e.g., a posting to a password-protected online discussion group) may become public at a much later date, should the archived information become publicly accessible (as has happened on occasion in the past). (British Psychological Association, 2013, pp. 6–7)

The passage above highlights the lack of clarity over whether an online space is public or private. Certain social media platforms are seen as inherently private spaces, for instance, Facebook, whereas others are seen as public spaces for online communication to take place, for example, Twitter. It is important to note that a key difference between platforms, such as Facebook and Twitter, is that most content that is shared on Twitter is publicly accessible via the Twitter API and/or via data resellers, whereas the majority of Facebook is considered private and that data from Facebook are normally only made available at an aggregate level. The public and private distinctions are important when researching online spaces as in addition to ethical implications the public may react negatively if they feel that researchers are intruding on their privacy. It is also important to note that Twitter profiles and tweets are, by default, set to public visibility and, consequently, Twitter could be considered more of a public space compared to Facebook. However, the extent to which individual users of Twitter are aware of this or moderate their behavior on Twitter to account for this is debatable.

Informed Consent

Traditional conceptions of informed consent may be challenged when using social media data. For example, in our own project looking at infectious disease outbreaks on Twitter, it has not been possible to obtain informed content from users. When researching social media platforms, such as Twitter, researchers may be working with large datasets in which it would be difficult to obtain informed consent from all users that are part of a dataset. Additionally, it may not be possible to reach Twitter users because when they are approached for informed consent via a tweet or a direct message, they simply may not reply or may no longer be maintaining their account. Some of the earliest health-based research on Twitter (Chew & Eysenbach, 2010) analyzed tweets at an aggregate level due to the difficulty of obtaining informed consent. However, it is important to consider thoroughly possible issues around consent as a study on Facebook (Kramer, Guillory, & Hancock, 2014) was criticized for a lack of informed consent (Arthur, 2014; Panger, 2014).

In our own Ph.D. project, we found that it would be very difficult to obtain informed consent from Twitter users to use their tweets. For instance, in one of the case studies that forms part of the Ph.D., which looks at tweets related to Swine Flu from 2009, there are over 7,000 tweets that were analyzed. The first issue was related feasibility, that is, that it would be very labor intensive to individually ask each user whether or not they would to take part in the research. The second issue is that, considering the outbreak occurred in 2009, the rate of potential responses was likely to be low. The users who tweeted in 2009 might have left the platform, or may take a long time to reply, which would fall beyond the scale of the project. Issues over informed consent highlight the need for researchers to work alongside social media companies, for instance, asking users at the sign-up phase whether they are OK with their content being used for research purposes. Or more generally, displaying a pop up that allows social media users to opt of research projects.

Legal Concerns

Twitter's Terms of Service and Privacy Policy are documents that govern how users may access and use the Twitter platform (Weller, Bruns, Burgess, Mahrt, & Puschmann, 2014; Zimmer & Proferes, 2014). By agreeing to Twitter's terms and service agreement, users will consent for their information to be collected and used by third parties (Twitter, 2016a). For example, the privacy policy notes that

> What you say on the Twitter Services may be viewed all around the world instantly. You are what you Tweet! (Twitter, 2016A)

The Twitter terms of service notes that

> You agree that this license includes the right for Twitter to provide, promote, and improve the Services and to make Content submitted to or through the Services available to other companies, organizations or individuals who partner with Twitter for the syndication, broadcast, distribution or publication of such Content on other media and services, subject to our terms and conditions for such Content use. (Twitter, 2016B)

A justification often provided by those working in an academic context with Twitter data with regard to the ethical and legal implications of using data without informed consent is that the reuse of data is permitted by Twitter's Terms and service as well as within the privacy policy. However, it is important to note that the act of scraping tweets or downloading tweets from Twitter's Advance Search will contravene Twitter's Terms and Conditions, therefore, voiding any protection these policies are likely to offer. This procedure would bypass retrieving data from Twitter's APIs and would allow Twitter to see who has retrieved data from the platform. As a consequence, this practice is expressively discouraged by Twitter:

> [...] scraping the Services without the prior consent of Twitter is expressly prohibited (Twitter, 2016B)

Additionally, reproducing tweets but removing user IDs, or altering tweets significantly will contravene Twitter's User Development Policy, which requires tweets to be published in full. However, academic researchers could argue that the policy is frequently breached and that Twitter has never taken any action due to the breaches. This is not to say that Twitter may never take action, nor that they will not take retrospective action, or that doing this is ethical. It is important for researchers to take the time to read user agreements for social media platforms as they govern what practices are permissible and provide guidance on publishing posts. Twitter users may be concerned about who owns tweets and whether users have the right of ownership and copyright of tweets that they post. However, in practice, many tweets would not be considered under copyright law because, in most cases, tweets are not original messages (Shinen Law Corporation, n.d.). Therefore, researchers may need to act 'more ethically' than other investigators for professional reasons. Moreover, this also highlights the power of social media platforms whom not only control access to data but whom also dictate how results of research projects are presented. For that reason, there is a definite need for researchers to engage with social companies for academic use of data.

PREVIOUS WORK

A NatCen Report

A report published by NatCen Social Research examined users' views toward research using social media, this was split across four focus groups, two paired, and two one-to-one in-depth interviews. The report found that the views of participants fell into three categories: skepticism, acceptance, and ambiguity. Moreover, they found that the views varied greatly depending on the context within which the research was taking place, and also of the participant's knowledge and awareness of social media websites (Beninger, Fry, Jago, Lepps, Nass, & Silvester, 2014).

Beninger et al.'s study also found that participants expressed concern about the quality of social media research and that these concerns were grouped under the research principles of validity and representativeness (2014). More specifically, the concerns related to four key points:

1. Those who post online may behave differently when they engage with social media platforms compared with how they behave in real life.
2. Views on social media platforms may be more exaggerated due to the anonymity afforded by online communication. Therefore, any research findings which use social media data may lead to inaccurate conclusions of a topic of study.
3. Comments that are posted on social media websites may be impulsive and may not necessarily reflect a participant's viewpoint when in a more measured state of mind.
4. Social media profiles may not always be accurate and without any further context they may lead to inaccurate information and findings.

In their report, Beninger et al. (2014) suggested that traditional ethical principles such as consent, anonymity, and avoiding undue harm should also be applied to social media research. Moreover, participants provided reasons for and against upholding the principles of informed consent and anonymity. With regard to those who felt that consent and anonymity are unnecessary, two chief reasons were provided. First, it was noted that the responsibility falls on end users to decide on how privately to post and whether to post at all. Second, it was noted that as long as the site owners make it clear that social media posts may be public, as well as the level of their being public, then consent and anonymity are unnecessary. Twitter is a platform where, by default, posts are set as public, and it could be argued that the responsibility falls on the end users to alter the settings of their accounts if they wish them to be more private.

With regard to those participants who felt that informed consent was necessary, there were nine reasons, as described below (Beninger et al., 2014):

• It is morally and legally required
• To promote trust between the researcher and the participants
• When researchers are quoting a username alongside a social media post

- When a post is no longer recent, it was noted that it would be important to ascertain whether the participant still holds the same view
- When researchers seek to publish photographs or other images
- If a social media post is considered particularly sensitive and/or personal
- In order to ascertain whether a user intended to post publicly
- If the social media post would be used to generate a profit
- In order for users to determine both the quality and purpose of the research

In terms of the users who thought that anonymity is required on social media platforms, there were at least three key reasons. First, participants felt that this was particularly necessary when informed consent was not gained. Second, some felt that anonymity is needed in order to avoid harm including judgments and/or potential ridicule. A third reason that participants felt that anonymity is needed was to preserve and/or protect personal or professional reputations.

Overall, it was found that there were at least four factors that would influence participants' views and expectations related to informed consent and anonymity, depending on the context of the research. The four factors identified consisted of the following:

- The mode and the content of the post that would also include written content, any photographs appended to social media posts, and also the sensitivity of the content
- The platform being researched because certain platforms are seen as more private (Facebook) than others (Twitter)
- The expectations users may have when posting to a particular social media platform
- The nature of the research including the organization the researcher is affiliated to along with the purpose of the research

Beninger et al. (2014) summarized a number of suggestions for improving research practices by drawing on discussions with participants. They noted that these suggestions should not be taken as rules and may not always be appropriate in all circumstances, but that they can be considered in the design stage of studies that use social media data. Table 1 from Beninger et al. (2014) outlines a number of suggestions for improving research practices.

Looking more specifically at examining the recommendations above in relation to Twitter, for recruitment, researchers could be more transparent by indicating that they are academic researchers on their Twitter biographies. Researchers could also include a link to their academic page, and examples of previous work. It may also be a good idea to ask whether users are happy

Table 1. Suggestions for Improving Research Practices:
From Sampling to Reporting.

Research stage	Aim	Activity
Recruitment	To appear legitimate, accommodate different user types and be transparent in your purpose and aims in order to ethically recruit participants to online and social media research.	• Ask the preferred mode of communication once a participant is recruited • Approach possible participants over the platform being used in the research (rather than email) • Be transparent in recruitment materials. Consider including your affiliation, web link to verify your idea (e.g., biography on organizational website), aims • Explicitly state the security and privacy terms in recruitment materials of the platform the research will involve • Explain where you obtained a participants contact details (i.e., Searched Facebook for public profiles) • Include a link to a company webpage; examples of previous work; transparent about research aims
Collecting or generating data	To improve representativeness of findings, and to understand the privacy risks of a platform used in a study in order to uphold protection and trust of participants.	• Recognizing differing views on what is legally permitted to be collected compared to what some may consider their intellectual property • Take time to consider the openness of a platform you are using and whether steps can be taken to gain trust of users (i.e., if a closed chatroom consider introducing yourself and state your research purposes and ask participants to opt into your research) • Acknowledge the different ways users engage online, how they create, share and observe, and how your data may include a specific view or type of user

Table 1. (*Continued*)

Research stage	Aim	Activity
Reporting results	To protect the identity and reputation of participants, maintain their trust in the value of the research and contribute to the progression of the field by being open and honest in reporting.	• Testing the traceability of a tweet or post and taking responsible steps to inform the user and to protect their identity, if desired. Options include paraphrasing instead of verbatim or using quote but no handle/user name. • Where reasonable, seek informed consent to use verbatim quotes, images, or video such as through direct tweets • Acknowledging limitations of the representativeness and validity of your findings • Explicitly stating the platform used (i.e., from Facebook rather than generally saying social media)

Recreated in Microsoft Word from Beninger, A. K., Fry, A., Jago, N., Lepps, H., Nass, L., & Silvester, H. (2014). *Research using social media; users' views.* NatCen Social Research. [Online] Retrieved from http://www.natcen.ac.uk/media/282288/p0639-research-using-social-media-report-final-190214.pdf\nhttp://www.natcen.ac.uk. Accessed on 28 November 2015.

to be contacted via Twitter, or whether they would like to be contacted using a different communication platform. In regards to collecting or generating data, it will be important to carefully consider whether any tweets contain content that has copyright restrictions and/or which has implications for intellectual property. Moreover, on Twitter academics may wish to consider how Twitter users engage with the platform, for instance, whether this is in a public or private capacity. Researchers may also wish to see whether there are methods of Twitter users opting into the research before it begins. In regards to reporting results researchers may wish to anonymize tweets and to search for the tweet in Twitter's advance search to ensure the user is not findable. It would also be advisable to state the social media platform used and to report on the limitations in regards to the representativeness of the data.

An Ipsos Mori Report

As a part of the Wisdom of the Crowd project, an ethical review was conducted on large-scale, aggregated analysis of social media data some-times termed as 'social listening' (Ranco, Aleksovski, Caldarelli, Grčar, &

Mozetič, 2015). In order to develop the report, three types of research were conducted. First, the authors conducted a survey online of 1,250 adults aged between 16 and 75 which sought to develop a better understanding of how people perceived the use of social media data for research, as well as how useful social media research can be. Second, three qualitative workshops were conducted in which participants discussed how social media content could be used and 'the principles of ethical social media research' (Ranco et al., 2015, p. 9). The third type of analysis was a statistical analysis of the survey.

The report itself focused on three key stages:

1. Secondary research – a review of the current literature related to social media research was conducted along with the ethical, legal, and regulatory implications.
2. Primary research – interviews and discussions were held with experts and users in order to better understand issues raised at stage one.
3. The final stage of the project sought to develop a set of 'best practice' recommendations by combining findings from stages 1 and 2.

The first two recommendations related to increasing awareness of social media research in order to build trust with the public. The first recommendation was that researchers should aim for transparency when doing research that involves social media analysis. When it is possible, details of the research project should be provided online with an outline of whose data is going to be collected, as well the purposes for which it will be used. The second recommendation stated that social media companies should ensure that they continue to review their terms and conditions in order to simplify the possible uses of the data. Twitter makes its data open and accessible to anyone with an Internet connection, and anyone is able to build large datasets of tweets for marketing purposes. However, this may not be known to Twitter users, and this information may also be forgotten. A further recommendation could be for social media companies to remind Twitter users that their data may be accessed and used by third parties.

Recommendations three to five were based on the option of opting out (Ranco et al., 2015) of social media research. This recommendation argues that researchers should ensure that there are systems in place that allow users to opt-out of specific social media research. For instance, having the ability for members of the public to submit their email address, or user id, in order to be excluded from social media research which is being conducted by an organization. They recommended that research organizations would need to work with analytics platforms. This recommendation could be difficult to achieve in practice because social media companies may be unwilling to give an option to opt out of social media research.

Recommendations six to seven were based on 'minimizing unnecessary personal data collection' (Ranco et al., 2015, p. 14), that is, researchers should question whether the extent to which the data they are collecting are necessary for a research project. The recommendation also suggested that researchers should remove names, or user handles from sight, strip out any other identifiable data, remove metadata which are not relevant for a project, create generalized groupings, and to develop specific metrics to analyze data rather to rely on standard algorithms. This is a particularly valid recommendation toward research on Twitter because, often, social media analytics tools are capable of retrieving vast quantities of meta-data. A further suggestion would be for software developers to develop mechanisms of selecting the metadata to retrieve and metadata should be left out.

Recommendations eight to ten were based on not including anyone under the age of 16 in their research social media (Ranco et al., 2015). This is because, currently, there is no method of removing minors, that is, those under the age of 18, from social media research. This recommendation stated that researchers should derive the age of social media users from the content that they post. This is a perfectly valid recommendation; however, there would be clear issues over the reliability and accuracy of such an approach, and an approach that would be very labor intensive.

Recommendations 11–16 were based around 'permission for publication' (Ranco et al., 2015, p. 16). Specifically, these recommendations concerned some of the following:

• Projects on social media must consider whether there is really a need to publish posts verbatim and projects that desire to display verbatim text should gain approval from an internal ethics review.
• Researchers should contact individual social media users if they would like to cite their posts in their original format.

Additionally, it was recommended that regulatory bodies should try to formulate clearer definitions of brands on social media. For example, some people may reasonably expect that those who have relatively large social media followings would expect to have less privacy than those who have a smaller following. Currently, some social media platforms prohibit the altering of posts at the publication stage. Here, it was also recommended that social media organizations should alter their developer guidelines in order to provide researchers with the flexibility of altering the social media content, in order to anonymize Tweets and prevent their being used in search engines to identify users.

Recommendations 17–18 were based on the definition of 'private' and note that that it is the responsibility of researchers to ensure that they have a good understanding of whether data that have been collected are public or private. Here, it was noted that analysis of private content should be approved via an internal ethics review. This recommendation is only likely to apply to Twitter research if private accounts or Direct Messages were to be studied.

Recommendation 19 was based on 'establishing ethics reviews for social media research' (Ranco et al., 2015, p.17). It was noted that social media companies should provide clarification on whether users are happy with privately shared data being used for research. Moreover, it was noted that researchers should try to understand the potential harm to participants and to identify possible steps that could put in place in order to meet user expectations and to also protect users from harm.

Academic and Industry Perspectives

In an academic setting, it is widely considered a cornerstone of research integrity and research quality to have considered the ethical implications of research, especially within the fields of social research. Bryman (2008) noted at least three areas of ethical concern that must be considered: informed consent, invasion of privacy, and the risk of deception (Bryman, 2008). He also noted that, within social research, consideration must also be given to legal aspects of holding personal data on others, such as the UK Data Protection Act (1998) or, for that matter, European or international directives. Higher educational organizations may well have a dedicated research ethics committee or Institutional review board that could offer guidelines regarding research ethics. Research may need to pass through a research ethics committee, whose role it is to protect research participants from potential harm, institutions from potential negative attention and reputational risk, as well as the researchers themselves. All of these principles apply to social media research because, essentially, the majority of content on online spaces such as Twitter is curated by people, with the exception of organizational, news, and automated Twitter accounts.

Broadly speaking, industry perspectives on social media research and research ethics may differ from that of academic research. In industry, it is rare to find research ethics committees, and there is more of a focus around the legality of the research being undertaken, and whether the users have shared posts publicly. It is important to note that while an individual researcher or organization may have met their legal obligations, the ethical concerns may still persist, and these should not be considered in isolation of each other. One of Twitter's revenue streams is via the reselling of its data to third parties, and these data are often used by advertisers to target users with products. Therefore, public posts may be considered by some to be 'fair game,' because analytical tools for analyzing social media data are readily available. To provide an example of some of the differences between academic and industry research, we can examine the #SpeakBeautiful campaign launched by Dove. An advertising campaign, called #SpeakBeautiful, saw Dove enter into a partnership with Twitter in order to send nonautomated responses to negative tweets which were sent by women with the aim of empowering the users in order for them to speak with 'more confidence, optimism and kindness about beauty online' (Nudd, 2015). Dove and Twitter may argue that Twitter data are publicly available, and that users check a terms and conditions tick-box when registering for Twitter. However, boyd & Crawford (2012) noted that, for academic researchers, it is not sufficient to state that using social media data is ethical just because the data are accessible.

The next section outlines two further case studies based on anonymized accounts of real research projects. These case studies hope to highlight that it is not possible to take a fixed position in relation to research on Twitter as different projects will have different aims and study different phenomena. However, it will be possible to identify patterns and principles that cut-across social media research in the case studies outlined below.

CASE STUDIES

Case Study 1 – Analyzing Mentions of a Terrorist Group

Imagine a study wished to understand better how users talk about terrorist organizations by analyzing hashtags in support, and against, the organization. It might be decided that the topic of interest is of a highly sensitive nature because if the tweeters were identified, it could place them at risk of serious harm, for example, from people or organizations with opposing views. There are issues over protecting the anonymity of the participants, and issues over informed consent, and whether there is likely to be any under

18 years that would be tweeting. Due to the immediacy of the research, it could also pose a security threat. It could be argued that the research should not take place at all, as the risks of the research might outweigh any benefits. If a research project of this nature were to go ahead, then the anonymity of the participants must be protected, the analysis performed should be of an aggregate nature, and data must be stored securely. In such cases, direct quotes should not be utilized as these could compromise the anonymity of Twitter users. Additionally, the method of analysis should aim to uphold the anonymity of Twitter users, and examine the themes that emerge from the data and report on aggregated trends without drawing attention to individual Twitter users. There would also be issues over publishing the dataset of tweets; however, according to Twitter's terms of service agreement, it is not possible to share datasets. However, sharing tweet Identification Numbers (IDs) is permissible, and this is particularly useful for academics as it allows research to be reproduced. However, the researchers in this case may not wish to release tweet IDs due to the potential risk of harm.

Case Study 2 – Examining Correlations of Followers

Imagine another proposed study that seeks to examine the correlations between the number of Twitter followers a company has and its worth on the stock exchange. The project would not collect Twitter data in itself, but would examine the number of followers a particular organization had. This case study is distinct from the previous case studies in that the researchers are not retrieving data generated by human participants. This is one of the major ethical debates in social media research, that is, identifying what counts as a human subject (Metcalf & Crawford, 2016).

It is important to note that not all research on Twitter will analyze the content of tweets, because Twitter has over 20 metadata fields. Research on Twitter, for instance, has been used to predict when to buy or sell stock corresponding to whether there has been a peak in tweets (Ranco, Aleksovski, Caldarelli, Grčar, & Mozetič, 2015). There may be data that has recorded how a user engages with Twitter, for instance, their likes, shares, retweets, followers and so forth. Regardless of whether a research study would make use of tweet content, there would still be issues over informed consent, and how the results were likely to be used and perceived by Twitter users. In this particular case study, there would be ethical issues on how the result would impact the organization.

Case Study 3 – Using Network Visualizations to Analyze a Hashtag
Relating to Sensitive Topics

Imagine a further study that seeks to use a popular network visualization tool in order to analyze a hashtag dedicated to particular views on sensitive topics, for example, abortion and sexuality. There are two versions of the visualization, an online and an offline capability. In the online visualization, Twitter users would be fully identifiable and their tweets would be visible via an interactive interface. The tweets and users would be clustered based upon their opinions, which may draw attention to individuals who may otherwise be lost in a crowd. Furthermore, the online version of the network visualization would display the Twitter handles of the individuals, whereas the offline network visualization would produce a network graph where users would be identifiable, but which would have the functionality of anonymizing Twitter users. In both the online and offline capabilities, there are issues over protecting the anonymity of the participants, and issues over informed consent, and whether there is likely to be any under 18 years that would be tweeting. In an academic context, it would be advisable to use an offline version to produce the network visualization and to only identify users who would have consented for their Twitter ID, and tweet, to be identified as holding a position within the network. This is because although the users tweeting using a particular hashtag would understand that their tweets may reach a larger audience, this is a sensitive area and could have a potentially negative impact on participants.

There have been some real-life examples of controversies regarding the use of social media data, as illustrated below.

Samaritans Radar Application

The Samaritans Radar Application was an online application which was designed to monitor tweets on Twitter matching a specific set of keywords such as 'kill myself' or 'end it all' (Lee, 2014). The application was designed to then send an alert if it was to spot anyone who may have been struggling to cope. The application marketed itself by suggesting that it gave Twitter users a second chance in seeing tweets that may have been missed (Lee, 2014; Samaritans Radar, 2016).

When news broke of the release of the application on Twitter, there was a large negative reaction with Twitter users being concerned about their privacy. Samaritans released a number of announcements noting that there was a Whitelist that could prevent tweets from being monitored. Another announcement noted that the app was in development for over a year and had been tested with a number of user groups from young people with mental health issues, Samaritans' volunteers, social media platforms, and other organizations. They also noted that they had worked with academic experts from the Universities of Glasgow and Cardiff on the project.

Further issues were raised over data protection laws, and whether the app would act as a data controller. Samaritans sought legal advice and argued that they would not act as a data controller, or processor of information. Moreover, they argued that, even if they were judged to be a data controller, they would be exempt from data protection laws. Those on Twitter felt that their online community i.e., their safe space to share honest thoughts and feelings had been breached.

Despite the reassurances offered by the Samaritans Radar App, shortly after its release (9 days), the application was suspended, and Samaritans offered a full apology alongside a support page for anyone whom had been negatively affected by the launch of the application. Ultimately, Twitter users believed that collecting and sharing their data without their express permission infringed their right to privacy. This case study highlights the importance of understanding how users view their privacy on online spaces. Lee (2014) noted that a lesson could be learned by those whom may develop similar apps in the future to ensure that their testing groups will reflect the wider Twitter ecosystem. Moreover, this case study highlighted the issues that, although tweets can be accessed publicly, Twitter users could expect a certain level of privacy when engaging on the platform.

Facebook Emotion Study

An experimental study sought to exclude certain elements from 689,003 peoples' news feed that were around 0.04% of all Facebook users during a week in 2012 (Arthur, 2014). The experiment manipulated two groups of Facebook users to assess whether their emotional states, which were measured by posting behaviors, would be affected by the emotional expressions of others (Arthur, 2014; Kramer et al., 2014). Kramer (2014), an author of the paper wrote in a Facebook post, in defense of the paper, that

> We felt that it was important to investigate the common worry that seeing friends post positive content leads to people feeling negative or left out. At the same time, we were concerned that exposure to friends' negativity might lead people to avoid visiting Facebook.

The study received a lot of negative publicity because of the methods that were used by the researchers. In particular, this concerned the decision related to not approaching participants for informed consent. Some researchers argued that consent was not necessary as the study was unlikely to cause significant harm to participants, and that the study was important contribution to developing new knowledge (Kleinsman & Buckley, 2015).

Facebook displays advertising on its platform that attempts to alter people's buying habits by trying to make them buy a product and/or service from advertisers; this is part of Facebook's business model. However, users may know that the adverts that they see are targeted and come to expect this from a free service. Conversely, in this context, users were affected without having prior knowledge or giving informed consent. This case study, at the very least, highlighted the need to consider whether a particular type of social media research will require informed consent.

Common Themes across Case Studies

There are a number of cross-cutting themes across the case studies that have been outlined, and these issues may need to be considered when undertaking social media research. For example, in case study 1 and case study 3, the central issue was based on the risk of harm to social media users. This is because if users were identified mentioning a terrorist group and/or a sensitive topic, then they may be at an increased risk of harm from those who may hold opposing views. In case study 2, an issue that was highlighted was related to the difficulty of identifying whether a study contained human participants. The final two case studies related to the Samaritans Radar Application and the Facebook Emotion study that highlight how issues of informed consent can arise in social media research. The purpose of outlining these distinct case studies was to highlight how even among different topics it would be possible to identify patterns and principles that cut-across social media research.

ETHICAL PRACTICALITIES FOR A RESEARCH ETHICS APPLICATION FOR THE UNIVERSITY OF SHEFFIELD

The authors of this chapter form part of a team that is undertaking a novel Ph.D. study that is using Twitter data related to infectious disease outbreaks as a primary data source. The research team obtained research ethics approval in accordance with the research ethics policy at the University of Sheffield (https://www.sheffield.ac.uk/polopoly_fs/1.112642!/file/Full-Ethics-Policy. pdf). This section outlines the steps and arguments that were made in order to obtain research ethics approval.

Initial Steps

The team proposed in the ethics application that data on Twitter could be considered to be public because anyone with Internet access can access content on Twitter. There is no need to subscribe, enter a password, or pay to access the data. One of the first questions raised was whether ethics approval was required for the project because, seemingly, Twitter data were in the public domain.

It was noted that ethical approval was required because the data are generated by people, and individuals may be identifiable from the data. In addition, when the data related to infectious disease outbreaks are analyzed issues may emerge from the data that could draw attention to groups, individuals, and trends. This would be beyond what would normally be expected from engagement on these platforms. For example, someone who was in conversation with another user on Twitter may tell a joke about Swine Flu believing that it would eventually disappear. In addition, people may post tweets when they are under distress, for instance, while experiencing an infectious disease, believing for their post to have disappeared, or simply having forgot about it.

Potential Participants

The application stated that all captured and relevant tweets would be analyzed, that is, those relating to relevant epidemics and pandemics or other health-related topics. These tweets could be posted by any user with a Twitter account, for example, anyone from the general public or from an organization. It was decided that tweets from public figures with Twitter accounts would not be examined intentionally; however, their tweets may co-incidentally be a part of the data captured. Tweets with geographical locations (geotag data) would only be analyzed at an aggregate level. It was also made clear in the application that Tweets with geographical locations would not be used to identify individual users.

Informed Consent

In the project, it was decided that it would not be practicable to gain informed consent to analyze tweets as a sample of tweets may contain in excess of a hundred thousand items. However, during the analysis of tweets, it may become apparent that tweets from a user or a set of users were of particular interest. In this case, if it would be useful to quote the content of the user(s) verbatim, for example, for the purpose of reporting and substantiating the results, or for the user IDs to be indicated, for example, in the Ph.D. thesis or in a publication, then informed consent would be sought retrospectively. In the case of Twitter, this would involve sending a tweet to the user with details of the study and requesting permission to quote their Tweet.

However, it was noted that it may be difficult to obtain consent via participant information sheets and consent forms as users may not wish to reveal their email address or click on links to participant information sheets and consent forms. Therefore, in this situation, it was argued that it may be necessary to accept a Tweet or saying 'Yes' or similarly suggesting that quotes from the Tweet could be used. In some instances, the researcher may have to gain consent via a Tweet, email, etc. The application noted that one of the researchers had a public Twitter account that could be used for this. However, in order to gain consent electronically, it was argued that the researcher would ensure that the person giving consent was the rightful owner of a Twitter account.

The research project, although having procedures in place for quoting tweets in research, as outlined above, took the ethical standpoint of not quoting tweets or disclosing nonpublic usernames, unless with the permission of the user. The reason for taking this decision is that those users tweeting, although they may be doing so in a public space, may not be aware that their tweets are being used for academic research. Although Twitter's terms and conditions state that user data may be redistributed or used for other purposes, a survey once found as few as 18% of users may actually read terms conditions agreements (Zimmer & Proferes, 2014).

Potential Harm to Participants and Data Confidentiality

With regard to data confidentiality and back-up, it was noted that data would be kept on two secure password-protected laptops alongside a university backed-up secure research server. Individual tweets would not be published without informed consent. In the case of Twitter's hash tag(s), generated by users for an infectious disease outbreak, there was the possibility of identifying participants through de-identification techniques, that is, by searching for the hashtag using a search engine and locating participants. It was argued that, if this was to occur, the risk to the end users would be low as the captured data did generally not fall under the category of being a highly sensitive topic, unless it related to the health of an individual, for example, suffering with the Ebola Virus Disease.

Data Storage

Related to the above, the ethics application outlined who would have access to the data and how they would be stored. It was decided that the lead researcher would have control of, and act as the custodian for, the data captured from Twitter (note this is not the same as being the data controller, as defined under English law). The analysis of the data would be conducted by the lead researcher and would take place in the researcher's place of study and home. It was argued that the data would not be analyzed in places deemed as public. The data would be stored on two password protected laptops, which themselves would be stored securely when not in use. The ethics application also noted that certain data might need to be shared with the supervisors for marking or for administrative use.

Issues Encountered

In addition to a number of ethical issues that were faced, there were also legal considerations, issues surrounding the retrieval of datasets, issues around cost of data, and dealing with tweets that were spam or fictitious accounts. It is important to understand the limitations of Twitter data, and the issues below also have implications for conducting, these challenges are described below (Ahmed, 2015b):

1. As highlighted in this chapter there were a number of ethical issues that we encountered around obtaining informed consent due to the large volume of tweets that were retrieved for the project. Moreover, as mentioned earlier, we also faced specific moral challenges related to whether we could publish tweets in publications that refer to user handles that can identify Twitter users. We decided not to gain informed consent from Twitter users, but with the proviso of not reporting user-handles and/or tweet verbatim. Tweets that were reported in the results were carefully reworded.

2. We had to consider legal issues, that is, the sharing of Twitter datasets is prohibited by Twitter's API Terms of Service (Twitter, 2012). However, we found that we could release tweet *Identification Numbers*, when required, so that other researchers could retrieve a similar dataset. We were also transparent with the date of retrieval for the data that we collected. As to allow other researchers the ability to retrieve data from a similar time period.

3. We were aware that there was likely to be missing data at the point data retrieval, for instance, when retrieving data using the keyword 'Swine Flu,' this would only retrieve data from users whom had used that specific keyword. If a user sent out a tweet that mentioned Swine Flu, without using the keyword, our data retrieval system would miss this. Issues around data retrieval have potential to lead to a biased sample, and this can also occur by the choice of language.

4. We also faced issues over the cost of data, as historical Twitter data can cost a lot of money depending on the query terms used to retrieve data as well and the time period of data retrieval.

5. There is also the issue of representivity as Twitter users are not representative of the national offline population. Further than this, Twitter users are not representative of Internet users, and Twitter data are not representative of Twitter users. This is because not all users will tweet about a topic of interest, such as, Swine Flu and those that do will belong to a very specific group of users.

6. On Twitter we found that there was a lot of spam such as link-baiting which occurred in popular hashtags. Moreover, we also found that there were a lot of fictitious accounts on Twitter, and we are aware that celebrities, politicians among others are likely to purchase retweet, favorite or user packages to increase their brand presence. This type of content and accounts are likely to affect the validity and reliability of results.

CONCLUSION

This chapter has provided an overview of existing literature in order to inform those whom may be undertaking social media research. It then outlined a number of industry and academic case studies in order to highlight the challenges that may arise, and finally it provided an overview of the steps that were described to gain ethics approval for a Ph.D. project using Twitter as a primary source of data. An advantage of using Twitter data for academic research is that it may be possible to retrieve data at a faster rate than it might take to run a survey or a series of interviews.

Emerging news stories, crisis events, and political discourses, for example, can all now be studied almost as soon as they occur. Researchers are now able to examine reactions or sentiments to most major events via social media data without the need to worry about the accuracy of participant's memories in recalling how they felt during an event. Therefore, social media research can be said to avoid one of the central problems facing qualitative research: chiefly that of interviewer bias (McKee, 2013).

However, although social media as a source of data may have benefits over traditional qualitative research data, as highlighted throughout this chapter, it brings with it its own challenges. There are a number of overlapping ethical and methodological issues to social media research that must be carefully considered, and researchers must reflect on whether data from social media platforms can sufficiently address the research question of a project.

REFERENCES

About (n.d.). *About Twitter, Inc.* [Online]. Retrieved from https://about.twitter.com/company. Accessed on 29 March 2016.

Ahmed, W. (2015a). [Online]. *Using Twitter as a data source: An overview of current social media research tools LSE Impact of Social Sciences blog.* Retrieved from http://blogs.lse.ac.uk/impactofsocialsciences/2012/04/19/blog-tweeting-papers-worth-it/ 10 July 2015. Accessed on 11 July 2015.

Ahmed, W. (2015b). [Online]. *Challenges of using Twitter as a data source: An overview of current resources LSE Impact of Social Sciences blog.* Retrieved from http://blogs.lse.ac.uk/impactofsocialsciences/2015/09/28/challenges-of-using-twitter-as-a-data-source-resources/ 28 September 2015. Accessed on 11 July 2015.

Arthur, C. (2014). [Online]. Facebook emotion study breached ethical guidelines, researchers say. *The Guardian.* Retrieved from https://www.theguardian.com/technology/2014/jun/30/facebook-emotion-study-breached-ethical-guidelines-researchers-say. Accessed on 11 August 2016.

Beninger, A. K., Fry, A., Jago, N., Lepps, H., Nass, L. & Silvester, H. (2014). Research using social media; users' views. *NatCen Social Research.* [Online]. Retrieved from http://www.natcen.ac.uk/media/282288/p0639-research-using-social-media-report-final-190214.pdf. Accessed on 28 November 2015.

boyd, D., & Crawford, K (2012). Critical questions for big data. *Information, Communication and Society*, *15*(5), 662–679.

British Psychological Society (2013). [Online]. *Ethics guidelines for internet-mediated research.* Retrieved from http://www.bps.org.uk/system/files/Public%20files/inf206-guidelines-for-internet-mediated-research.pdf. Accessed on 02 October 2016.

Bryman, A. (2008). *Social research methods. Social research* (Vol. 3). doi:10.4135/9781849209939

Cameron, M. A., Power, R., Robinson, B., & Yin, J. (2012). Emergency situation awareness from twitter for crisis management. *Proceedings of the 21st International Conference Companion on World Wide Web – WWW '12 Companion*, ACM Press, New York, NY (p. 695). doi:10.1145/2187980.2188183

Chaffey, D. (2016). Global social media research summary. 2016. Retrieved from: http://c.ymcdn. com/sites/www.productstewardship.us/resource/resmgr/Phone_Books/Global_Social_ Media_Statisti.pdf. Accessed on 30 September 2017.

Chew, C., & Eysenbach, G. (2010). Pandemics in the age of Twitter: Content analysis of tweets during the 2009 H1N1 outbreak. *PLoS ONE, 5*(11), e14118.

Chorus. (n.d.). *Project site for the Chorus Twitter analytics tool suite*. [Online]. Retrieved from http://chorusanalytics.co.uk/. Accessed on 11 December 2016.

Discovertext.com, (n.d.). [Online]. Retrieved from https://www.discovertext.com/. Accessed on 15 December 2016.

Golder, S. A. & Macy, M. W. (2014). Digital footprints: Opportunities and challenges for online social research. *Annual Review of Sociology, 40*(1), 129–152.

Gupta, A., Joshi, A., & Kumaraguru, P. (2012). Identifying and characterizing user communities on Twitter during crisis events. *Proceedings of the 2012 Workshop on Data-Driven User Behavioral Modeling and Mining from Social Media* (pp. 23–26). doi:10.1145/2390131.2390142

Kleinsman, J., & Buckley, S. (2015). Facebook study: A little bit unethical but worth it? *Journal of Bioethical Inquiry, 12*(2), 179–182.

Kramer, A. D. I. (2014). [Online]. [*Untitled Facebook post, June 29, 2014.*] Retrieved from https: //www.facebook.com/akramer/posts/10152987150867796 Accessed on 14 August 2016.

Kramer, A. D. I., Guillory, J. E., & Hancock J. T. (2014). Experimental evidence of massive-scale emotional contagion through social networks. *Proceedings of the National Academy of Sciences, 111*(24), 8788–8790.

Lachlan, K. A., Spence, P. R., Lin, X., Najarian, K., & Del Greco, M. (2015). Social media and crisis management: CERC, search strategies, and Twitter content. *Computers in Human Behavior*. doi:10.1016/j.chb.2015.05.027

Lee, N. (2014). The Lancet Technology: November, 2014. *The Lancet, 384*(9958), 1917.

Merchant, R. M., Elmer, S., & Lurie, N. (2011). Integrating social media into emergency-preparedness efforts. *New England Journal of Medicine, 365*(4), 289–291.

Metcalf, J., & Crawford, K. (2016). Where are human subjects in big data research? The emerging ethics divide. *Big Data and Society, 3*(1), 1–14.

Macy, M., Mejova, Y. & Weber, I. (2015). *Twitter : A digital socioscope*. New York, NY: Cambridge University Press.

McKee, R. (2013). Ethical issues in using social media for health and health care Research. *Health Policy, 110*(2), 298–301.

Mendoza, M., Poblete, B., & Castillo, C. (2010). Twitter under crisis. *Proceedings of the First Workshop on Social Media Analytics – SOMA '10*, New York, NY: ACM Press (pp. 71–79). doi:10.1145/1964858.1964869

Mozdeh (n.d.). *Mozdeh Twitter Time Series Analysis*. [Online]. Retrieved from http://mozdeh. wlv.ac.uk/. Accessed on 14 January 2016.

Nudd, T. (2015). [Online]. *Dove and Twitter team up to address hateful tweets about beauty on Oscar Night*. AdWeek. Retrieved from http://www.adweek.com/news/advertising-branding/dove-and-twitter-team-address-hateful-tweets-about-beauty-oscar-night-163040. Accessed on 02 October 2016.

OECD. (2016). [Online]. *Internet access (indicator)*. Retrieved from https://data.oecd.org/ict/ internet-access.htm. Accessed on 14 August 2016. doi: 10.1787/69c2b997-en.

Panger, G. (2014). *Why the Facebook experiment is Lousy social science. Medium.* Retrieved from https://medium.com/@gpanger/why-the-facebook-experiment-is-lousy-social-science-8083cbef3aee#.xxqym5ltd. Accessed on 14 December 2016.

Procter, R., Vis, F., & Voss, A. (2013). Reading the riots on Twitter: Methodological innovation for the analysis of big data. *International Journal of Social Research Methodology, 16*(3), 197–214. doi:10.1080/13645579.2013.774172

Purohit, H., Hampton, A., Shalin, V. L., Sheth, A. P., Flach, J., & Bhatt, S. (2013). What kind of #conversation is Twitter? Mining #psycholinguistic cues for emergency coordination. *Computers in Human Behavior, 29*(6), 2438–2447. doi:10.1016/j.chb.2013.05.007

Ranco, G., Aleksovski, D., Caldarelli, G., Grčar, M., & Mozetič I. (2015). The effects of Twitter sentiment on stock price returns. *PLoS ONE, 10*(9), e0138441.

Samaritans Radar (2016). [Online]. *Samaritans.org.* Retrieved from http://www.samaritans.org/ how-we-can-help-you/supporting-someone-online/samaritans-radar. Accessed on 02 October 2016.

Shinen Law Corporation. (n.d.). *Twitterlogical: The misunderstandings of ownership.* [Online]. Retrieved from http://www.canyoucopyrightatweet.com/. Accessed on 08 October 2016.

Simon, T., Goldberg, A., Aharonson-Daniel, L., Leykin, D., & Adini, B. (2014). Twitter in the cross fire — The use of social media in the Westgate Mall terror attack in Kenya. *PloS ONE, 9*(8), e104136. doi:10.1371/journal.pone.0104136

Smith, M., Milic-Frayling, N., Shneiderman, B., Mendes Rodrigues, E., Leskovec, J., & Dunne, C. (2010). NodeXL: A free and open network overview, discovery and exploration add-in for Excel 2007/2010.

Tomer, S., Avishay, G, & Bruria, A. (2015). Socializing in emergencies – A review of the use of social media in emergency situations, *International Journal of Information Management, 35*(5), 609–619. Retrieved from http://www.sciencedirect.com/science/article/pii/ S0268401215000638. Accessed on 07/10/16.

Townsend, L., & Wallace, C. (2016). [Online] *Social media research: A guide to ethics.* The University of Aberdeen. Retrieved from http://www.dotrural.ac.uk/socialmediaresearch-ethics.pdf. Accessed on 15 August 2016.

Twitter. (2012). *Twitter / Twitter terms of service. Twitter.com.* Retrieved from https:// twitter.com/ tos. Accessed on 02 October 2016.

Twitter. (2016a). [Online]. *Twitter privacy policy. Twitter.com.* Retrieved from https:// twitter.com/ privacy. Accessed on 02 October 2016.

Twitter. (2016b). *Twitter. Twitter terms of service. Twitter.com.* Retrieved from https:// twitter.com/ tos. Accessed on 02 October 2016.

Weller, K., Bruns, A., Burgess, J., Mahrt, M., & Puschmann, C. (Eds.). (2014). *Twitter and society.* New York, NY: Peter Lang.

What APIs Are And Why They're Important. (2013). [Online] *Readwrite.* Retrieved from http:// readwrite.com/2013/09/19/api-defined/. Accessed on 02 October 2016.

Woodfield, K., Morrell, G., Metzler, K., Blank, G., Salmons, J., Finnegan, J., & Lucraft, M. (2013). Blurring the Boundaries? New social media, new social research: Developing a network to explore the issues faced by researchers negotiating the new research landscape of online social media platforms. NCRM Paper. NCRM.

Zimmer, M., & Proferes, N. (2014). Privacy on Twitter, Twitter on privacy. In S. Jones (Ed.), *Twitter and Society* (pp. 55–67). New York, NY: Peter Lang.

CHAPTER 5

GETTING TO YES: INFORMED CONSENT IN QUALITATIVE SOCIAL MEDIA RESEARCH

Janet Salmons

ABSTRACT

When a study involves human participants, researchers need to ensure their safety and protect their identities. How do potential participants know what they are agreeing to contribute, and how and why the research is being conducted? Informed consent describes the process and agreements that answer such questions. Conventional consent protocols focused on presearch discussions between the researcher and the potential participant, resulting in a signed document that verified the agreement. In research conducted with, on, or through social media, there are fewer opportunities for conversational explanations of formal documents. Simply posting legalistic documents is ineffective because Internet users typically do not read such materials before verifying agreement. Researchers need to understand communities, contexts, and communication styles of target participants and settings in order to provide information in familiar, user-friendly ways. Based on a review of literature about informed consent, and a study of current practices used by companies that need to verify agreements online, practical research suggestions are offered. Qualitative researchers who

The Ethics of Online Research
Advances in Research Ethics and Integrity, Volume 2, 109–134
ISSN: 2398-6018/doi:10.1108/S2398-601820180000002005

want to collect data through active interactions with human participants will find these examples and recommendations of use when designing their studies.

Keywords: Human participants; informed consent; research ethics; ethical online research

INTRODUCTION

There are many ways to collect data in, with, or through social media – and some entail interacting directly with individuals or using their personally identifiable information. No matter how many posts we read or how rich the archives or databases, sometimes we need to dig more deeply into the back stories and probe perspectives of the users. We need a trustworthy answer from the person behind the screen.

For such studies, informed consent is typically required by regulatory bodies, academic institutions, or research funders. Informed consent might be recommended by professional societies serving the discipline and associated journals, or by professional standards. This chapter will explore challenges and opportunities for qualitative researchers who due to one or more of these reasons, must inform human participants about the nature of the study and potential risks, and document agreements before the study can proceed. Such researchers have goals similar to those of software, application, and platform providers who must confirm customers' willingness to accept terms of service. Examples from research and software communities are surveyed to determine respectful and effective ways to use online tools to inform participants and make sure that they understand how their information will be used.

CONSENT WITH HUMAN PARTICIPANTS IN SOCIAL MEDIA: DEFINING KEY TERMS

While research characteristics vary across professions and disciplines, and procedures for reviewing and approving research proposals vary across countries, the definitions of terms used in discussions of ethics and consent are remarkably consistent. (See suggested readings at the end of this chapter for links to ethics guidelines, from the United States, Europe, the United Kingdom, South Africa, Australia and Canada, and from national and international professional societies.) Terms used throughout this chapter are defined here to provide a common language for discussing ethical decision-making related to informed consent.

Social Media and Social Networking

Social media refers to the online places where we engage in *social networking*.

> The term **social media** refers to websites, online platforms or applications that allow for one-to-one, one-to-many, or many-to-many synchronous or asynchronous interactions between users who can create, archive, and retrieve user-generated content. (Salmons, 2014)

Social media allows users to define and create groups, lists or circles of 'friends' or 'followers' who have access to content and can participate in dialogue. In social media, the user is producer; communication is interactive and networked with fluid roles between those who generate and receive content (Bechmann & Lomborg, 2013). In this chapter, I describe these activities as 'social networking.'

Communications possibilities differ depending on the social media platform. Many-to-many crowd features, one-to-many, and one-to-one communications characterize most social media platforms. Some include synchronous and asynchronous modes. Individuals can synchronously chat using text messaging or video conferencing. Asynchronous communications include posting to discussion threads or boards for friends or the public to see and discuss, or leaving personal notes to individuals, whenever they login. In addition to written communications, social media sites encourage exchange of visual material, including drawings, photographs, graphics, and/or video. All of these forms can be harnessed for communication with participants throughout the study.

Human Participants

The definition for the term *human participant* used in this chapter was drawn from the US Common Code (HHS, 2005), and further explained by the University of Washington Human Subjects Division ('Does Your Research Involve Human Subjects,' 2012):

> A human participant is a living individual about whom an investigator conducting research obtains (1) data or samples through intervention or interaction with individual(s), or (2) identifiable private information.

Living means that the subject is alive at the time of the research, according to applicable local and national regulations.

About whom means the data or information relates to the person. Asking individuals what they think about something is almost always about the person.

Intervention includes both physical procedures by which data are gathered, and manipulations of the subject or the subject's environment that are performed for research purposes.

Interaction includes communication or interpersonal contact between investigator and subject.

Identifiable the identity of the subject is or may readily be ascertained by the investigator or associated with the information.

Private information includes information about behavior that occurs in a context in which an individual can reasonably expect that no observation or recording is taking place, and information which has been provided for specific purposes by an individual and which the individual can reasonably expect will not be made public.

For our purposes, the human participant is the person on the other side of the monitor, the 'user' with a mobile device who is typing on the keyboard, chatting on a video call, or uploading images or files (Salmons, 2016b). The human may be represented or expressed online by graphic representations or avatars, pseudonyms or screen names.

Informed Consent

A comprehensive definition of informed consent was articulated by the UK Economic and Social Research Council (ESRC), with additional details from the European Commission:

Informed consent entails giving sufficient information about the research and ensuring that there is no explicit or implicit coercion so that prospective participants can make an informed and free decision on their possible involvement. Information should be provided in a form that is comprehensible and accessible to participants, typically in written form (or in a form that participants can access after the end of the research interaction), and time should be allowed for the participants to consider their choices and to discuss their decision with others if appropriate. The consent forms should be signed off by the research participants to indicate consent. (ESRC, 2015, p. 29)

[I]nformed consent is meant to guarantee the voluntary participation in research and is probably the most important procedure to address privacy issues in research. Informed consent consists of three components: adequate information, voluntariness and competence. This implies that, prior to consenting to participation, participants should be clearly informed of the research goals, possible adverse events, possibilities to refuse participation or withdraw from the research, at any time, and without consequences. Research participants must also be competent to understand the information and should be fully aware of the consequences of their consent. Although informed consent is often seen in the context of clinical research, this principle is important for all types of research, including the social sciences. (EC, 2013, p. 13)

The term *informed consent* is often used generally to describe both the process researchers engage in to ensure that individuals are informed about the study and the record verifying their consent to participate in the study. Important elements of the agreement include adequate information, as well as assurance that the individual is competent to agree and will do so voluntarily.

Adequate information. To state the obvious: if participants were not informed, they did not authentically consent. About what exactly do researchers need to inform participants? It is beneficial to the researcher, as well as the participant when they both understand and agree to expectations for the type, timing, setting, and duration of the interaction. Participants should also know how resulting data and findings will be used.

Participants should be informed of any foreseeable risk or discomfort, including that harm, loss, or damages that could occur, including physical, psychological, social, economic, and/or legal risks (Owens, 2010). The potential harm for participants in social sciences and the humanities are, in general, more subtle than those associated with medical or other types of research. Harms may be of a psychological nature and/or linked to how cultures and/or and ethnicities are represented in the community (Romare & Collste, 2015). Risks related to technology-oriented types of research studies are largely informational, primarily from the inappropriate or inadvertent disclosure of information and not from the research interventions themselves (HHS, 2017, p. 7152).

Participants should also be informed about any benefits from making a contribution to scientific knowledge; tangible benefits for the participants (i.e., food, money, and medical/mental health services); insight, training, learning, role modeling, empowerment, and future opportunities; psychosocial benefits (i.e., altruism, favorable attention, and increased self-esteem); kinship benefits (i.e., closeness to people or reduction of alienation); and community benefits (i.e., policies and public documentation) (Owens, 2010, p. 603).

Voluntariness of Participation and Competence to Agree

Potential participants must freely and voluntarily agree to the conditions and expectations of the study. Research participants should be made aware of their right to refuse participation for whatever reason they wish and withdraw from the study without penalty or repercussions (BSA, 2002, p. 3). Researchers should clarify the point at which it will not be feasible to withdraw because analysis and/or publication. (This is a requirement for those researchers under the aegis of the European Commission.)

Individuals must be free to choose to participate without substantial influence, coercion, or control by others, including the researcher. Researchers need to demonstrate that they will treat individual participants as autonomous agents who can decide for themselves whether and to what extent they wish their personal information and interactions to be studied (Stern, 2009). Voluntary consent also means the signatory is capable of providing consent, and is of legal age, and if not, parental consent was acquired.

Certainly, many components of a consent agreement for an online study are comparable to agreements for studies carried out face-to-face. People are people, and deserve the same respect whether they talk in an office or chat on social media. However, a consent agreement for online research additionally answers questions specific to characteristics of the online setting or communications technology. For example, a study that involves collecting images or artifacts must address ownership and permissions not needed in text-only data collection. If the researcher intends to use a webcam, avatars, or other special tools or applications, the expectations should be clearly spelled out in the agreement discussion and form.

SOCIAL MEDIA AND QUALITATIVE RESEARCH: GENERATING DATA THROUGH INTERACTIONS WITH CONSENTING PARTICIPANTS

Negotiating Consent

Qualitative researchers use interviews, focus groups, participant observation, narratives and diaries, written questionnaires, and arts-based and creative methods when they interact with human participants. Researchers can use the interactive capabilities of social media to carry out such data collection online – and we will explore some examples later in this chapter. Whether the person meets with, talks to, chats or texts, or plays games with the researcher, whether the person writes about, photographs, or draws responses to the researcher's prompts or questions, they are human participants. Is the researcher's responsibility to take care in designing the study and to communicate how this individual will be protected from harm when voluntarily consenting to participate in the research.

Researchers seeking informed consent need to make clear to potential participants what material they will collect and how material about them and/or from them will be used. In addition to data collected in a direct interaction between the researcher and the participant, it is essential to include in the consent discussion any potential use of material the participant has posted on the social media site(s). To err on the side of ethical research behavior, participants can be given the option to disallow online profiles, images, or other specific material they have posted on social media pages to be used as data.

Possible topics to negotiate include the types of quotations or paraphrases that might be drawn from interview narratives, as well as the kinds of publications or presentations the researcher intends to develop after analyzing the data. Additionally, how participants' identities will be protected is a critical part of information they need to understand before signing an agreement.

Not surprisingly, in online research, the researcher often carries out these consent negotiations online. The shift from a paper agreement discussed and signed in person to an online agreement submitted electronically is more complex than it may appear. In person, a researcher can perceive whether the individual is uncomfortable, and offer reassurance. The researcher can take extra steps to build rapport and make sure any concerns have been addressed. Researchers cannot assume that by simply posting a consent agreement and collecting a signature or other verification means the participant read and understood it. Even when follow-up information is offered, the participant may be reluctant to contact the researcher.

Users of software and social media are familiar with agreements posted online. They have learned how to move through as quickly as possible to find and tick the box that allows them to proceed to the desired activity. Savvy users might scan the agreement for specific items related to privacy or data sharing with third-party vendors, but most will simply scroll and click. This is not the kind of 'agreement' process that could satisfy the needs of the ethical researcher. The ethical researcher wants more than a tacit approval, because we need to know the participants' preferences in regard to the ways we will communicate during the study, the types of data we can collect in online interactions with participants, what ways we can use it, as well as how and where we can publish it. We must go beyond simply informing participants of the study essentials; we need to establish credibility and trust with participants so they will complete the steps needed to collect quality data.

These obstacles have been widely recognized, but with quickly changing technology and usage patterns, professional societies, editors, and academics review boards have had a difficult time determining the best approaches and developing explicit guidelines. Trevisan and Reilly (2014, p. 1133) suggest that 'discipline-grounded ethical reflexivity' can help researchers plan and respond to complex research situations. Similarly, the Association of Internet Researchers Guidelines (2012) advocate a 'bottom-up, case-based approach to research ethics, one that emphasizes that ethical judgment must be based on a sensible examination of the unique object and circumstances of a study, its research questions, the data involved, the expected analysis and reporting of results, along with the possible ethical dilemmas arising from the case' (Lomborg, 2013, p. 22).

Experienced researchers may have the judgment necessary to adapt established approaches into ethical designs for research using social media, and proposals that can be approved by the relevant oversight bodies and accepted for publication. However, as the noted in the RESPECT Code of Practice for Socio-Economic Research, 'carrying out socioeconomic research in an ethical manner involves balancing a number of different principles which often lie in tension with each other' (*RESPECT Code of practice for socio-economic research*). Student and novice researchers are often caught between vague and changing sets of rules that insufficiently address issues unique to the digital environment and conventionally minded research ethics reviewers who do not understand what the researchers are doing and why.

Intrepid online researchers are developing innovative ways to verify agreement with participants. Their examples offer legitimization of this emerging field, and models for others to use as the basis for their own reflexive development of ethical values. By exploring the specific issues and ethical questions associated with online inquiry and ways to address them, this chapter recommends well-founded approaches to use when obtaining consent for studies that involve recruiting and collecting data from human participants.

Credibility, Trust, and Consent

The informed consent form or letter formalizes study participation. A signature on the consent agreement 'serves as a proxy indicator of the participant's trust in the researcher' (Rallis & Rossman, 2012, p. 64). In an online study researchers and participants typically do not meet, and participants may not be familiar with the academic institution or agency, the researcher represents.

All research needs to demonstrate the trustworthiness of the researcher (Bulpitt & Martin, 2010), but in online research, it is critical to success. If a potential participant searches for the researcher's name and does not discover evidence of scholarship, it will be difficult to build trust in the research project. As Reich discovered, online sleuthing can go both ways:

> I was surprised to learn that after sending invitations to participate in my study, potential participants were quick to research me before responding. Skepticism of research and researchers is well described when studying elite populations (Ostrander, 1993); however, technology will has made it much easier for potential subjects to scrutinize researchers. As they contacted me, they often mentioned they had already reviewed my earlier research, read my book online, or checked my university credentials to see if I was fair and could be trusted. (Reich, 2014, p. 400)

Researchers can learn from Reich's experience and make an effort to convey messages that will demonstrate trustworthiness to potential participants so they are confident the researcher will be respectful, protect anonymity and data, and observe stated parameters for what data will be collected, and how it will be used. Cassell suggested that researchers and participants are doing 'identity work' because we intentionally use our identities to present ourselves in a way that is appropriate to the study (Cassell, 2005).

Online identity awareness is especially important for new researchers, who may need to put in extra effort to create a separate online identity associated with the study – apart from personal and social identities, researchers can create an online space and email account dedicated to the research. Depending on the nature of the research and likely interest of research population, this could be a blog or page(s) on social networking sites, or series of media clips. Links to the researcher's academic institution or other publications can convey integrity and authenticity of the researcher. Alternatively, the researcher can offer webinars or host online discussions about issues related to the study to build a scholarly reputation. When potential participants search for the researcher and find evidence that verifies the authenticity of the study, they may, hopefully, be more inclined to sign the needed agreements and contribute meaningfully to the study

Beyond the Agreement Document

Importantly, the signature (whether physical or electronic) even in the case of direct communication with participants, as is the focus of this chapter, is not the end of communication between researcher(s) and participants in online research. Stanford University explicitly states that 'obtaining written informed consent from a potential participant is more than just a signature on a form' ('Human subjects research and IRB,' 2016). Stanford (2016) advises its researchers to use the consent document 'as a guide for the verbal explanation of the study' and the 'basis for ongoing meaningful exchange between the researcher and the participant' (p. 2).

Too often, universities and other sponsors of research weight the focus almost entirely on a formal informed consent agreement that must be signed before the study can proceed with participants. This preresearch practice is sometimes called an 'anticipatory review.' An anticipatory focus may not be well suited to online research, which does not always proceed according to a preset plan (Miller, Birch, Mauthner, & Jessop, 2012). Miller points out that anticipatory review can make ethics approval a 'curiously disconnected facet of a research project's life' (Miller, 2012, p. 30). This perspective emphasizes the importance of an iterative process throughout the study (Guillemin & Gillam, 2004; Miller, 2012). That said if the research design or proposal is not approved because consent is not verified before data collection begins, the researcher will not have the opportunity to observe how the issues unfold. To avoid this dilemma, it is essential for researchers to make every effort to consider possible dilemmas that could involve participants and taken steps needed to ensure they are protected from undue risk.

VERIFYING AGREEMENTS ONLINE: CHALLENGES AND LESSONS FROM TECHNOLOGY USER AGREEMENTS

Software, applications, and membership-oriented sites typically ask users to verify agreement with terms of service, privacy, data use, and other policies. The End-User Licensing Agreement (EULA) is important to those who are selling products, services, or access to privileged information. Like a research consent agreement, the commercial enterprise wants to verify that the user is aware of the particular expectations, and at the same time, they want to protect themselves from liability, legal actions, as well as from negative messages from unhappy customers distributed over social media. Software companies have funds, legal advisors, and staff, and can allocate to the development of effective agreements. What can researchers learn from them?

Two of the most common types of EULAs are called *clickwrap* and *browsewrap* (Brehm & Lee, 2015). Brehm and Lee explain that

Clickwrap agreements require a user to affirmatively click a box on the website acknowledging agreement to the terms of service, which are often available in a scrolling text box, before the user is allowed to proceed. Browsewrap agreements have hyperlinked terms of use that are typically found on a separate webpage, which the user does not have to visit to continue using the website or its services. (para 4)

Since browsewrap agreement verbiage exists on another page, the company can change the agreement without the knowledge of prior users – a step considered unacceptable in the European Union (Webber & Rubin, 2011). To ensure that the EULA can be enforced in Europe, the recommended approach is to include a link to the EULA and require an affirmative 'click-accept' of the EULA when the app is first opened by a user on his or her device to demonstrate that the EULA was accepted (McLean & Wells, 2016). Similarly, courts in the United States have upheld clickwrap or click-through agreements but have ruled on number of cases that no contract is formed between the parties using a browsewrap approach since no action needs to be taken by the user to indicate agreement to the terms (Brehm & Lee, 2015). In a 2001 case in England, the Law Commission concluded that clicking on a website button can demonstrate consent to the terms of an agreement in a commercial transaction (Webber & Rubin, 2011). In the European Union E-commerce Directive (2000/31/EC), Article 9 states that any kind of agreement (including EULAs) can be validly concluded electronically (Webber & Rubin, 2011).

In some online situations, a hybrid approach is used, that is, the user must click to agree to terms in order to proceed, but the terms of agreement are not immediately visible. To be available, the user must click to read them on a separate screen. While this makes team inconvenient, asking the user to take an action that demonstrates 'constructive assent' is a critical factor.

Brehm and Lee (2015) recommend that

- There is a check-box that users must click adjacent to an affirmation similar to, 'By clicking on the box, you are indicating that you have read and agree to the Terms of Use.'
- The webpage is designed so that if the user does not check the box manifesting assent to the terms, the user cannot proceed in the transaction.
- In addition to a check-box that users must click, the terms of use are available either in a nearby scrolling text box or a nearby hyperlink.
- Any hyperlink of the terms is obvious, for example, 'Terms of Use' is underlined and has decent size lettering and visible coloring (not small lettering and not obfuscatory coloring).

Legal issues aside, will users read and understand the materials before they check to verify their agreement? Further, while a clickwrap approach might work on a website or blog where users are accustomed to reading text, it might not be feasible for researchers to present text-heavy agreements if they are researching in a visually oriented virtual world or game. Kunze (2008) studied EULAs or terms of service agreements (TOS) in such environments. He observes that

> These agreements are typically extremely long, and use more legalese than plain language. Because EULAs are written poorly, the user will not comprehend the terms or understand what he is agreeing to, and thus is unlikely make a rational, informed choice regarding his virtual world selection and participation. Ultimately, given the length of the document and the confusing language, most readers abandon reading these agreements altogether. (p. 109)

To promote more careful reading of agreements, Kunze recommends concise, plainly written agreements that customers can understand (Kunze, 2008). Chee, Taylor, and de Castell (2012) underscored this point:

> Can we agree about the role of agreements? When one clicks 'I Agree' after being presented with what is often a dense, multiscreen wall of prose, to what is one really agreeing? What are the implications of obtaining this type of agreement as a condition of participation in online communities in virtual world games and play? (p. 497)

Chee et al. (2012) conducted small qualitative studies to establish 'a kind of barometer' about how much of the EULA participants read before playing a game in a virtual world, and to what extent they understood them. Not surprisingly, only 3% said they read the entire agreement (Chee et al., 2012). While the participants had not taken the time to review the agreement, when Chee et al. asked them a question about one of the provisions of the agreement – access to their data by a third-party – a majority said no. Written comments made in notes to the researchers echoed Kunze's (2008) points: the EULA should be simpler and easier to follow and read. Chee et al. raise a critical point:

> [If] anyone who has clicked through from the software installation screens into the game is now a 'consenting research subject,' albeit one with no voice, no right to clearly explained information about how and by whom and for what purposes one's information will be used, and no right to withdraw without loss. (p. 504)

In such situations does the user want to play the game or operate the application, agreement is the only option available to the user.

Moran, Luger, and Rodden also explored alternatives to the clickwrap style of consent for ubiquitous computing systems. Moran et al. see the checkboxes as inadequate 'due to their focus on a single moment of consent, which is a concept that seems out of place in large scale, dynamic, real-time and complex information systems' (2014, p. 636). A challenge they point to is that the operation of these systems is hidden from users' view, behind the interface the typical user sees. Users may know that information is being collected about them behind the screen, but since it is not obvious, they may not grasp the extent of the risks involved. To make the invisible understandable so users make a real choice when consenting, Moran et al. (2014) advocate using short animated visuals to illustrate the significance of users' choices. They also recognize that users have different skill sets and abilities to understand technologies, meaning users have different thresholds for when they can be deemed adequately informed (p. 638). Tools exist that allow companies to provide dynamic content, for example, 'allowing the provision of more comprehensive descriptions on how the technology works to technical users, whilst having simpler framings for non-technical users' (Moran et al., 2014, p. 638).

Kay and Terry similarly pointed to the value of visual means of consent, through 'narrative pictograms, illustrative diagrams designed to convey the abstract concepts of software agreements' (2010, p. 2175). Kay and Terry worked from the assumption that visuals have the advantage over written agreements because they do not require the ability to read English-language documents (and do not require software companies to translate documents into diverse local languages). The study showed that participants understood the agreements best when the pictograms were complemented with text.

Waddell, Auriemma, and Sundar studied the effect of a paraphrased EULA and forced-exposure EULA, as compared with traditional EULA, on users' attitudes, attention, and comprehension (2016, p. 5252). In the paraphrased EULA, the terms were displayed using the large fonts, bullet-point statements and practical, nonlegal language. The forced-exposure option required participants to scroll through not only the entire page of conventional style but also before the terms of service could be accepted. A typical click-through agreement was the third option. The findings showed that

> the paraphrased EULA elicited more positive attitudes and longer exposure times than the traditional EULA. Furthermore, our results show that attitudes and EULA comprehension were positively related. By comparison, the forced exposure condition did not affect EULA attitudes or comprehension relative to control. (p. 5255)

The findings of this small study point to not only more time spent on the clean graphic style used in what is called the paraphrased agreement, but importantly, participants also demonstrated more understanding of its meaning.

The examples presented here show that while more research is certainly needed about comprehension and concurrence with EULAs, those studying this dilemma agree to some common recommendations:

- The click-through or clickwrap approach is not effective, without other considerations for the way the content is presented.
- Written information should be presented using clear, simple language in a concise format.
- Visuals, whether graphic design of text-based information or the use of pictures and diagrams, promote comprehension.

How do scholarly and social researchers who need to convey consent agreements to participants avoid creating documents that do not achieve the goal of informing participants?

THE ONLINE CONSENT PROCESS AND SCHOLARLY SOCIAL SCIENCE RESEARCH

When studies are conducted online, researchers may look for alternatives to the paper-and-pen form of agreement and consider the same options as software developers. The clickwrap versus browsewrap distinction is present in the noncommercial world of social research.

In the CITI module used to train the US researchers in Internet research ethics protocols, the clickwrap type of online form is noted as an acceptable approach (Hicks, 2011). Participants can be asked to indicate agreement with a check box ('I accept') in an email returned online to the researcher or on a Web form posted on a research forum or site (Markham, Buchanan, & Committee, 2011). Researchers intending to ascribe to institutional rules might use a browsewrap type of an approach with a link to the agreement found on the researcher's or the institution's website. Given what we have learned about the mixed success of clickwrap options, are they a viable solution for scholarly and social science researchers?

Instead of making the mistake of expecting potential participants to read, digest, and sign long and complex agreement forms, online researchers may want to use the visual, interactive communication styles common online to inform and engage potential participants. In Fig. 1, Dr. Bowser used a blog post with embedded link to an interactive questionnaire to achieve consent with participants for an online study.

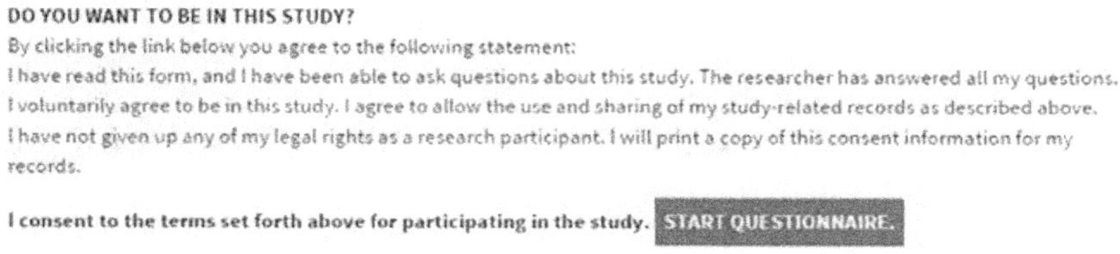

DO YOU WANT TO BE IN THIS STUDY?

By clicking the link below you agree to the following statement:

I have read this form, and I have been able to ask questions about this study. The researcher has answered all my questions.
I voluntarily agree to be in this study. I agree to allow the use and sharing of my study-related records as described above.
I have not given up any of my legal rights as a research participant. I will print a copy of this consent information for my records.

I consent to the terms set forth above for participating in the study. START QUESTIONNAIRE.

Fig. 1. Clickwrap Consent for Online Social Research.

To ensure that all materials describing the study, including all of the implications of the consent agreement, are understood, the researcher may want to provide the information in multiple formats. Rowbotham et al. suggests that options enable participants to hear, view, or read the consent form at their own pace (Rowbotham, Astin, Greene, & Cummings, 2013, p. 1). Do you will how researchers are putting new ethical approaches into practice when conducting studies in social media?

AUTHENTIC INFORMED CONSENT IN ONLINE INQUIRIES: A FEW EXEMPLARS

The first example, 'How Consumers Persuade Each Other: Rhetorical Strategies of Interpersonal Influence in Online Communities,' (Scaraboto, Rossi, & Costa, 2012) demonstrates a thoughtful process for obtaining consent to collect observational data from an online discussion group on a social networking site. Drawing on the Netnography methods described by Kozinets and Herring (Herring, 2007; Kozinets, 2010), Scaraboto et al. (2012) organized the study in four stages: (1) defining the field, (2) entering the field, (3) collecting data, and (4) analyzing data (p. 252). As the first stage, they tried to define the field and narrow down the community best suited to the study. They conducted what they termed 'unobtrusive observation' on a number of online communities that fit the study's criteria. They did not request permission or consent in these communities because they did not interact or collect data. Through this process, they identified a suitable research site. Next, to enter the field of this community they reviewed the community's norms, functions, and styles of participation that allowed them to have a meaningful dialogue with the community owner and obtain consent.

Once a consent agreement was signed with the community owner, Scaraboto et al. (2012) posted a note on the discussion board describing the research project and requesting the consent of all members to collect data for academic purposes (pp. 252–253). This thread was left open and stuck to the top of the forum throughout the period of observation on the site, in essence as an opt-out choice. No concerns or negative responses from community members were registered. The researchers were accessible to members of the community and could answer any questions and address any concerns that emerged over the course of the study (pp. 252–253). Researchers took the time needed to build trust and cooperation with the community owner and used the conventions of the group to interact with its members, rather than expecting group members to grasp academic conventions.

The second exemplar also used a two-stage process of unobtrusive observation followed by a request for consent. In the article 'Online Facebook Focus Group Research of Hard-to-Reach Participants' (Lijadi & van Schalkwyk, 2015). Lijadi & van Schalkwyk (2015) presented their research about adults whose childhood included multiple cultural perspectives. In the first stage of the study, researchers visited relevant Facebook discussion groups. They selected groups based on said inclusion criteria. Research information and succinct recruitment messages were posted (p. 3). After reviewing the information, individuals willing to participate sent private messages to the researchers. Researchers followed up with a consent form, a biographic questionnaire, and an invitation to accept a 'friend' request from the researchers (p. 4). While this hybrid clickwrap and browsewrap type of process required multiple steps, again, the researchers adapted to the modes of interaction common to the group, rather than intervening with a process members might have found obtrusive.

The third exemplar demonstrates the possibilities for immersion of the researcher into the research setting. Dr. Jaime Banks is a scholar focused on researching avatars, virtual worlds, and games. Such games are visually oriented, and highly interactive. Text is used minimally, embedded within the visual elements of the game. To conduct a study on *World of Warcraft (WoW)*, Banks used these conventions and stylistic elements such as typical typefaces with lighter text on dark backgrounds to engage potential participants (Banks, 2015c, personal communication). Players were invited to visit this game-like website with informed consent information and a screening survey with items measuring demographics, gameplay habits, and thoughts, feelings, and memories regarding a favorite *WoW* avatar.

To build credibility and establish an identity as a researcher for a study of avatars by interacting within the game, she took the role of an avatar:

> I offered information about my own gaming practices as a way of establishing a bit of familiarity/credibility. Online gamers are a suspicious bunch, which is warranted given the prevalence of hackers/gold farmers and griefers [...] [I posted] a brief bio that included my academic and gaming info (to make myself vulnerable first, so that they'd hopefully feel comfortable with doing it themselves), along with my contact information, personal web site, department site, and academia.edu web site, and then c) a section where they could 'sign up now' by taking the initial survey. (Banks, 2015c, personal communication)

These approaches were successful, and she was able to gain consent for participation in online interviews and use of images from the game:

> Participants were told during the consent process that I would be recording our conversations and that, during the play interview, I would be capturing video and stills of the game interface but would mask all identifying information associated with the avatar. Since there's no way to tell what could happen during gameplay sessions (the world and other players are not predictable), I asked them to complete an addendum following the play interview, disallowing or allowing me to use the images captured in publications resulting from the interviews. (Banks, 2015c, personal communication)

Numerous journal articles and presentations (Banks, 2015a, 2015b; Banks & Bowman, 2014; Banks & Martey, 2015) were based on the successful data collection of this study, and Banks continues to conduct research in and about virtual environments and games.

The fourth exemplar shows a way to use social commenting tools with online consent forms. In the article, 'Social Annotation Valence: The Impact on Online Informed Consent Beliefs and Behavior,' researchers explored the response of potential participants to electronic forms that included comments made by other participants. Balestra et al. recognized that, when researchers and potential participants negotiate agreements online, informal conversations are missing (Balestra, Shaer, Okerlund, Westendorf, Ball, & Nov, 2016). They wondered whether to actually attach it. I don't think it's quite yet but almost is a letter and

> [A] computer-supported social environment could enable individuals deliberating on their consent decision to connect with each other, share information, formulate and evaluate different perspectives, and ultimately understand the risks and benefits of the research beyond the scope of one-on-one dialogue with a research staff member. (p. 197)

People are accustomed to reading the comments of other users of software or applications, or other consumers who are considering or have purchased products online. Balestra et al. wanted to use the same kinds of approach in the consent process by allowing potential participants to read and make comments. The researchers recognized the risk involved when users post, erroneous information in the comments, possibly influencing participants to change their minds about contributing to the study.

Balestra et al. conducted the study to evaluate "participants' perceptions of the extent to which they felt informed when they made their consent decisions, the extent to which they felt that they understood the content of the consent form, and the extent to which they trusted the organization seeking consent" (p. 198). They constructed a social consent form that included comment boxes with social annotations in the margins of the screen. Positive and negative annotations were selected for the study instrument. Balestra et al. found that the consent rate did not change with the use of annotations, however, potential participants reported that they felt more informed, compared to the control group without access to annotations (Balestra et al., 2016).

The fifth example, 'Social media and peer feedback: What do students really think about using Wiki and Facebook as platforms for peer feedback?' Was a mixed methods study that used qualitative and quantitative, online and face-to-face data collection (Demirbilek, 2015). Students completed a written informed consent agreement, after the study was explained, and they were given an option to participate or decline.

Demirbilek (2015) conducted the study with a group of his own students, which allowed him the flexibility to provide training in the specific digital skills needed to carry out the activities he wanted to investigate. He wanted to study how students perceive giving and receiving peer feedback using social media, and whether there are there differences in how students perceive Wiki and Facebook as platforms for peer feedback? He also wanted to understand the students' experiences, benefits, issues, and challenges associated with peer feedback activity through Wiki and Facebook. Demirbilek (2015) asked participants to carry out a series of activities on an assigned platform, either Facebook or on a closed wiki site. In addition to observing their participation during the course of the study, he also collected data with a quantitative online questionnaire, and conducted face-to-face interviews at the conclusion of the project.

LESSONS FROM THE EXEMPLARS

All of these exemplars demonstrate the value of qualitative research with consenting participants, and important lessons can be discerned from the ways the studies were described in the cited articles. A limitation to this analysis is the lack of detailed descriptions for the actual consent negotiation and agreement processes each researcher used.

First, when researchers build in an initial stage to 'define the field,' as Scaraboto et al. (2012) and Lijadi and van Schalkwyk (2015) did, they can observe ways that the target population or demographic groups typically communicate electronically. At this stage, the researchers did not interact with anyone or collect any data – they simply visited sites and opened groups to determine the best setting for their studies. Even so, this stage of the research can inform the researcher's choice of familiar technologies and styles for consent negotiation as well as data collection. It is unrealistic to expect that potential participants will acquire new digital literacy skills in order to access the consent agreement form. Given what can be learned through visiting potential research sites, choices for the consent agreement could include minimizing text and presenting key information related to study participation visually with images, media, graphics, or infographics. Depending on the type of site, and institutional ethics requirements, permission may be needed from the group moderator or owner spelling out the specific activities to be observed.

Second, researchers can learn from Banks exemplar and be attentive to creating an appropriate re identity online in order to build credibility and trust. While Banks created a game avatar, other options include creating a simple website, blog, or page on a social networking site. Banks demonstrated the usefulness of including links to an educational institution, funding agency, or other relevant affiliation, as well as any publications that verify authenticity. At the same time, Banks showed her knowledge of the game and shared personal characteristics that might have helped potential participants realize why she was interested in learning more.

Third, Balestra et al. (2016) demonstrated the use of interaction modes common to the target population, and/or community. This team created a research hub that provided the necessary information in engaging and interactive ways. Other approaches included providing information in smaller increments that allowed the users to click through to the next item once they have read or viewed each segment of information.

Fourth, Demirbilek (2015) showed that social media and social networking activities do not have to be studied in the wild, they can be explored using protected environments with a known group of participants.

SUMMARY

Ethical decision-making, including the consent process, is anything but linear in qualitative research, whether conducted online or face-to-face. It is complex and typically involves multiple stakeholders often with contradictory perspectives. Online researchers must consider not only the protection of consenting participants who may have multiple identities or may voluntarily reveal information about themselves that extends beyond the topics and issues germane to the study. Online researchers also need to understand and respect the cultures and norms of online communities, discussion groups, and other kinds of electronic research settings. (See the relationships illustrated in Figure 2 and considerations for consent laid out in Table 1.)

Researchers who plan to collect data, and ultimately publish findings based on data collected from human participants online are compelled to address a set of inter-related challenges:

- Protecting human subjects and their multiple identities and representations in cyberspace.
- Building trust and credibility. This process may begin with discussion group moderators, online community owners, and other gatekeepers before the researchers are able to reach individual members with recruitment messages.
- Using communication styles, including visuals were media, to inform participants before the study and informing participants during the study. Successful research exemplars demonstrate the value of careful (and sometimes lengthy) observation to learn how individuals interact and the norms and conventions of the site or group. Researchers mirror, to the extent possible, these approaches – rather than expect the participants to adopt the communication styles academic or social researchers might be accustomed to using.
- Researchers must reconcile the requirements and expectations of institutional or ethics review boards with the cultures and norms of the social networking sites or online communities being studied.

Fig. 2.   Online Research Ethics: Interrelated Issues (Salmons, 2017).

ADDITIONAL RESOURCES

Ethics Materials and Guidelines

International:
HHS. (2017). *International compilation of human research standards.* Office for Human Research Protections U.S. Department of Health and Human Services, Washington, D.C.: Retrieved from https://www.hhs.gov/ohrp/sites/default/files/international-compilation-of-human-research-standards-2017.pdf

Africa:
HSRC. (2017). *Code of research ethics.* Human Sciences Research Council, Pretoria: Retrieved from http://www.hsrc.ac.za/en/about/research-ethics/code-of-research-ethics

Australia:
Australian code for the responsible conduct of research. (2007). Retrieved from http://www.nhmrc.gov.au/index.htm

Canada:
TCPS. (2005). *TriCouncil policy statement: ethical conduct for research involving humans.* Canadian institutes of health research, natural sciences and engineering research Council of Canada, social sciences and humanities research Council of Canada, Ottawa: Retrieved from http://www.pre.ethics.gc.ca/archives/tcps-eptc/docs/TCPS%20October%202005_E.pdf

Europe:
EC. (2013). *European Commission: Ethics for researchers.* Retrieved from http://ec.europa.eu/research/participants/data/ref/fp7/89888/ethics-for-researchers_en.pdf

Romare, J., & Collste, G. (2015). *Principles and approaches in ethics assessment human subjects research.* Retrieved from Linköping University: file:///C:/Users/dream_000/Documents/ethics/codes/1.d-Human-subjects-research.pdf

United Kingdom:
ESRC. (2017). *The research ethics guidebook: A resource for social scientists.* London: Retrieved from http://www.ethicsguidebook.ac.uk

ESRC. (2015). *ESRC Framework for research ethics.* Retrieved from http://www.esrc.ac.uk/_images/framework-for-research-ethics-09-12_tcm8-4586.pdf

ESRC. (2015). *Framework for research ethics,* London: Economic and Social Research Council, Retrieved from http://www.esrc.ac.uk/files/funding/guidance-for-applicants/esrc-framework-for-research-ethics-2015

United States:
HHS. (2005). Code of Federal Regulations: Protection of human subjects, Part 46 C.F.R.

Table 1.   Questions to Ask in the Consent Agreement (Salmons, 2016a).

Questions to Answer in the Consent Agreement for Face-to-Face Research	Considerations and Questions Relevant to Agreements for Online Research
• Who is conducting the study: identity of researcher(s)? Is there an affiliation with an institution, agency or a funder?	• Where can a potential participant learn about the researcher and verify that the study is legitimate? Can you include links to the researcher's page or blog that contains credible information about the researcher and the study? Can you include links to any affiliated institution or agency, including contact information for the research supervisor if the researcher is a student?

How can researchers be contacted at any time to answer pertinent questions about the research and the participant's rights?

What is the purpose of the study?

What rights does the participant have to withdraw from the study at any time without penalty?

• Will interactions with the researcher be recorded? How will recordings be protected from distribution?	• Will interactions with the researcher be recorded, saved, or archived online? Will the researcher download original files for any recordings, interview chat records or posts, and delete them from commercial servers to ensure they are safe from hacking or public release.
• Can the participant review transcripts, images or media collected or generated, and correct information provided?	• Can participants review transcripts or recordings – will you send links or attached documents? Does the participant have the digital skills needed to access materials in this way?
	• How will participants communicate any corrections? By email? Are participants expected to make changes on documents and return them; if these approaches require technology skills the participant does not have, are there alternative ways to convey any requested changes?
• What does the study entail in terms of duration, time commitment, and types of interactions (1–1 with researcher or as part of a group)?	• What does the study entail in terms of duration, time commitment, and types of interactions (1–1 with researcher or as part of a group)? If in a group, how will the individual's identity protected?
	• What types of technologies will be used for communications with the researcher and/or for participant–participant communication associated with data collection activities?
• How will the researcher ensure protection of confidentiality and anonymity of the data?	• How will the researcher ensure protection of confidentiality and anonymity of data collected online? Is personal information contained in metadata?

How will the data be used? Where will findings be published? What procedures will be used in cases of incidental findings?

What are the risks or potential risks associated with participation?

What are potential benefits associated with participation?

Here are some additional recommendations researchers can adapt to the particular needs of the study and the characteristics of the population:

Informing Participants

Before the study:

- Introduce yourself in a friendly, personable way.
- Generate interest in study participation.
- Let potential participants know what you need from them to achieve the purpose of the study. Communicate specifics about time, technology access, or other requirements.
- Reassure potential participants about protection of data, anonymity, etc. Let them know where you plan to publish the results. For example, will the study findings be available to the general public, or to professionals and academics only?

During the study:

- Give timely reminders about follow-up interviews, observations, or member checking steps.
- Address any changes in the study that vary from those in original consent agreement.
- Signal emergent directions such as new questions to discuss in follow-up interviews or observations.
- Reiterate any anticipated uses of data in publications or presentations.

Additional questions to ask when evaluating potential ethical risks in an online study:

- Will the investigator(s) be collecting sensitive information? If so, do additional measures need to be taken to protect the confidentiality of the data through coding, destruction of identifying information, and/or limiting access to the raw data?
- Should documentation of consent be waived to protect confidentiality? If so, what are the requirements of the academic institution or other oversight body?
- Are safeguards in place to protect confidentiality of the participant at all stages of the study, including publication?

- Can the researcher ensure that data will not be used for purposes other than those the participant consented to in the agreement? If the researcher wants to repurpose the data, can the participant be reached to update the agreement?

REFERENCES

Balestra, M., Shaer, O., Okerlund, J., Westendorf, L., Ball, M., & Nov, O. (2016). Social anno-tation valence: The impact on online informed consent beliefs and behavior. *Journal of Medical Internet Research*, *18*(7), e197. doi:10.2196/jmir.5662

Banks, J. (2015a). Multimodal, multiplex, multispatial: A network model of the self. *New Media & Society*, *19*(3), 419–438. doi:10.1177/1461444815606616

Banks, J. (2015b). Object, Me, Symbiote, Other: A social typology of player-avatar relationships. *First Monday*, *20*(2).

Banks, J., & Bowman, N. D. (2014). Avatars are (sometimes) people too: Linguistic indica-tors of parasocial and social ties in player–avatar relationships. *New Media & Society*. doi:1461444814554898

Banks, J., & Martey, R. M. (2015). *Multiphrenic Mages? Examining assumptions of the postmod-ern self in an online gaming context*. Paper presented at the International Communication Association, San Juan, Puerto Rico.

Bechmann, A., & Lomborg, S. (2013). Mapping actor roles in social media: Different perspec-tives on value creation in theories of user participation. *New Media & Society*, *15*(5), 765–781. doi:10.1177/1461444812462853

Brehm, A. S., & Lee, C. D. (2015). 'Click here to accept the terms of service.' *Communications Law*, *31*(1). Retrieved from American Bar Association website: http://www.americanbar .org/publications/communications_lawyer/2015/january/click_here.html

Brehm, A. S., & Lee, C. D. (2015). Click here to accept the terms of service. *Communications Law* (Vol. 31): American Bar Association.

BSA. (2002). *British sociological association: Ethical guidelines*. London: Retrieved from https:// www.britsoc.co.uk/media/23902/statementofethicalpractice.pdf

Bulpitt, H., & Martin, P. J. (2010). Who am I and what am I doing? Becoming a qualitative research interviewer. *Nurse Researcher*, *17*(3), 7–16.

Cassell, C. (2005). Creating the interviewer: Identity work in the management research process. *Qualitative Research*, *5*(2), 167–179.

Chee, F. M., Taylor, N. T., & de Castell, S. (2012). Re-Mediating research ethics: End-User License Agreements in online games. *Bulletin of Science, Technology & Society*, *32*(6), 497–506. doi:10.1177/0270467612469074

Demirbilek, M. (2015). Social media and peer feedback: What do students really think about using Wiki and Facebook as platforms for peer feedback? *Active Learning in Higher Education*, *16*(3), 211–224. doi:10.1177/1469787415589530

Does Your Research Involve Human Subjects. (2012). *UW Human Subjects Division*. Retrieved from http://www.washington.edu/research/hsd/topics/Does+Your+Research+Involve+ Human+Subjects#fed

EC. (2013). *European Commission: Ethics for researchers*. Retrieved from http://ec.europa.eu/ research/participants/data/ref/fp7/89888/ethics-for-researchers_en.pdf

ESRC. (2015). *Framework for research ethics* London: Economic and Social Research Council. Retrieved from http://www.esrc.ac.uk/files/funding/guidance-for-applicants/esrc-frame-work-for-research-ethics-2015/

Guillemin, M., & Gillam, L. (2004). Ethics, reflexivity, and 'ethically important moments' in research *Qualitative Inquiry*, *10*(2), 261–280. doi:10.1177/1077800403262360

Herring, S. (2007). A faceted classification scheme for computer-mediated discourse. *Language@ Internet*, *4*(1), 1–37.

Code of Federal Regulations: Protection of human subjects, Part 46 C.F.R. (2005).

HHS. (2017). *Federal policy for the protection of human subjects*. Washington, DC: Government Publishing Office. Retrieved from https://www.hhs.gov/ohrp/regulations-and-policy/regulations/common-rule/.

Hicks, L. (2011). *Internet research*. Miami.

Human Subjects Research and IRB. (2016). Retrieved from Stanford University: https://human-subjects.stanford.edu/new/resources/consent/

Kay, M., & Terry, M. (2010). *Communicating software agreement content using narrative pictograms*. Paper presented at the CHI 2010, Atlanta.

Kozinets, R. (2010). *Netnography: Doing ethnographic research online*. Thousand Oaks, CA: Sage.

Kunze, J. T. (2008). Regulating virtual realms optimally: The model end user license agreement. *Northwestern Journal of Technology and Intellectual Property*, *7*(Fall), Article 7.

Lijadi, A. A., & van Schalkwyk, G. J. (2015). Online Facebook focus group research of hard-to-reach participants. *International Journal of Qualitative Methods*, *14*(5), 1–9. doi:10.1177/1609406915621383.

Lomborg, S. (2013). Personal internet archives and ethics. *Research Ethics*, *9*(1), 20–31. doi:10.1177/1747016112459450

Markham, A., Buchanan, E., & Committee, A. E. W. (2011). *Ethical decision-making and Internet research: 2011*. Recommendations from the AoIR Ethics Working Committee (DRAFT Document). Retrieved from http://aoirethics.ijire.net/

McLean, S., & Wells, S. (2016). Launching a mobile app in Europe? Seven things to consider when drafting the terms & conditions *Socially Aware: The law and business and social media*, (January 27). Retrieved from http://www.sociallyawareblog.com

Miller, T. (2012). Reconfiguring research relationships: Regulation, new technologies and doing ethical research. In T. Miller, M. Birch, M. Mauthner, & J. Jessop (Eds.), *Ethics in qualitative research* (2nd ed.). London: Sage Publications.

Miller, T., Birch, M., Mauthner, M., & Jessop, J. (Eds.). (2012). *Ethics in qualitative research* (Second ed.). London: Sage Publications.

Moran, S., Lugar, E., & Rodden, T. (2014). *An emerging tool kit for attaining informed consent in UbiComp*. Paper presented at the UbiComp '14, Seattle.

Owens, R. L. (2010). Informed consent. In N. Salkind (Ed.), *Encyclopedia of Research Design* (pp. 603–608). Thousand Oaks, CA: SAGE Publications, Inc.

Rallis, S. F., & Rossman, G. B. (2012). *The research journey: Introduction to inquiry*. New York, NY: Guilford Press.

Reich, J. A. (2014). Old methods and new technologies: Social media and shifts in power in qualitative research. *Ethnography*, *16*(4), 394–415. *RESPECT Code of practice for socio-economic research*. doi:10.1177/1466138114552949

Romare, J., & Collste, G. (2015). *Principles and approaches in ethics assessment human subjects research*. Retrieved from Linköping University: file:///C:/Users/dream_000/Documents/ethics/codes/1.d-Human-subjects-research.pdf

Rowbotham, M. C., Astin, J., Greene, K., & Cummings, S. R. (2013). Interactive informed consent: Randomized comparison with paper consents. *PLoS ONE*, *8*(3), 1–6. doi:10.1371/journal.pone.0058603

Salmons, J. (2014). *New social media, new social science... and new ethical issues!* Retrieved from London: http://nsmnss.blogspot.com/2014/02/new-social-media-new-social-science-and.html

Salmons, J. (2016a). *Doing qualitative research online*. London: SAGE Publications.

Salmons, J. (2016b). Using social media in data collection: Designing studies with the qualitative e-research framework. In A. Quan-Haase (Ed.), *The SAGE Handbook of Social Media Research Methods* London: SAGE Publications.

Scaraboto, D., Rossi, C. A. V., & Costa, D. (2012). How consumers persuade each other: Rhetorical strategies of interpersonal influence in online communities. *Brazilian Administration Review (BAR)*, *9*(3), 246–267.

Stern, S. R. (2009). How notions of privacy influence research choices: A response to Malin Sveningsson. In A. N. Markham & N. K. Baym (Eds.), *Internet inquiry: Conversations about method*. Thousand Oaks: Sage.

Trevisan, F., & Reilly, P. (2014). Ethical dilemmas in researching sensitive issues online: Lessons from the study of British disability dissent networks. *Information, Communication & Society*, *17*(9), 1131–1146. doi:10.1080/1369118X.2014.889188.

Waddell, T. F., Auriemma, J. R., & Sundar, S. S. (2016). *Make it simple, or force users to read?: Paraphrased design improves comprehension of end user license agreements*. Paper presented at the Proceedings of the 2016 CHI Conference on Human Factors in Computing Systems, Santa Clara, California, USA.

Webber, M., & Rubin, L. (2011). Liability matters under end user licence agreements. *E-Commerce Law and Policy*, *13*(04).

CHAPTER 6

THE TROUBLE WITH TINDER: THE ETHICAL COMPLEXITIES OF RESEARCHING LOCATION-AWARE SOCIAL DISCOVERY APPS

Jenna Condie, Garth Lean and Brittany Wilcockson

ABSTRACT

This chapter explores the ethical complexities of researching location-aware social discovery Smartphone applications (apps) and how they mediate contemporary experiences of travel. We highlight the context-specific approach required to carrying out research on Tinder, a location-aware app that enables people to connect with others in close proximity to them. By journeying through the early stages of our research project, we demonstrate how ethical considerations and dilemmas began long before our project became a project. We discuss the pulls toward data extraction/mining of user-generated content (i.e., Tinder user profiles) within digital social research and the ethical challenges of using this data for research purposes. We focus particularly on issues of informed consent, privacy, and copyright, and the differences between manual and automated data mining/extraction techniques. Excerpts from our university ethics application are included to demonstrate how our research sits uneasily within standardized

The Ethics of Online Research
Advances in Research Ethics and Integrity, Volume 2, 135–158
Copyright © 2018 by Emerald Publishing Limited
All rights of reproduction in any form reserved
ISSN: 2398-6018/doi:10.1108/S2398-601820180000002006

ethical protocols. Our moves away from a 'big data' approach to more 'traditional' and participatory methodologies are located within questions of epistemology and ontology including our commitment to practicing a feminist research ethic. Our chapter concludes with the lessons learned in the aim to push forward with research in challenging online spaces and with new data sources.

Keywords: Big data; apps; Smartphone applications; user-generated content; feminist research; data extraction

INTRODUCTION

As digital technologies and new media platforms rapidly emerge, academics rush to research them, ourselves included. The huge volumes of data generated by our everyday digital activities represent opportunities for researchers across many disciplines in the quest for knowledge production and impact. In this chapter, we critically reflect upon the methodological decisions made in designing a research project to explore how location-aware social discovery smartphone applications (apps) mediate contemporary travel experiences. We focus specifically on Tinder, a location-aware smartphone application (app), marketed as a social discovery app that 'empowers users around the world to create new connections that otherwise might never have been possible' (Tinder, 2016a). Tinder is primarily known and used as a dating site where people swipe through profiles of other users in close proximity to them. Given Tinder's prominence and its market positioning for use while travelling (including it's recent 'Passport' feature that enables users to change locations ahead of travelling to a destination), it offers an appropriate research context for understanding how location-aware technologies mediate contemporary travel experiences.

When we first started talking about our Tinder research to colleagues and peers, some found it trivial and perhaps not worthy of serious study. Admittedly, we are perhaps caught up in the rush to research the trending and the popular, but we also 'take Tinder's silliness seriously' (Mason, 2016, p. 4). Tinder has been widely framed within popular discourses as a 'hook up' app designed to facilitate casual sexual encounters, contributing to a supposed 'dating apocalypse' (Sales, 2015). Yet at the same time, 'hook up' apps have become more commonplace and normalized, so much so that they now mean much more than a 'hook up' app (Hsiao & Dillahunt, 2017; MacKee, 2016; Mason, 2016; Sumter, Vandenbosch, & Ligtenberg, 2017). The varied motivations for use such as finding casual and romantic partners, making new friendships, and for entertainment purposes (Sumter et al., 2017), inform our adoption of the broader term 'social discovery' to refer to Tinder and apps that enable new social connections based on locational information. From exploring how newcomers to an area gain social capital (Hsiao & Dillahunt, 2017) to understanding how Tinder functions as a serious relationship app for gay men (MacKee, 2016), 'social discovery' apps now mediate many every-day, ordinary social connections, and can therefore indicate the future of our mobile (location-aware) communications (de Souza e Silva, 2013).

Our journey through the stages of the research project and the ethical deci-sions and pivots along the way reflect our changing epistemological and onto-logical positions as to how to carry out such research and how we understand our topic of inquiry. In theorizing Tinder as a social space and a data source, we demonstrate how user-generated content as data slots uneasily into the standardized ethical protocols to which university research boards and pro-fessional research organizations require adherence. We include an analysis of our university ethics application for this research project and the subsequent amendments submitted as our ethical approach toward the research evolved. This enables us to identify the constraints of University ethics panels on crea-tive and alternative practices across new digital terrains. We conclude with our commitment to a feminist research ethic to ensure that the research we carry out attends to, and addresses, the inequalities of the web. A final aim of this chapter is to offer practical solutions for researchers to push forward with research in challenging online spaces and new data sources.

WHEN RESEARCH IDEAS ORIGINATE FROM PERSONAL EXPERIENCES

The idea to explore how people use location-aware digital technologies while travelling originates from personal experiences. New to Australia and the online dating scene, I (Jenna) ventured onto the Tinder platform, set up a profile, and started 'swiping right' on other users' profiles. The popular dating app is gami-fied and encourages you to 'keep playing.' I did. When other users also 'swipe right' on your profile, there is a 'match,' which enables private messaging so you can then chat directly. When using Tinder, I inevitably considered the social interactions it makes possible through the lens of a researcher interested in social media and identity. I noticed the conventions around how people present themselves on the platform through a combination of visual images and written text, and I quickly learned the protocols for avoiding unwanted sexual advances and unpleasant interactions. I also noticed that many of the people using the app were travelling for various purposes such as work, leisure, holidays, and backpacking. This was largely due to my location in the popular travel destination of Sydney in New South Wales. Tinder gave me a useful insight not only into who resides in my new city but also who is travelling through it from elsewhere. I was amazed at how far and wide they said they came from. What are they doing here? Who do they want to encounter as they go? How do they use place to portray who they are to others, their online identities? I discussed the use of Tinder for travel with Garth who researches travel and mobilities[1] and the idea to explore 'Tinder tourism' or 'Tinder travel' took form.

I (Garth) was initially reluctant to engage in the research topic. While my knowledge of Tinder was limited, everything I had read had portrayed it in a negative light: a casual sex app jeopardizing the future of 'traditional' relationships. Unlike Jenna, I was not a part of social circles using these apps. After persistence from Jenna, we eventually met to discuss project ideas. An Internet search during the meeting revealed the breadth of the phenomenon: we quickly discovered a plethora of blogs and media detailing the exploits of 'Tinder Tourists.' We were convinced that Tinder was a topic that warranted further enquiry, so we devised a plan to apply for an internal research grant from our department.

Prior to formally launching our project, Jenna urged me to join Tinder and similar apps so I could get an idea of how they worked and how travelers were using them in Sydney. At first, I was quite anxious about this. I had taught thousands of students at Western Sydney University. If not by a student, I had visions of being discovered on what I still conceptualized as a 'hook-up' app by colleagues or friends. As such, I initially set up a photo-less fake profile. However, it did not take long to dispel the taboos of Tinder that I had imagined. Once I saw that people were on there for a range of intentions, I set up a new profile with my real details albeit with a direct caveat that I was on Tinder for the purposes of research (which I also felt necessary in terms of ethical practices). Indeed, it was seeing the profile of colleagues and a former student that helped to normalize being on the app.

My (Garth) research methods often incorporate autoethnography, and it was important for me to get a sense of how the applications worked and the types of interactions had. In the early stages of the research, I added myself to Tinder and several other location-aware social discovery smartphone apps: Bumble, Happn, and Backpackr. This was enabled more easily by being single at the time and not having to explain this reasoning to a significant other. Ethical considerations raised their head periodically. For instance, one woman's first communication with me on Bumble was 'I am so ready to be used for academic purposes.' I signed up for 'Tinder Plus,' a paid service that allowed me to change my geographic locations on the app to anywhere around the world. As a geographer and travel researcher (and 'travel addict'), the app became a form of travel in itself. It was an opportunity for me to explore local communities anywhere I liked (albeit communities of women), and to meet people across the globe.

Ethical considerations of carrying out this research, therefore, began long before we submitted an application to our university's Human Research Ethics Committee. Although I (Jenna) encouraged Garth to join the 'hook up' apps, as the project moved from idea to actuality, I contemplated removing my profiles. I felt uncomfortable being on Tinder and researching Tinder at the same time. The professional context of running a research project presented identity 'trouble' (Wetherell, 1998) in my personal use of the app when my bio read 'I research platforms like this' and received replies such as 'am I now a case study?' The honest answer to that becomes '[well]…maybe!' With a background training in psychology, I still carry the baggage that is scientized, detached, and objective research (also see Burman, 1997), although I am unloading it, piece by piece. I found Garth's approach to setting up a researcher profile difficult to imitate as I was concerned about my safety and being easily located 'in real life.' In hindsight, perhaps this was the first piece of evidence to support a gendered examination of Tinder.

Researching Tinder has presented many ethical dilemmas due in part to what it represents as an online site of sociality: its primary purpose for online dating, but its reputation as a 'hook up' app for casual sex. In contrast, if we had been developing a research project on Facebook or Twitter, for example, such dilemmas would look very different across both professional and personal contexts. It was difficult to find precedent for ethical research practices in relation to Tinder given that the platform is, at present, under-researched. As such, our reflections here on our research project highlight the need to take a context-specific approach to designing research in online spaces, a key recommendation from the Association of Internet Researchers (AOIR)'s ethical guidance (Markham & Buchanan, 2012). We now turn to consider Tinder as a social space in order to contextualize our approach to researching how people use this platform within its wider 'social media ecosystem' (Van Dijck, 2013). Our reflections on Tinder and the research methods that we have engaged with throughout this project to date constitute 'uncomfortable reflexivity' by 'leaving what is unfamiliar, unfamiliar' (Pillow, 2003, p. 117) and thus contributing to 'Critical Data Studies' (Dalton, Taylor, & Thatcher, 2016), a nuanced debate and concentrated research effort focusing on where we are going with our research practices in an era marked by digitalization.

TINDER AS A RESEARCH CONTEXT

With predictions of 'distal futures' (Boellstroff, 2013) framing current research agendas around digital forms of knowledge production, issues of power inevitably come to the fore. According to Tinder's website, there are 1.4 billion 'swipes' and 26 million 'matches' per day (Tinder, 2016), which translates not only to a lot of time spent 'tindering' but also to a lot of data for social analysis. For researchers increasingly concerned with the 'digital,' Tinder presents 'an archive for thinking about socially mediated digital spaces' (Mason, 2016, p. 4). The wealth of data created by our digital activities has gone hand in hand with the rise of 'big data' research (Boyd & Crawford, 2012). The pull toward data mining/extraction and a quantified approach was strong for us, given the availability of data and the prominent position that 'big data' holds across industry and academia (Boellstorff, 2013). Our initial approach to researching Tinder was subsequently influenced by its archival potential and also by its 'big-ness.' At the start of our project, we proposed to carry out a quantitative content analysis[2] of Tinder user profiles to determine the prevalence of 'Tinder travel' as a social phenomenon. Despite various forms of evidence that people were using Tinder and other 'social discovery' apps while traveling in the form of blog posts and news articles on the subject, as well as social media posts on platforms such as Twitter, Instagram, and Facebook, we still set out to measure its prevalence.

Perhaps our initial approach also enabled us to not quite 'be there' in an ethnographic sense (Pink, Horst, Postill, Hjorth, Lewis, & Tacchi, 2015) and subsequently navigate Tinder 'trouble' with a detached form of data collection. Influenced by a Goffmanesque understanding of self-presentation in the digital world (Bullingham & Vasconcelos, 2013; Goffman, 1959; Hermans, 2004), another reason for analyzing Tinder user profiles was to understand how people present themselves online in the contexts of travel and mobility. However, as we learned more about 'social discovery' apps, particularly from research studies that contribute to 'gay Internet studies' (MacKee, 2016), we began to develop an 'onto-epistem-ology' (Barad, 2003) grounded within techno-feminist literature, which emphasizes the materiality of the social relations that digital technologies render and reproduce. Such theoretical leanings aim to go beyond binary understandings of the online and the offline as essentially distinct from one another (Morrow, Hawkins, & Kern, 2015). When the materiality of Tinder matters, user profiles become more than digital representations, and this should shape how researchers approach them as a potential data source. Furthermore, when social discover apps become 'material actants that modify the practices and encounters they enable in quite specific, potentially impactful, ways' (Race, 2015, p. 256), our research questions move toward exploring not just how apps such as Tinder mediate travel but also how travel mediates Tinder use.

Questions of epistemology and ontology therefore need to be prioritized from the outset in terms of 'what do these data represent and what claims can be made from them?' (Tinati, Halford, Carr, & Pope, 2014, p. 664). We want to draw attention to the 'material specificity' (Race, 2015) of 'social discovery' apps and how they mediate new social encounters. Alone, user profiles tell only part of the story. As we have moved forward with our research, our use of more participatory, critical, and feminist methodologies place us in a stronger position to better attend to how Tinder 'exists within (and therefore reflects and reproduces at times) problematic social structures' (Morrow et al., 2015, p. 257). The value of doing so has already been demonstrated. For example, Mason's (2016) study shows how Tinder user's use images of themselves in humanitarian and volunteering situations to attract potential 'matches,' which reproduces hierarchies of race. Furthermore, Race (2015) also notes that even participation in 'hook up' cultures entails various forms of privilege at the level of access: access to the Internet, a smartphone, and private spaces in which to have new sexual encounters.

The structure of Tinder in terms of its architecture and design also require consideration. For example, Tinder reinforces gender binaries in that it rests on the segregation of men and women. There are only two choices for your own gender identity – male or female. Tinder's hetero-normative advertising campaigns signal its primary target market of straight men and women. Indeed, Tinder's marketing heavily influenced our approach to researching Tinder within the contexts of travel and mobilities. Tinder also use travel[3] as the key narrative to market the premium version 'Tinder Plus,' which has a 'Passport' feature enabling users to change their geolocations and engage in digital forms of travel. While issues of privilege and social inequalities were not our initial focus, they cannot be ignored given the privileged contexts of travel and how the interactions made possible through the app are not exempt from existing social structures. If we had stayed on course to do a quantified 'big data' study, 'categories of race, gender, class, disability, and sexuality become fixed leaving little room for interrogating the forms of power that create and compose them and apply value to them in the first place' (O'Connell, 2016, p. 84).

Location-aware technologies such as Tinder arguably 'strengthen people's connections to their surrounding space' thus creating new social implications for its use in public spaces (de Souza e Silva, 2013, p. 117). You might be sitting at home swiping on Tinder through profiles of people in close proximity such as your neighbors and people you know and interact with daily. You might be in a cafe and your profile shows up on a passerby's phone, and they recognize you. Tinder can therefore be theorized as a public space (de Souza e Silva, 2013), which in turn has implications for the ways in which we research the app, and how we approach it as a data source.

A final point to make is that 'social discovery' apps do not operate in a silo. For example, Tinder is used as a relationship app for gay men, which can be understood further in relation to Grindr, which maintains its status as the most popular 'hook up' app (Race, 2015). Each app operates within the wider 'ecosystem' (van Dijck, 2013) of other socially mediated spaces that facilitate new encounters. Although Tinder holds a central position within the 'social discovery' landscape, what it means and represents is relative to other 'social discovery' apps. In Tinder's case, its competition for online dating (e.g., Bumble, Happn) and travel (e.g., Couchsurfing, Backpackr) contribute to how it develops and changes both representationally and architecturally.

We now explore some of the key ethical issues across our research journey to date. It is important to note that this project is ongoing, and this chapter, therefore, acts as 'writing as inquiry' as part of our commitment to engaging with a feminist research ethic, potentially to make amends for our initial 'big data' approach. As 'the terrain of research and ethics is quickly shifting beneath our feet' (O'Connell, 2016, p. 69), we focus heavily on the initial 'big data' methods of analyzing Tinder user profiles that we proposed given the range of ethical issues that we have since come to understand through a feminist lens. We include excerpts from our first ethics application for the purposes of critical reflection and analysis of the ethical issues in play. The methods we have turned to, and are turning to, are then discussed.

ANALYZING TINDER USER PROFILES

In the first instance, we gained ethical approval from our University's Human Research Ethics Committee for a two-staged research design consisting of (1) a content analysis of Tinder user profiles, and (2) an online questionnaire. While the online questionnaire[4] was relatively straightforward in terms of meeting standard ethical protocols, the content analysis of Tinder user profiles was much more challenging to address within the ethical framework set out by the National Ethical Approval Form (NEAF). The NEAF is a web-based application form designed by the National Health and Medical Research Council that Australian institutions are encouraged to use in their human research ethics systems. The ethical framework within which our institution operates, including the NEAF, is not a 'neutral framework, but rather enshrines a value laden paradigm,' one which is framed by positivist and biomedical epistemologies and methodologies (Pitt, 2014, p. 319). Thus the ethics paradigm currently dominant within academia leaves little room for new and alternative ethical practices to emerge, but it also restricts the possibility of beginning a research project within an alternative ethical framework from the outset (e.g. Pitt, 2014; Tolich & Fitzgerald, 2006). This is particularly pertinent with regards to digital social research, where many of the 'status quo' ethical protocols are difficult to achieve. As such, we looked toward a range of ethical guidance that has been developed specifically for digital research from learned societies such as the AOIR (Markham & Buchanan, 2012), the British Psychological Society (2013), New Social Media, New Social Science (Salmons, 2014). We also drew upon recently published guidance from Townsend and Wallace (2016).

The excerpt below is from our NEAF application where we respond to questions of 'Participation Experience' and raise informed consent as a key ethical issue associated with carrying out a content analysis of Tinder user profiles (Fig. 1).

The 'Participation Experience' section of the NEAF orientates toward the use of research methods that involve participants directly in the data collection/generation stages of research. As Townsend and Wallace (2016) note, informed consent has often been designed into well-established social research methods such as an information sheet and tick box consent options in questionnaires for example. When analyzing user-generated online content, the data has already been created and gaining informed consent by traditional means is problematic, particularly with larger samples (Townsend & Wallace, 2016). Asking for informed consent is more difficult, if not impossible, on

---

Provide a concise detailed description, in not more than 200 words, in terms which are easily understood by the lay reader of what the participation will involve

The purpose of the content analysis is to gain an understanding of the prevalence of users who are using Tinder while travelling, to identify different travel purposes (e.g., from 'backpacker' to 'visiting Sydney for the weekend'), and to examine how users are positioning themselves within narratives of travel on the Tinder platform. Participation in this aspect of the study has technically already occurred. This component of the project is retrospective – that is, the data (user profile content) for collection and analysis already exists. Therefore, while participants are technically participating in the project in the sense that their data is included in the study, this participation is not active.

Fig. 1.   Our Response in the 'Participation Experience' Section of Our Ethics Application.

Tinder due to the platforms design. We would have to 'match' with users in order to contact them directly for their informed consent.

Issues of informed consent interrelate with issues of privacy and copyright. We justified the waiving of informed consent by considering Tinder user profiles as publicly available through interpretations of the Australian Copyright Act 1968 (New South Wales) and the Privacy and Personal Information Act 1998 (New South Wales). The excerpt below includes our response as to why informed consent was 'impracticable' for the content analysis and how the data can be considered to be public. In drafting our response, we sought guidance from within our university to identify the acts we needed to address and in turn, our interpretations of those acts. It is important to note here that we initially applied to carry out a manual approach to the content analysis, which would involve swiping through Tinder user profiles within a 10 km radius of Sydney city center and analyzing the profiles according to a quantitative coding scheme. This would not produce a record of users' profiles (Fig. 2).

Tinder and other 'social discovery' apps provide an interesting case for understanding online data as public. Alongside the arguments we made earlier about Tinder as a social space that encompasses the 'virtual-material' (Morrow et al.,

---

Why is it impracticable to seek consent?

It is impracticable to seek consent as the project is retrospective – the data (user profile content) has already been generated. Therefore, the consideration of consent would only apply to data reproduction (use of data in research analyses). It is argued the data resides in the public domain (it is published on the Internet and openly accessible to anyone who signs up to the application) and is thus subject to the Australian Copyright Act, which allows for the reproduction of such data for fair dealings (including research purposes) without consent.

Furthermore, the research does not intend to record or reproduce any data that could be considered personal subject to the Privacy and Personal Information Act 1998 (NSW); and following does not intend to record or reproduce data that could lead to the identification of participants at any stage of the project.

Therefore, it is argued that it is impracticable to seek consent, as the consent only applies to the reproduction of data that has already been generated and resides in a public domain – which is therefore subject to the Copyright Act 1968 (NSW) and the Privacy and Personal Information Act 1998 (NSW). It is understood that the use of this *data, within this context, would be allowed for under the provisions of these acts without consent.*

Fig. 2. Our Response within the 'Consent Process' Section of the NEAF.

2015), and how location-aware technologies present social implications for people in public spaces (de Souza e Silva, 2013), Tinder gives a sense of privacy in that profiles are not visible to everyone. User profiles are discoverable to people who have downloaded the app that meet the user's search criteria (e.g., gender, age range) and their geolocational settings. This limited publicity is reinforced by Tinder profiles not being searchable in the ways that profiles are for other 'mainstream' social media platforms (e.g., Facebook, Twitter). At the same time, Tinder has recently introduced a number of features that make profiles more public. Tinder users can connect their profiles to other social media platforms (e.g., you can include links to your Spotify or Instagram accounts), 'recommend' another user by sharing their profile with someone else, and group swipe with your Facebook friends. There is also an option to claim a username for a webpage that you can use to direct people to your Tinder profile. Users have agency in making themselves more discoverable. For example, placing usernames and handles for other social media platforms (e.g., Instagram and Snapchat) is relatively common on the app. Even so, Tinder users are unlikely to create a profile and contribute their information to it with the expectation that researchers will use their profiles as data. Recent surveys have shown that when asked, people are more likely to say no than yes to their online data being used for research purposes (see Ipsos Mori's 'Wisdom of the Crowd' Report, Evans, Ginnis, & Bartlett, 2015) and NatCen's 'Research using Social Media; Users' Views' Report (Beninger, Fry, Jago, Lepps, Nass, & Silvester, 2014 for overviews). Just because data is available and accessible does not necessarily mean it is 'fair go' for research purposes.

We sought direction from past research on 'social discovery' apps to explore how informed consent has been addressed with regards to the types of data that had been collected and analyzed in such studies. We found precedent for the analysis of user-generated online content in digital anthropological research, particularly 'gay Internet studies' (MacKee, 2016) where informed consent is not always possible or expected, particularly when ethnographic methods such as participant observation and autoethnographic insights are central. For example, Race (2015) carried out an insider-ethnography to examine the new genres of sexual interactions made possible by 'hook up' apps Grindr and Scruff. This study involved historical and textual data analysis, which included screen shots of personal conversations the researcher had had with users of the apps. No formal ethical approval was sought to have such conversations as Race (2015) argues:

> nothing should prevent bona fide participants in sexual cultures from representing their experiences of these cultures in scholarly venues and using these reflections to inform their analysis. (p. 258)

Furthermore, these conversations were historical and institutional ethics processes are not geared toward granting retrospective approval. Race (2015) removed all identifying information from the screenshots included in his analysis. We planned to anonymize users' profiles by presenting data analysis in aggregated form, which enabled us to pursue a detached form of research that aligns with standardized ethical protocols.

That we did not move toward a more ethnographic approach, drawing upon our own adventures in 'social discovery' apps perhaps reflects our attempts to not 'be there' in an ethnographic sense (Pink et al., 2015) and to remain detached from the research. When framed as participant observation, the relationship between researcher and participant is often acknowledged as blurred but most importantly, it is acknowledged. This stands in contrast to our initial stance on researcher–participant relationships and perhaps the expectations of university ethics panels. In the NEAF section on 'Relationship of researchers/investigators to participants,' we position ourselves as completely detached from participants (Fig. 3).

We firmly claimed that no relationships would exist between participants and research team members during the research, completely separating the researcher and researched. Yet in practice, it became clear that this goal was unachievable as to see user profiles, we have to log into Tinder via Facebook using our personal Facebook accounts. Those social networks therefore become connected in the process. Using our own geolocations to generate data inevitably means that people we know or might know in the future are included in our sample. The interconnectedness of social media is, therefore, something that should be acknowledged within digital social research and given space for within ethics review processes.

After gaining ethical approval for a manual approach for the content analysis of Tinder user profiles, we discovered an automated way to collect data using an Application Programming Interface (API), which was also approved by our University's Human Research Ethics Committee. This would involve using our own Facebook accounts to access Tinder data (Fig. 4).

Specify the nature of any existing relationship or one likely to rise during the research, between the potential participants and any member of the research team or an organization involved in the research

There are no existing relationships or ones likely to arise during the research between potential participants and members of the research team and/or organization.

Fig. 3. Excerpt from Our Initial Ethics Application Addressing the Nature of Relationships within the Study.

'While these data are classed as *publically* available under the Privacy and Personal Information Protection Act 1988 (NSW), Tinder's Terms of Service (ToS) state that users of the platform should not "use any robot, spider, site search/ retrieval application, or other manual or automatic device or process to retrieve, index, "data mine," or in any way reproduce or circumvent the navigational structure or presentation of the Service or its contents." Having reviewed Tinder's ToS in full, Tinder is focused on preventing the commercial use of their application and/or the use of their application that brings detriment to users. Indeed, Tinder has recently added a function that allows users to share data on their platform with non-Tinder users. Our use of the application is not for commercial purposes, and the data management procedures we have in place will address any potential harm which could come to individuals through using publicly available data obtained through the application (see the attached record management plan). There is a precedent for the collection of research data via a geolocation applications (Grindr) using the same methods proposed in this study, and with similar ToS stipulations from Grindr (see: (Birnholtz, Fitzpatrick, Handel, & Brubaker, 2014; Zytko, Lingel, Birnholtz, & Ellison, 2015).'

Fig. 4.   An Excerpt from Our Amendment to Use an Automated Approach.

Going from a manual to an automated process results in the creation of a record or dataset, which heightened the issues around informed consent and rights to anonymity as we move from the reasonable likelihood of seeing someone on a social discovery app (and then analyzing their profiles according to a coding scheme) to creating a permanent record outside of the context within which is was created. The API also strongly provoked another key issue around the legalities of extracting Tinder user profiles and creating a data record outside of the app. We examined Tinder's Terms of Service where there is a specific statement related to 'data mining':

> You will not: use any robot, spider, site search/retrieval application, or other manual or automatic device or process to retrieve, index, 'data mine,' or in any way reproduce or circumvent the navigational structure or presentation of the Service or its contents. (Tinder, 2016b)

In comparison to a manual approach, using an API makes it difficult to argue that we are not breaking Tinder's Terms of Service. However, as Bruns (2013) notes 'scholars in the academy have shown remarkable resilience and inventiveness in working around these restrictions and limitations, if at times by bending the rules of what social media APIs allow them to do' (n.p).

We argued that Tinder's ToS were geared toward commercial appropria-tions of their service, as opposed to academic research. ToS are increasing problematic for academic researchers as social media organizations enforce a hierarchy of those who can access social media data and those who cannot (Bruns, 2013). Social media companies increasingly act as commercial gate-keepers blocking and/or making it difficult to access data for the purposes of social research (Boellstorff, 2013; O'Connell, 2016).

Around the time we gained ethical approval to use an API, a high profile incident of 'data mining' hit the news headlines. Not a research study but an act carried out in the name of 'open data.' the release of 70,000 users' data from OKCupid, an online dating site, onto an 'open science' platform (the data have now been removed) demonstrated for us, how not to go about digital social research (see Markham, 2016, for a deeper ethical consideration of this case). However, we continued to justify to ourselves and to our university's Human Research Ethics Committee that analyzing Tinder user profiles, whether man-ual or automatic, record or no record, was justified as the data was in the public domain. We also stated that we would not open the data as in the OKCupid case to avoid de-anonymization of parts of the dataset. However not releas-ing and sharing data with other researchers presents another ethical issue with regards to a 'restricted culture of research findings' (Boyd & Crawford, 2012, p. 674). There are also implications for establishing the authenticity and cred-ibility of the research among (social) scientific communities.

Writing this chapter now, it is difficult to identify when we made the deci-sion to not analyze Tinder user profiles. We pushed forward with the API approach to test the waters. Attending and presenting at a conference on Social Media Ethics was a key event in our ethical pivot toward more par-ticipatory research methods, particularly the discussions that emerged there around informed consent and rights to privacy. Another key factor in the decision not to pursue content analysis of Tinder user profiles relates to the open source of API available via Github (a website where programmers share code). The API available to automatically extract Tinder user profiles was called 'The Hoes.' The name of the API indicates that other people who are extracting data from Tinder are doing so for reasons much less ethical than our own. What are we complicit in if we use an API that has the misogynistic label 'The Hoes'? The existence of this API reflects the problematic wide-spread abuse of women in digitally mediated spaces and how existing social inequalities are reproduced in the ways we use the web and its data. Questions around who created the API and their motives for doing so provide support for Tinder's ToS and the need for data security given the abusive ways in which personal data can be used.

After much consideration and debate, we shelved our 'big data' approach given the ethical issues that are difficult to balance out to justify extracting Tinder user profiles. Furthermore, we started to question why we even wanted this data. Put simply, we originally wanted to understand how people present themselves online. There are other ways to do that without 'dispossessing' (O'Connell, 2016) people of their own data. One of the many arguments for analyzing user-generated content as data is that such data is in the public domain. We used that argument ourselves in order to gain ethical approval. We now discuss the alternative ways to know about 'Tinder travel' that we have explored and used since. The methods we now use align more closely with a feminist research ethic and a more contextualized approach to understanding how people use 'social discovery' apps while travelling.

RELYING ON TRADITIONAL METHODS FOR PARTICIPANT RECRUITMENT

The online questionnaire has been a constant presence within our research project, but it has remained in the background within ethical considerations and reflections. This is largely because it enables us to be detached, objective researchers carrying out the kind of digital social research that is perhaps more 'ideal' (Pitt, 2014) within dominant research ethics paradigms. More importantly though is that recruiting people to participate in the online questionnaire has been difficult. At the time of writing, we have 23 respondents despite widespread promotion of the project across social media platforms and in online travel forums. While these contributions to our research are indeed invaluable, we are receiving rather short responses to our survey's open questions. Here are some examples of participants' questionnaire responses:

> It was easy to get matches as a foreigner. Away field advantage. I used Tinder to meet local girls – most of whom I would not have access to otherwise. It was also helpful to meet English-speaking expats who become friends.

> Was the same as using them [apps] in England, good to meet people and fun for short periods of time.

> I used the app [Tinder] to meet new people in the area I was visiting. I was looking to experience the area as locals do and I asked for ideas about what to do/see, etc. I met several people but I ended up meeting up with one person several times and having a short romantic relationship with them. This individual took me on hikes, showed me local hole-in-the-wall restaurants, taught me about local culture, and was a great ambassador for the area. I found the experience fantastic but confusing as I had never had such an 'open' relationship with someone before.

These responses raise many more questions and open up many other lines of inquiry. As such, we asked survey participants for their contact details should they want to participate in future research most likely in the form of online interviews. We supervised a psychology honors student project that involved interviewing participants from the online questionnaire who had agreed to take part in further stages of our research project. Participants were also recruited through other means such as personal networks and by contacting bloggers who have written on the topic of 'Tinder travel.' Our methodological decision here echoes that of other researchers who have used qualitative interviews alongside other methods to research social discovery apps (e.g., Miguel, 2016; Race, 2015). It also arguably reflects the prominence of 'multi-modal' approaches often employed within social digital research to understand the relations between the 'online' and the 'offline' (Miguel, 2016). To date, the interview data generated is providing insights particularly around gendered travel (e.g., women place more emphasis on issues of safety and risk) and around nationality (e.g., national identities become more salient in the context of travel in other countries).

Having to rely on interviews to get sufficient data on 'Tinder travel' has led us to question the value of the online questionnaire as a 'go to' method within (digital) social research. An online questionnaire is relatively easy and quick to complete, but why would someone really want to do it? What do they get out of research participation? Tyldum (2012) notes that research ethics training assumes respondents who participate in research do so 'for the sake of research and the common good' (p. 199). Our information sheet reproduces that assumption (see Fig. 5).

Tyldum (2012) argues that in practice, participant altruism is rare and that 'pressure' is often needed to increase research participation. Rather than 'pressure,' we have turned toward an approach that attempts to make research participation an enjoyable digital experience and something that participants might find beneficial. We have begun to prioritize how people are learning about and making sense of their digitally mediated travel experiences, which

---

What specific benefits will I receive for participating?

There are no specific benefits of taking part in the study except for your contribution to knowledge on this topic.

Fig. 5.   Section from Our Information Sheet that Refers to the Benefits of Research Participation.

Gubrium and Turner (2009) argue is a necessity for any social research project.

CREATING A DIGITAL STORYTELLING MAP

Mimicking the long-standing traditions of documenting travel and tourism in a paper journal, or diary, and more recently, the popular genre of travel blogging (Ting, Ting, & Hsiao, 2014; Volo, 2010), we have developed an online mapping tool that is currently in prototype stage (and at the time of writing is still to be submitted to our university's Human Research Ethics Committee). Our idea is that travelers, whether currently travelling or not, might engage with a more open, storied approach to research participation: an approach that also enables them to read other participants' stories of 'Tinder travel.' In moving toward a 'digital storytelling' method, we hope to align with how 'increasingly, the public is using MMP [multi-modal media production] to publicly document, comment upon, and create their own meaning of events around them' (Gubrium & Turner, 2009, p. 469). This move also reflects the current shifts toward storytelling and the 'turn to narrative' within the human sciences (Reissman, 2008).

We are also drawing upon the principles of user experience (UX) design that permeate technology industries in the quest to create positive digital experiences. As such, this raises another set of ethical considerations when considered from a techno-feminist perspective where digital technologies may design in the social inequalities we now seek to address, given that the tools available to us are made within a largely male-dominated sector (Morrow et al., 2015). Thus, we need to think ethically about the design of our digital storytelling map. The design so far has been a complex process as we have acted as a client for our university's computer science undergraduate degree for a group of students completing their professional experience final-year project. For us, this process has highlighted that as social researchers, we would benefit from developing our own programming and web design skills to do create and produce new digital research tools. Furthermore, as the student team was working toward an assessed piece of work with strict parameters, potential research participants were not included within the design stages for this prototype. We do plan to test the prototype to refine the tool before collecting data with it in the future.

We also worked with a student team from our university's web design undergraduate course where a student team developed a brand identity for our project (see Figs. 6 and 7). The result is 'The TinDA[5] Diaries,' an online digitally mediated space that aims to reflect the ways in which people now share their experiences.

Fig. 6.   Overarching Project Logo.

Fig. 7.   Digital Storytelling Map Logo.

In "The TinDA Diaries,' participants can pin their digitally mediated travel stories on the map, read other participants stories, and potentially (ethics permitting) share posts onto other social media platforms, which then locates the digital storytelling map within the wider social media ecosystem. As de Souza e Silva (2013) forecasts, smartphones with location-aware apps and services are increasingly the norm. By tapping into this norm, we hope to encourage a different form of research participation in our study.

However, another set of ethical issues rise up when research participation moves into a more public online sphere. When we requested an ethics amendment to ask our online questionnaire participants if we could publish their stories on our website, our university ethics committee questioned this move. Our ethics panel queried the link between an individual's data and communicating the projects focus to participants to facilitate participant recruitment. In relation to the digital storytelling map, issues around anonymity are particularly important as participants may choose to forgo their rights to anonymity or they may inadvertently compromise their anonymity and that of others in the telling of their relational and spatial stories. As such, we have designed in a moderation system to anonymize any information that may identify other people within participants' stories. Within this moderation process, we might change a named person for a pseudonym or adjust the pinned location of a story. While moderation shifts ownership of stories from participants to researchers, this design feature balances the needs to ensure rights to anonymity and confidentiality and extend those rights to others mentioned within participants' stories. The moderation function is perhaps made more important if we include a 'share' feature within our digital storytelling map, which would enable participants and users of our site to share posts onto other social media platforms, mainly Facebook and Twitter. We have to consider how a share feature shapes the stories told. For example, how does a story change if it written with the participants Facebook audience in mind? How does a share feature compromise attempts at confidentiality and anonymity?

While a share feature might reflect the ways in which people share their experiences in contemporary times, sharing content also reflects a more commercialized approach to participant recruitment. As researchers, we are often competing for our research projects to be seen and interacted with amongst a wealth of information that appears in prospective participants' social media newsfeeds. Researchers often share links to their research via their own profiles but that does not necessarily mean that their social networks reach the people they need to take part in their studies. A share button on our digital storytelling map would enact a snowball approach to sampling. The power of this approach, influenced by marketing and commercial strategies, also requires ethical consideration. While the digital storytelling map circumvents some of the issues with extracting data from social media platforms and restrictive Terms of Service, we are now in the 'business' of creating tools, which presents issues of power dynamics for our research practices. It is crucial that future work on this tool engages prospective participants as co-designers to ensure that a feminist research ethics of care is in action when participants' stories are made public in this way.

CONCLUSION

This chapter reflects our commitment to a feminist research ethic and to interrogate our research practices. We hope that our revised research approach to 'social discovery' apps demonstrates our 'commitment to inquiry about how we inquire' (Ackerly & True, 2008, p. 635) through our writing and our 'outing' (Finlay, 2002) of both researchers and research methods. *Such* reflexivity has enabled us to consider the process of knowledge production (Reed, Miller, Nnawulezi, & Valenti, 2012), to examine the pull toward 'big data' and to reject it for more participatory methods. While these participatory methods raise another set of ethical issues, by committing to feminist principles of research ethics, we are becoming the kinds of digital social researchers we want to be. Therefore, our ethical considerations of researching Tinder and other 'social discovery' apps do not stop here. We must remain as aware as possible of the potential for reinforcing hierarchical power relationships with the participants in our research (Morrow et al., 2015).

In writing this chapter, it is evident that we have been disciplined to operate within the 'status quo,' which meant that our responses and claims made within our NEAF were designed to 'get through' the system. As digital social researchers who navigate complex digitally mediated spaces, we need to take a concerted effort to change the ethics systems in place and champion for a system that allows for alternative approaches to research participation, data generation, and researcher-participant relations.

We might have saved ourselves time and energy if we had theorized Tinder more fully as a social space and as a data source from the outset. By locating our research within epistemological and ontological frames that then guide the research methodology, we might have arrived at a more feminist, participatory approach sooner. Indeed, the key lessons learned can be summarized as follows:

- When research ideas stem from personal experiences, the potential for autoethnographic methods should not be overlooked. In retrospect, we could have started to keep a detailed journal and screenshots, for example. Working through the identity 'trouble' presented when personal and professional uses of a platform or online space overlap may generate insightful research findings.
- Writing about the ethics of this research project and the different ways in which to carry out our research emphasizes how ethical considerations are dynamic processes that begin before a project commences and change as a project progresses. Reflexivity is a key tool for ethical research in new digital spaces.
- Although we recognize that 'big data' approaches to researching Tinder and other 'social discovery' apps could prove useful, we should have resisted the appeal of data mining/extraction in the first instance. We should have theorized Tinder more fully as a social space and considered the range of potential ways to generate data within digital social research contexts.
- Pinning down epistemological and ontological positions early on, particularly in new research collaborations, would have saved us time and energy in terms of making a more informed decision as to the methodological approach to take.
- Social media guidance from learned societies is a useful starting point in terms of addressing ethical issues within digital social research for the purposes of gaining ethical approval. However, the discussions we had with colleagues and peers around ethical challenges and dilemmas have been particularly useful for us as we move our research forward in an ethical manner.
- Dating mining/extracting user-generated content raises a number of ethical concerns such as informed consent and issues of privacy and copyright.

The accumulation of ethical issues compromised the kinds of researchers we wanted to be. However, given the variability across apps/platforms/spaces, a context-specific approach to digital social research should be used to address how participants feel about their content being used as data.
* As we move toward more 'traditional' and participatory storytelling methods within our research, different ethical considerations arise. Our inquiries into the ways in which we proceed with our research project do not stop here.

Far from a fad or gimmick, Tinder represents the rising popularity of location-aware mobile services made possible by the enhanced capabilities of smartphones to locate nearby things including people. While we may be researching the trending, it seems likely that Tinder will be a notable event on the timeline in the history of location-aware mobile communications and the emergence of 'social discovery' apps. Critical reflection on the ways in which we theorize Tinder as a social space and a data source must be prioritized as the future of social relations and encounters may well lie in location-aware technologies.

NOTES

1. The study of mobilities includes 'research on the combined movements of people, objects, and information in all of their complex relational dynamics' (Sheller, 2014, p. 1).
2. We initially gained ethical approval to carry out a manual content analysis of Tinder user profiles by swiping through profiles on the app with a quantitative coding scheme. We later submitted an amendment to automate this process using an Application Programming Interface (API). We discuss these methods in greater detail later on in the chapter.
3. In Tinder's main video advertisement, the protagonist, a young woman from Manhattan, changes her location to select local travel 'companions' in advance of arriving in London and Paris (Tinder, 2014).
4. We discuss the online questionnaire in more detail later in this chapter.
5. TinDA is an acronym of our wider research project 'Travel in Digital Age.'

REFERENCES

Ackerly, B., & True, J. (2008). Reflexivity in practice: Power and ethics in feminist research on international relations. *International Studies Review*. Retrieved from http://isr.oxfordjournals.org/content/10/4/693.abstract

Barad, K. (2003). Posthumanist performativity: Toward an understanding of how matter comes to matter. *Signs, 28*(3), 801–831. Retrieved from https://doi.org/10.1086/345321

Beninger, K., Fry, A., Jago, N., Lepps, H., Nass, L., & Silvester, H. (2014). *Research using Social Media; Users' Views*. London. Retrieved from http://www.natcen.ac.uk/media/282288/p0639-r esearch-using-social-media-report-final-190214.pdf

Birnholtz, J., Fitzpatrick, C., Handel, M., & Brubaker, J. R. (2014). Identity, Identification and Identifiability: The language of self-presentation on a location-based mobile dating App. *To Appear in Proceedings MobileHCI 2014*, 3–12. Retrieved from https: //doi.org/http://dx.doi.org/10.1145/2628363.2628406

Boellstorff, T. (2013). Making big data, in theory. *First Monday*. Retrieved from http://first monday.org/ojs/index.php/fm/article/view/4869/3750

Boyd, D., & Crawford, K. (2012). Critical questions for big data: Provocations for a cultural, technological, and scholarly phenomenon. *Information, Communication & Society, 15*(5), 662–679. Retrieved from https://doi.org/10.1080/1369118X.2012.678878

British Psychological Society. (2013). *Ethics guidelines for internet-mediated research. British Psychological Society*. Retrieved from https://doi.org/INF206/1.2013

Bruns, A. (2013). Faster than the speed of print: Reconciling 'big data' social media analysis and academic scholarship. *First Monday, 18*(10). Retrieved from https://doi. org/10.5210%2Ffm.v18i10.4879

Bullingham, L., & Vasconcelos, A. (2013). 'The presentation of self in the online world': Goffman and the study of online identities. *Journal of Information Science, 39*(1), 101–112. Retrieved from https://doi.org/10.1177/0165551512470051

Burman, E. (1997). Minding the gap: Positivism, psychology, and the politics of qualitative methods. *Journal of Social Issues, 53*(4), 785–801.

Dalton, C. M., Taylor, L., & Thatcher, J. (2016). Critical Data Studies: A dialog on data and space. *Big Data & Society, 3*(1), 1–9. Retrieved from https://doi.org/10.1177/2053951716648346

de Souza e Silva, A. (2013). Location-aware mobile technologies: Historical, social and spatial approaches. *Mobile Media & Communication, 1*(1), 116–121. Retrieved from https://doi. org/10.1177/2050157912459492

Evans, H., Ginnis, S., & Bartlett, J. (2015). *#SocialEthics A guide to embedding ethics in social media research*. London. Retrieved from https://www.ipsos-mori.com/Assets/Docs/Publications/i m-demos-social-ethics-in-social-media-research.pdf

Finlay, L. (2002). 'Outing' the researcher: The provenance, process, and practice of reflexivity. *Qualitative Health Research, 12*(4), 531–545.

Goffman, E. (1959). *The presentation of self in everyday life*. London: Penguin Books.

Gubrium, A., & Turner, K. (2009). Digital storytelling as an emergent method for social research and practice. In S. Hesse-Biber (Ed.), *The handbook of emergent technologies in social research*. Oxford: Oxford Unversity. Retrieved from https://works.bepress.com/aline_gubrium/5/download/

Hermans, H. (2004). Introduction: The dialogical self in a global and digital age. *Identity: An International Journal of Theory and Research, 4*(4), 297–320.

Hsiao, J., & Dillahunt, T. (2017). People-nearby applications: How newcomers move their relationships offline and develop social and cultural capital. *Proceedings of CSCW 2017*. Retrieved from https://www.researchgate.net/profile/Chiao_Yin_Hsiao/publication/308148080_People-Nearby_Applications_How_Newcomers_Move_Their_Relationships_Offline_and_ Develop_Social_and_Cultural_Capital/links/57db414108ae5292a376a2ba.pdf

MacKee, F. (2016). Social media in gay London: Tinder as an alternative to hook-up Apps. *Social Media + Society, 2*(3). Retrieved from https://doi.org/10.1177/2056305116662186

Markham, A. (2016). OKCupid data release fiasco: It's time to rethink ethics education. *School of Communication and Culture,*

Markham, A. & Buchanan, E. (2012). Ethical decision-making and Internet Research Recommendations from the AoIR Ethics Working Committee. *Recommendations from the AoIR Ethics Working Committee (Version 2.0)*, 19. Retrieved from https://doi.org/ Retrieved from www.aoir.org

Mason, C. (2016). Tinder and humanitarian hook-ups: the erotics of social media racism. *Feminist Media Studies*. Retrieved from https://doi.org/10.1080/14680777.2015.113733

Miguel, C. (2016). Visual intimacy on social media: From selfies to the co-construction of intimacies through shared pictures. *Social Media + Society*, *2*(2), 2056305116641705. Retrieved from https://doi.org/10.1177/2056305116641705

Morrow, O., Hawkins, R., & Kern, L. (2015). Feminist research in online spaces. *Gender, Place & Culture*, *22*(4), 526–543. Retrieved from https://doi.org/10.1080/0966369X.2013.879108

O'Connell, A. (2016). My entire life is online: Informed consent, big data, and decolonial knowledge. *Intersectionalities: A Global Journal of Social*. Retrieved from http://journals.library. mun.ca/ojs/index.php/IJ/article/view/1523

Pillow, W. (2003). Confession, catharsis, or cure? Rethinking the uses of reflexivity as methodological power in qualitative research. *International Journal of Qualitative Studies in Education*, *16*(2), 22.

Pink, S., Horst, H., Postill, J., Hjorth, L., Lewis, T., & Tacchi, J. (2015). *Digital ethnography: principles and practice*. London: Sage.

Pitt, P. (2014). 'The project cannot be approved in its current form': feminist visual research meets the human research ethics committee. *The Australian Educational Researcher*. Retrieved from http://link.springer.com/article/10.1007/s13384-013-0136-6

Race, K. (2015). 'Party 'n' Play': Online hook-up devices and the emergence of PNP practices among gay men. *Sexualities*, *18*(3), 253–275. Retrieved from https://doi.org/10.1177/1363460714550913

Reed, S., Miller, R., Nnawulezi, N., & Valenti, M. (2012). Erecting closets and outing ourselves: Uncomfortable reflexivity and community-based research. *Journal of Community Psychology*, *40*(1), 11–26. Retrieved from https://doi.org/10.1002/jcop.20491

Reissman, C. (2008). *Narrative methods for the human sciences*. London: Sage.

Sales, N. J. (2015). Tinder and the dawn of the 'dating apocalypse.' *Vanity Fair*. Retrieved from http://www.vanityfair.com/culture/2015/08/tinder-hook-up-culture-end-of-dating

Salmons, J. (2014). *New Social Media, New Social Science… And New Ethical Issues!*

Sheller, M. (2014). The new mobilities paradigm for a live sociology. *Current Sociology*. Retrieved from http://csi.sagepub.com/content/early/2014/05/23/0011392114533211.abstract

Sumter, S., Vandenbosch, L., & Ligtenberg, L. (2017). Love me Tinder: Untangling emerging adults' motivations for using the dating application Tinder. *Telematics and Informatics*. Retrieved from http://www.sciencedirect.com/science/article/pii/S0736585316301216

Tinati, R., Halford, S., Carr, L., & Pope, C. (2014). Big data: Methodological challenges and approaches for sociological analysis. *Sociology*, *48*(4), 663–681. Retrieved from https://doi.org/10.1177/0038038513511561

Tinder. (2014). Tinder Plus. Retrieved from https://vimeo.com/111080451. Accessed on December 12, 2016.

Tinder. (2016a). About Tinder. Retrieved from https://www.gotinder.com/press. Accessed on December 12, 2016

Tinder. (2016b). Terms of Use. Retrieved from https://www.gotinder.com/terms. Accessed on December 12, 2016.

Ting, K., Ting, P., & Hsiao, P. (2014). Why are bloggers willing to share their thoughts via travel blogs? *International Journal of Technology Management 64*(1). Retrieved from https://doi.org/10.1504/IJTM.2014.059237

Tolich, M., & Fitzgerald, M. (2006). If ethics committees were designed for ethnography. *On human research ethics*. Retrieved from http://journals.sagepub.com/doi/abs/10.1525/jer.2006.1.2.71

Townsend, L. & Wallace, C. (2016). *Social media research: A guide to ethics*. Aberdeen.

Tyldum, G. (2012). Ethics or access? Balancing informed consent against the application of institutional, economic or emotional pressures in recruiting respondents for research. *International Journal of Social Research Methodology, 15*(3), 199–210.

Van Dijck, J. (2013). *The culture of connectivity: A critical history of social media*. Oxford: Oxford University Press.

Volo, S. (2010). Bloggers' reported tourist experiences: Their utility as a tourism data source and their effect on prospective tourists. *Journal of Vacation Marketing, 16*(4), 297–311. Retrieved from https://doi.org/10.1177/1356766710380884

Wetherell, M. (1998). Positioning and interpretative repertoires: Conversation analysis and post-structuralism in dialogue. *Discourse & Society, 9*(3), 387–412.

Zytko, D., Lingel, J., Birnholtz, J., & Ellison, N. (2015). Online dating as pandora's box: Methodological issues for the CSCW community. *Proceedings of the 18th*. Retrieved from http://dl.acm.org/citation.cfm?id=2699335

CHAPTER 7

ETHICAL CHALLENGES OF PUBLISHING AND SHARING SOCIAL MEDIA RESEARCH DATA

Libby Bishop and Daniel Gray

ABSTRACT

The focus of this chapter is the intersection of social media, publication, data sharing, and research ethics. By now there is an extensive literature on the use of social media in research. There is also excellent work on challenges of postpublication sharing of social media, primarily focused on legal restrictions, technical infrastructure, and documentation. This chapter attempts to build upon and extend this work by using cases to deepen the analysis of ethical issues arising from publishing and sharing social media data. Publishing will refer to the presentation of data extracts, aggregations, or summaries, while sharing refers to the practice of making the underlying data available postpublication for others to use. It will look at the ethical questions that arise both for researchers (or others) sharing data, and those who are using data that has been made available by others, emphasizing the inherently relational nature of data sharing. The ethical challenges researchers face when considering sharing user-generated content collected from social media platforms are the focus of the cases. The chapter begins by summarizing the general principles of

The Ethics of Online Research
Advances in Research Ethics and Integrity, Volume 2, 159–187
ISSN: 2398-6018/doi:10.1108/S2398-601820180000002007

research ethics, then identifies the specific ethical challenges from sharing social media data and positions these challenges in the context of these general principles. These challenges are then analyzed in more detail with cases from research projects that drew upon several different genres of social media. The chapter concludes with some recommendations for practical guidance and considers the future of ethical practice in sharing social media data.

Keywords: Data publication; Data sharing; Facebook; Internet research; research ethics; research integrity; social media; Twitter

INTRODUCTION

Early in 2016, 70,000 users of OK Cupid – a dating social media platform – had their details scraped and then made available by a researcher in a public data repository (Markham, 2016). The author in this case defended his actions, even after significant public protest. His defense rested on the claim that the data were 'already public' (Zimmer, 2010). Much of the debate has explored this issue of defining public and private. Indeed, the ambiguity of public/private boundary is one of the central points in the Association of Internet Researchers' guidance for online research (Markham & Buchanan, 2012).

Somewhat less emphasis was given to the fact that the author defended his actions as supporting the goal of open science. The credentials of the particular open repository emerged as questionable (it appeared to have been operated by the author; Markham, 2016); however, the value of open science remains as a legitimate objective. Early open initiatives focused on publications, but more recently, equally strong claims are made for open data (Concordat on Open Data, 2016).

One reason the case provoked so much public debate is because there are several compelling and conflicting ethical principles at work. Both protecting data subjects' privacy and opening data are defensible values. This is the nature of ethical dilemmas and makes them, for many, frustrating to think about because of the paucity of unambiguous answers.

This chapter looks at the ethical challenges researchers face when considering sharing user-generated content held on the social media platforms of Twitter and Facebook. It will be concerned with exposing data extracts in publications or other forms of dissemination and also with postpublication sharing, such as in data repositories and archives. It will look at the ethical questions that arise both for researchers sharing data and those who are using data that has been made available by others.

Data sharing can take many forms, ranging from informal sharing within teams, peer-to-peer sharing upon request, through to the most formal systems where data are deposited in archives or repositories for long-term curation (Van den Eynden & Bishop, 2014; Borgman, 2012). Ethics issues arise in all forms of sharing: informal sharing, when one researcher grants a one-off request from another for use of the original data, may avoid some privacy concerns because the researcher maintains personal control over who may have the data and how it is reused; however, issues of unequal access may arise if only selected requests are granted. Similarly, making data available through a repository may be more democratic, but careful consideration must be given to whether repository conditions match confidentiality commitments given to data subjects and possible risks from data linkage.

Based on the literature to date, as well as one of the author's experience with teaching ethics as part of data management workshops at the UK Data Service, there is considerable anxiety in the research community due to the uncertainty about data sharing, and specifically, social media. Other research has reached similar conclusions:

> We found social media data sharing to be fraught with insecurity, uncertainty and aggravation. Yet we also witnessed an intrinsic, often strong motivation to share data for the sake of improving access to social media data and to be able to develop and improve on methods in the fast developing field. (Weller & Kinder-Kurlanda, 2015, p. 36)

Better legal guidance would be helpful, of course, but given the fast-moving nature of big data research relative to the development of case law, a period of uncertainty and ambiguity is going to exist for some time. More and better collective moral reasoning about these questions by the research community (and data subjects and public) can help develop better ethical practice, and thereby benefit from the generosity of the many researchers who are motivated to share social media data for public benefit.

But there is even more at stake: aggregation of knowledge is aggregation of power (Schroeder, 2014). We justifiably subject such data aggregation to scrutiny when done by commercial and government entities (Schneier, 2015). But equally, we have to acknowledge the dual nature of this accumulation of knowledge. Sharing and archiving data contributes to this growing reservoir of knowledge.

Such aggregation of data and knowledge, and hence, power, raises at least two concerns. First, as data becomes a more valuable resource, access to it has implications for the 'digital divide,' that is, inequality resulting from access to digital resources. Conditions of data access, whether legal, technical, or other, have implications for who can benefit from growing repositories of data. Second, growing capabilities for data linkage mean that any entity holding data, particularly personal or sensitive data, has an increasingly difficult responsibility to protect such data from unauthorized linkage.

The chapter begins by reviewing the general principles of research ethics, then identifies several specific ethical challenges from sharing social media data. We analyze the challenges in more detail, using examples from research projects that used several different genres of social media. The conclusion provides some recommendations and suggestions for where practical guidance may be found and reflections on the future of ethical sharing of social media data.

BACKGROUND AND CONTEXT – RESEARCH ETHICS AND SHARING DATA

Principles for Human Subjects Research

Before turning to the principles, the use of the term 'human subjects' needs some justification. There is debate about the terminology, with some favoring the term 'participants,' and seeing the term 'subjects' as borrowing too heavily from medical research, at the cost of denying full agency to those engaging in research (Markham & Buchanan, 2012). We are using the term 'subjects' because it is more generic; there are many ways to provide data or engage with research other than being a participant. Moreover, there are definitions of 'subject' that convey agency 'subject versus object' rather than 'subject to.' Researchers and those they work with have complex relationships, not reducible to one being more agential or powerful than the other in all situations.

There is a rapidly growing literature on the research ethics of Internet-research, and social media specifically (Shilton & Sayles, 2016; Markham & Buchanan, 2012; Woodfield et al., 2013). Typical issues raised include:

- Informed consent, for example, can signing of terms of service of the platform provider be interpreted as fully informed consent?
- Privacy – can the content of public forums be considered public? Are sites where anyone can register deemed public? Is this true even if participants do not believe their data are public?
- What constitutes a human subject?

It is equally helpful to position these questions that are specific to Internet and social media research in the broader context of research ethics. There are three principles that are at the foundation of such guidance on ethical treatment of people, and the Association of Internet Researchers recommendations recognize the three from the Belmont Report (US Department of Health, Education and Welfare, 1978) as a useful modern synthesis (Markham & Buchanan, 2012, p. 4).

- **Respect** for persons – for their autonomy as human beings, not mere means, including respect for privacy.
- **Beneficence** – doing good. Research should do good, for individuals if possible, more generally by improving the knowledge and the public good. This recognizes that harm may be unavoidable, however, it must be minimized and justified.
- **Justice** – participation in, and gains from, research should be as equitable as possible.

In addition to these principles that address treatment of persons, there is a fourth one of 'research integrity,' which focuses on researchers' duties to peers and the public, including honesty and transparency (Iphofen, 2017).

Ethical Issues Specific to Sharing Social Media Data

The principle of respect implies respecting peoples' autonomy and not treating humans as mere means to other ends. It includes respect for privacy, including informational privacy. One central debate is over whether social media data are public, and if so, does that imply that they are available for unrestricted dissemination?

The legal case may be clear if users accepted the platform's terms of service (and these permit third-party sharing), but this still leaves ethical questions unresolved. There are several grounds for questioning data sharing, even if it is technically legal. First, users may not be aware of terms of service that authorize third-party sharing and may believe their data is more protected than it actually is. Acquisti, Brandimarte, and Loewenstein (2015) have reviewed the key literature on users' understanding of privacy. They conclude that uncertainty about privacy trade-offs, the context-sensitivity of privacy preferences, and the malleability of such preferences make it inappropriate to rely (solely) on expressed preferences of 'informed' or 'empowered' users for privacy protection. With such cautions in mind, it is still possible for empirical research to shed some light on users' preferences (Evans, Ginnis, & Bartlett, 2015; Williams, Burnap, & Sloan, 2017, Chapter 2, this volume). Again, such preferences are not necessarily determinative, but need to be factored into any ethical decision.

The second principle of beneficence raises further challenges, and these can be considered both for individuals and for groups. Placing a dataset where it is accessible, whether fully open or under forms of controlled access, must also consider the potential of the data to be linked with other sources, and any disclosure risks. Moreover, disclosure risk is greater due to this multi-dimensionality of data (OECD, 2016).

Furthermore, there are growing risks of collective, rather than individual harm. Whereas traditional ethics protections have focused on risks to individuals, the scale of social media data highlights risks of collective harms, for example, of discriminatory profiling by algorithms for insurance (Barocas & Nissenbaum, 2014) and predictive policing (Mayer-Schönberger & Cukier, 2013).

Finally, justice is relevant to sharing in several ways. There are issues of justice regarding data access (and data cannot be shared if access is not possible). If tools and infrastructures are of a scale and cost to be prohibitive to all except researchers at elite, well-resourced institutions, that is a problem of justice (Driscoll and Walker, 2014; Weller & Kinder-Kurlanda, 2016).

Second, restrictions that prevent data from being shared call into question if researchers' obligations to share benefits from research (especially publicly funded research) are being fully met. These restrictions may be part of the terms of service of social media companies, or these may be restrictions imposed as conditions when academics seek access to data by collaborating with social media companies. It is unlikely that fundamental, ethical obligations about transparency can be met under such restrictions.

If an original dataset on which published findings rest cannot be reproduced because the provider no longer makes it available, because of deletions (e.g., deleted tweets), or because the sampling cannot be reproduced (Thomson, 2016, p. 15), is it ethical to use such data for research? This might seem easy to answer with a resounding, no, but this issue is not simple. Many genres of research based on interpretivist foundations (usually) do not rest their validity on reproducibility, in contrast to positivist-based research (Mason, 2002). That said, there remains some consensus around the obligation for transparency, including revealing analytical processes and making data available, even if it is simultaneously acknowledged that exact replication is infeasible. This issue will be taken up in more detail in the specific cases below.

While this chapter will attempt to focus on ethical issues, the boundary between legal and ethical in this domain is sometimes not sharp. Increasingly, questions arise – is it ever ethical to violate laws, or terms of service, for research purposes? And it is clear to anyone attending conferences or reading blogs that for many researchers, violating a law or terms of service may not necessarily be considered unethical.

Sharing Data as an Ethical Act

While most ethics discussion of data sharing is concerned with risks to participants, it is worth highlighting ethical arguments *for* sharing data. First, while there are risks to participants, there is also a duty to value their time and contributions by making the most effective use of any data generated. This is true for any data, but is even more salient when data have been collected from vulnerable groups, such as the infirm or bereaved, or from hard-to-access groups such as elites or refugees.

Second, in keeping with the theme of research integrity noted above, making data available contributes to research transparency, contributing to fulfilling researchers' duties to the wider public. Given the current public sentiment questioning the value of experts, as well as declining trust in all public institutions, researchers should use every opportunity, such as being open with data, to attempt to restore and rebuild such trust. The Concordat on Open Research Data (2016) highlights as key reasons for opening data as 'securing public support for research funding and increasing public trust in research.' These arguments are also given by social media researchers when asked about their motivations to share data (Weller and Kinder-Kurlanda, forthcoming).

Social Media Data in Social Research

While there is little doubt that use of social media in research is growing, the scale of that growth may be somewhat exaggerated. Metzler, Kim, Allum, and Denman (2016) find that 9.8 percent (927 of 9412) of researchers surveyed have used social media, whereas the majority of big data research has been with administrative data (p. 1). Nonetheless, the number of publications naming social media in their title has grown from virtually zero to over 1,500 in 2013 (Weller, 2015).

There is extensive debate as to what, if anything, makes big data, or social media in particular, different from traditional research data. For technical debates, the features of volume, velocity, and variety are most relevant (Laney, 2001). However, for ethics, what is more germane is that social media data is not collected by researchers, for research purposes, and not in discrete data-sets (Halford, 2017, this volume; Metcalf, Keller, & boyd, 2016; OECD, 2016).

Big data is generated by many sources – social media websites, government offices, devices, and commercial transactions. In these cases, the data collection is not (usually) being done by academic researchers, and thus, is not subject to established procedures of Review Ethics Committees or codes of conduct of professional bodies that generally apply to academic researchers.

Moreover, social media and other big data are almost never being generated for research purposes. In most cases, research is not the primary purpose of data collection. It may be a secondary purpose, but most often, the data are not generated with the intent of using them for research. However, the standard research protections deployed to protect privacy – seeking informed consent and anonymizing data – take place at the point of collection or early in processing. And these forms of data do not routinely pass through these procedures.

The core issue then is that this 'wild' data is often generated, processed, analyzed, and disseminated outside the scope of ethical protections afforded by traditional research governance, creating what Barocas & Nissenbaum (2014) call an 'end run' around protocols for consent and anonymization.

There is already excellent work on challenges of sharing social media. By and large, these works – while identifying ethical issues – have primarily focused on other challenges such as legal restrictions, technical infrastructure, and documentation (Weller & Kinder-Kurlanda, 2015; Thomson, 2016). (For a significant exception that addresses ethics of sharing social media directly, see Weller and Kinder-Kurlanda, forthcoming). The cases in this chapter build upon and extend this work by focusing primarily on ethical issues of data sharing.

CASE ONE – TWITTER WITH AGGREGATED DATA

We will present three cases of sharing social media data, two from Twitter and a third from Facebook. The selection of these cases is justified because Twitter and Facebook seem to be the predominant sources of social media, based on publications (Weller, 2015). Giglietto, Rossi, & Bennato (2012) also make a convincing case that due to the significant differences in factors such as ease of access and privacy norms, it is a misnomer to talk about 'social media' as a unified source, and better to examine each platform on its own.

Our first examples are based on research being done at the Social Data Science Lab (SDSL) at Cardiff University using the Collaborative Online Social Media Observatory (COSMOS) software platform for collecting and analyzing data from Twitter.

The Social Data Science Lab at Cardiff University is an Economic and Social Research Council (ESRC) strategic 'Big Data' investment that brings together social, computer, political, health, statistical and mathematical scientists to study the methodological, theoretical, empirical and technical dimensions of New Forms of Data in social and policy contexts. This empirical social data science programme is complemented by a focus on ethics and the development of new methodological tools and technical/data solutions for the UK academic and public sectors. The Lab was established in 2015 and continues the successful COSMOS programme of research that ran between 2011–2015. The Lab's mission is to democratise access to big social data among the academic, private, public and third sectors, and to support real-time social data analytics for research, policy & practice. (Reproduced with minor edits from http://socialdatalab.net/)

The SDSL now runs the COSMOS platform for accessing and analyzing Twitter data. It is free to users conducting not-for-profit research from academia or the public sector. The SDSL complies with all provisions of Twitter's terms and conditions and developer policies. These conditions prohibit sharing machine-readable data and storing data in any cloud infrastructure. The implications of these and other constraints will be elaborated below.

Twitter and Journal Publication

Our first case is a study by Williams and Burnap (2015) from the SDSL at Cardiff University using Twitter. They wanted to find out if a terrorist act triggered an increase in cyberhate language in social media. They looked at tweets following the murder of Lee Rigby, a British soldier, in Woolwich in 2013. Data were collected via the Twitter streaming Application Programming Interface (API)-based trending keywords following the event (i.e., 'Woolwich'). Their dataset consisted of 427,330 tweets collected over 15 days following the murder.

They wanted to be able to show what cyberhate terms were being used, their frequency and geographical distribution. And this had to be done without disclosing identities – to protect participants. Sharing the data in the publication itself was not problematic; they used techniques of aggregating the data, frequency displays of word clouds, and mapping at a level of granularity so as not to be disclosive (see Fig. 1; Williams & Burnap, 2015).

Sharing social media data in the form of publication of results from data analysis may be somewhat constrained, but is not generally problematic. This is the case largely because the data are aggregated and thus any disclosure risk is negligible. Moreover, creative forms of data visualization enable findings to be communicated clearly, and this capacity is likely to increase as visualization tools improve.

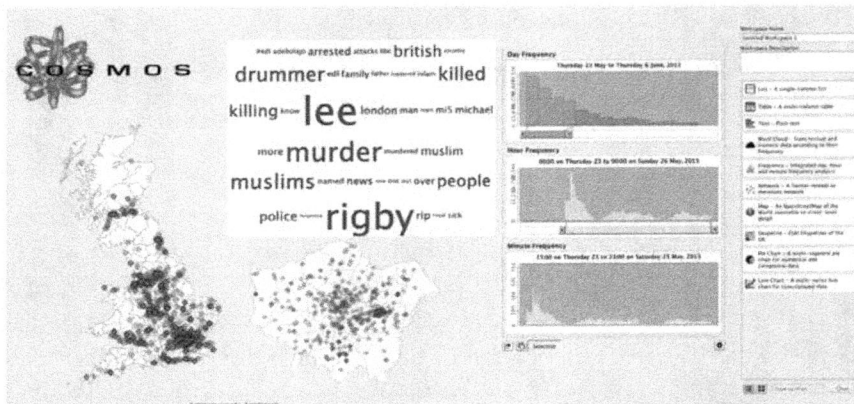

Fig 2: Woolwich Inventory Stage – COSMOS visualisation of twitter traffic during the first four days of collection (left to right: Geo-located tweets in UK & London, WordCloud of tweet content and Frequency of Tweets in the 15 day collection window)

Fig. 1.   COSMOS Visualization of Aggregated Twitter Data for Publication.
Source: Williams, M. L., & Burnap, P. 2015. Cyberhate on social media in the aftermath of Woolwich. *British Journal of Criminology*, *56*(2), 211–238. 10.1093/bjc/azv059.

Twitter and Sharing Data Underpinning a Publication

In another project (Sloan & Morgan, 2015) investigated whether 'there are any demographic differences between users who do or do not enable local services on Twitter?' and the same question was asked about geotagging. The journal that accepted the paper, *PLOS One*, requires data to be made available as a condition of publication.

However, in this case, the authors were unable to make the data available because of Twitter's policies. Twitter permits two forms of limited sharing: first, sharing is permissible for up to 50K tweets in a nonreadable form, such as pdf. Second, Twitter permits archiving tweet and user IDs. These IDs can, in principle, be rehydrated by secondary users who themselves access Twitter using an API.

To accommodate these restrictions, the authors made available a dataset of User IDs, and their derived demographic variables through figshare. The published paper has this accompanying statement of data availability:

Data Availability: The data is subject to Twitter Terms and Conditions which prevent redistributing most data collected from the 1% API beyond the research team. Twitter Terms and Conditions prevent the authors from openly sharing the metadata supplied by the API; therefore 'Dataset1' and 'Dataset2' contain only the user ID (which is acceptable) and the demographics the authors have derived: tweet language, gender, age and NS-SEC. Replication of this study can be conducted through individual researchers using user IDs to gather the Twitter-produced metadata that the authors cannot share as, according to the Terms and Conditions of Twitter, they are able to supply user IDs so that others can retrieve the same data from the Twitter API. The data can be accessed via figshare using the following links: Dataset1: http://dx.doi.org/10.6084/m9.figshare.1572291, Dataset2: http://dx.doi.org/10.6084/m9.figshare.1572292.

Arguments For and Against this Restriction

- The data sharing complies with Twitter's terms and conditions. This not only complies with the law but also demonstrates an effort to respect for research integrity and the transparency it requires.
- There is legitimate justification for Twitter's restrictions – to sustain its legal obligations to its users to delete their tweets if asked. If data are archived out of Twitter's control, they cannot keep that promise to users.
- This solution helps to maintain good relations between the SDSL and Twitter, which is important for continuing negotiations for better access for academic research (Thomson, 2016). These negotiations would not be possible if researchers were to arbitrarily violate terms and conditions. (It is also an argument for why other researchers should not take law-breaking lightly, however strongly they might disagree with a data providers' terms and conditions.)

However, this outcome is far from ideal and difficult ethical questions remain.

- Original and rehydrated datasets will, in all probability, not be identical because of deleted tweets, sampling variation, and other factors (Maddock, Starbird, & Mason, 2015).
- More importantly, the nature of the differences cannot be established, but are not likely to be random.
- Ongoing availability of data is at Twitter's discretion and subject to their policies, as well as change of ownership of the corporation. (This point was made early in 2017 when Twitter altered its policy and restricted sharing to 1.5 million Tweet IDs, later clarifying the change to exempt academics doing non-commercial research (Twitter, 2017)).
- This current practice does not fully meet requirements of research integrity by making data available for replication (OECD, 2016, p. 33; Schroeder, 2014).

To summarize, attempts to archive social media confront conflicting ethical principles involving research integrity and justice. Repositories such the UK Data Service and the German Data Archive for the Social Sciences at

GESIS are just beginning to curate such content, and the current practice is to hold only tweet and user IDs to enable rehydration, with no assurances that identical data will be produced. In special cases, more complete datasets are being held. Most often, these are tweets from public institutions or figures, such as in research about the German elections in 2013 (Kaczmirek & Mayr, 2015). Where holdings are more complete, they are done in exclusive partnerships, with limited or no data accessibility beyond the core team, as is happening at MIT's Media Lab (Thomson, 2016).

The ability to access data should be considered as another facet, or dimension, of the digital divide (boyd & Crawford, 2012). While in principle, the data may be available to anyone with the necessary technical skills (e.g., to access Twitter's API), in practice, data may not actually be available without partnership of some form with social media companies. Increasingly, the problem, then, is that the data necessary to replicate, reproduce, or validate research findings is in the hands of private entities (Borgman, 2016; Schroeder, 2014).

Of course, replication is not a universal standard across the social sciences (e.g., ethnography, much qualitative research), and it is certainly more often esteemed than executed. But the possibility of some kind of validation remains salient, and when this capacity is under private control it raises ethical concerns that should be made explicit by both those using data for research and those entities curating such data.

While this chapter's focus is on ethics, not law, this case demonstrates their connections. Law-abiding behavior in this case prohibits data sharing, making full transparency impossible. Replication, or even transparency, cannot be held up as absolute, inflexible criteria for ethical research. However, legal compliance has ethical consequences, revealing competing principles: researcher integrity (law-abiding behavior) versus more equitable access to data and scientific principle of replicability. And for Twitter data, prohibitions on data archiving conflicts with standards of research integrity, and when data access is exclusive, justice is compromised. The benefits to date have been great, and SDSL has contributed an open software platform, practical tools and guidance, and significant research findings. But the debate requires continual assessment of all dimensions of these trade-offs.

CASE TWO – TWITTER – PUBLISHING
UNANONYMIZED QUALITATIVE DATA

The second case addresses a different genre and use of Twitter data: the publication and sharing of full texts of tweets. Here again, Twitter's policies pose challenges for typical research ethics practice. While Twitter permits publishing of individual tweets (indeed encourages it), Twitter's terms and conditions require that third parties must publish tweet content in full with IDs, and cannot alter content in any way (Twitter, 2017). Obviously, this restriction makes anonymization or pseudonymization impossible. Of course, anonymization is not universal in social research. Exceptions include oral history, some participatory or action research, and much audio and visual data that would be rendered unusable for research if it were to be anonymized (Iphofen & Tolich, 2018 forthcoming).

This case is presented by Daniel Gray – now a Ph.D. student at Cardiff – who engaged reflexively with the COSMOS guidelines for social media research for his master's dissertation on misogynist speech on Twitter (Gray, 2015). Because the data had to remain identifiable, to comply with terms and conditions, COSMOS had developed a protocol (later incorporated into the SDSL Ethics Statement (Social Data Science Lab, 2017) to obtain informed consent by using the Twitter platform. That protocol was successfully used in Gray's research.

In 2015, I undertook a dissertation research project as part of my master's degree in social science research methods (Gray, 2015). This took the form of an attempt to apply a fine-grained qualitative critical discourse analysis to misogynistic/sexist and antifeminist user-generated content found on Twitter, collected through the Collaborative Online Social Media Observatory (COSMOS). Most of the project's themes were evident from the start: the expanded critique of sexist ideology in a novel discursive environment, the application of qualitative methods to a field of study where they were under-represented, and the testing of both the limitations and potentials of computational social data collection methods in discursive research. What emerged rather unexpectedly and took a prominent position both in the research process and its findings were the ethical issues and dilemmas raised by this kind of project.

These ethical issues are diverse: the role of institutional approaches to ethical social research, the limitations imposed on social media researchers by the architecture of platforms and the stipulations of their owners, the blurring of private and public contexts online, the presentation and sharing of potentially compromising or harmful user-generated data, and the tensions between the interests of critical research and the interests of the individuals whose actions are subject to critique. Here I illustrate the contours of these issues and explain how they shaped and continue to shape the research.

Institutional Ethics and Risk Assessments

The presence of unanonymized user data in the project meant incorporating the ethical framework developed by Williams et al. (2017a), the principle document being the COSMOS Risk Assessment (see Fig. 2). This document prescribed the forms of consent a researcher must obtain in order to present unanonymized tweets where the identification of users is a possibility, based on the nature of the account and the content of their tweet. In cases where the originator of a tweet appeared to be an individual rather than the public facing account of an organization, the framework requires obtaining consent when seeking to publish. Tweets containing sensitive, overly personal or abusive content are classified as 'high risk,' and require affirmative informed consent, while tweets without this degree of compromising content but still from individuals are classified as 'medium risk,' and though they still require contacting the users and seeking consent, a nonresponse can be interpreted as permission to publish.

This framework, which I had to adhere to as a requirement for ethical approval within the university, had a number of unexpected and important effects on my research. The potential difficulty of obtaining

---

Low risk – Tweet is from official/institutional account: Publish without seeking consent in most cases.

Medium risk – Tweets are from individual users and contain mundane information of a nonsensitive nature: Must contact the user (direct message/@mention/ email) informing them of the intent to publish; unless the user opts out consider as permission to publish.

High risk – Tweets are from individual users and contain sensitive information (overly personal, abusive etc.). Must contact the user (direct message/@mention/ email) and ask their permission to publish. Only publish if consent is received.

High risk – Tweet has been deleted precluding publication under Twitter Developer Agreement/Policy.

High Risk– Tweet is from a deleted account meaning it has been deleted precluding publication under Twitter Developer Agreement/Policy.

Fig. 2. COSMOS Risk Assessment.

informed affirmative consent from participants producing hateful content led me to focus on less hateful but still relevant tweets where users talked about feminism in more general terms. While this genre of discourse was still very relevant, my refocusing on it, nonetheless, illustrated the ways in which ethical frameworks can shape topics of inquiry. While many of the 'medium risk' sentiments expressed by these users about feminism and feminists were still problematic in an academic or activist context, I reasoned that in public discourse their language was very much in keeping with typical constructions of the subject, and as such would not be compromising to them if published. Indeed, the similarities between these sentiments about feminism and those observed historically in offline contexts (Edley & Wetherell, 2001) were one of the key findings of my project.

Those tweets classified as high risk tended to express negative sentiments in a kind of extreme invective language, in a similar fashion what has been classified as 'E-bile' by Jane (2014). These more hateful tweets included gendered slurs, and 'variously referred to [feminists] as "ugly c***s," "retarded c***s," and simply "c***s"' (Gray, 2015, p. 35), as well as in one case including a command that the constructed category of feminists ought to commit suicide. While these tweets were not obviously directed at a particular user or an individual, the content had an obviously abusive and hateful character to it, and as such was classified as high risk. Additionally, in most of these cases, the participants appeared to be using pictures of themselves for their display pictures, making them directly identifiable.

As an ethical framework, the COSMOS Risk Assessment expresses particular positions on the ethical priorities of social media research, and these positions shaped the conduct of the project in various ways. The framework has a very strong and central concern for the wellbeing of participants in situations where their content may be of a hateful, sensitive, and personally compromising nature. There is obvious justification for this concern. The production of hateful speech by identifiable individuals has the potential for real consequences, emblematic in the now much reported case of Justine Sacco, a public relations executive who made international headlines after posting an offensive tweet that went viral, causing lasting damage to her career (Salon, 2013). This transmission of offensive or compromising content out of a particular context without knowledge of the participant seemed to feature prominently in the priorities of my ethical approval, and the possibility, however remote, that this could happen because of academic republication is clearly a major concern.

From a critical perspective, however, this rigorous attention to harm and privacy has profound consequences. By requiring affirmative (opt-in) consent from those users who post the most serious and abusive content, the very act of producing hateful discourse is turned into a barrier to the scrutiny of this discourse. The perverse consequence of this measure is that it serves to privilege and protect the interests of those who produce hateful discourse over those who are subject to hateful discourse. As a researcher with explicitly critically orientated theoretical, analytical, and methodological dispositions, this is a highly problematic requirement for research that relies on the publishing of hateful user-generated content to achieve methodological integrity.

Limitations to Gaining Informed Consent on Twitter

Having accepted the requirements of the COSMOS Risk Assessment, I encountered several challenges when implementing it; issues that related to the actual practicalities of using Twitter as a communicative medium for contacting participants, as well as the implicit and explicit priorities of Twitter's developers and owners. These issues not only highlighted the practical challenges of attempting ethical social research in a structured social media environment but also clearly illustrated the public nature of Twitter as a platform.

Contacting participants directly became problematic. While I had intended to discreetly make contact, be open about my position as a researcher, and what participation entailed, it quickly became clear that Twitter does not prioritize discreet communication, and only allows direct private messaging between accounts that mutually follow each other. Establishing a mutual following was not practical for a number of reasons: a requirement of my ethical approval was that I use an anonymized profile to contact participants, and I reasoned that users would be disinclined to follow an anonymous profile with very few followers and little content. This was further complicated by the fact that narrow time constraints meant building a public profile and contacting users to ask for private contact was impractical.

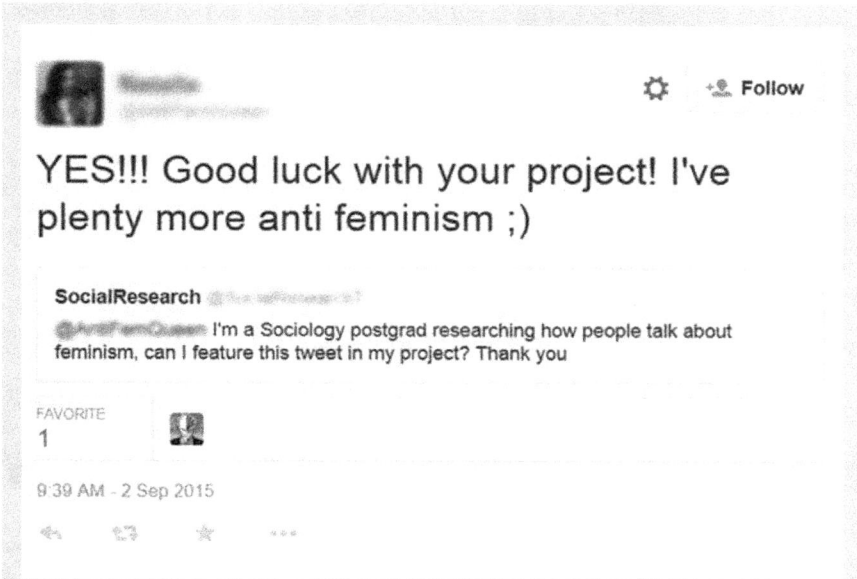

Fig. 3. Screenshot Featuring '140 character consent form' Tweet, and a Participant's Reply Giving (Apparently Enthusiastic) Affirmative Consent.

Due to these constraints, I relied on direct contact via tweeting to obtain consent (see Fig. 3). This consisted of replying to the specific tweets I wanted to feature in my research with my own tweet containing a very brief introduction and request for consent. This solution was far from ideal. Openly tweeting users meant that any of my participants could very easily follow a link to my profile, look at my activity and see the other participants, including the specific tweets I had selected. A highly problematic consequence of this situation is that it potentially allowed participants to contact each other. While some participants identified themselves as explicitly antifeminist, others produced less hostile and even ostensibly positive discourse about feminism. Given the highly antagonistic speech produced by the former category of participants, this method potentially produced even greater risk of participant harm than publishing without consent, but was still seen as preferable to treating initial publication as consent.

Another pertinent issue with this method is that rather than communicating with potential participants through private messages, which would have allowed me to give detailed information about my status as a researcher, the nature of my research and what participation would entail, I was left with what was in effect a '140-character consent form,' a significant portion of which was taken up with the given user's Twitter handle. Clearly, this kind of communicative method is not ideal for informing participants of the possibilities for harm, and the specifics of what taking part entails that are necessary for achieving informed consent.

In practice, consent in this project was managed pragmatically. Potential participants received replies to the tweets I intended to feature, giving the best outline I could of my status, intentions, and their option to withdraw. Contrary to my assumptions, no participants actively refused to give consent; some did not reply to my message, while other responses ranged from straightforward agreement to apparent enthusiasm. While this was a very ad hoc process, the way these issues were resolved and negotiated presents potentially interesting opportunities for future developments in the consent process on Twitter. Future research may explore such methods as transforming the consent process into a conversation between the researcher and potential participants, or treating these conversations as another level of qualitative data related to how consent is negotiated in such a structured and mediated environment.

Twitter Design, Privacy, and Publicity

While these barriers to discreet contact were immediately present in the interface of Twitter, the underlying architecture and approaches toward privacy, publicity, and communication that shape the development and design of Twitter also contribute to a medium that is somewhat at odds with researcher approaches to privacy and consent. From the perspective of a critical researcher Twitter can and should be seen as possibly the most open communicative medium in history. Twitter is designed as a system that avoids more opaque and user-controlled forms of privacy that have been present in other systems of communication online. In this context, the discretion and anonymity afforded in other settings is absent: tweets cannot be directed to certain users and not others, they cannot be hidden, users are encouraged to post under their own names in an identifiable way, to share their geolocational data, even direct messaging is designed to be able to direct text at large groups of people.

From this perspective, Twitter can be seen as a medium that assumes the whole world as speaker and audience and allows instantaneous communication in a medium that prioritizes moving content exponentially quickly between users in a very public manner, to reach as many users as is possible. Users are directed to share, reply, comment, favorite, link, follow, unfollow, and promote themselves and others in the most public way possible. While the medium has features that allow users to prioritize viewing the content of other particular users, and direct their communication via hashtags, the underlying logic is still to make content as visible as possible. Through these logics of design, Twitter is orientated toward a discursive environment that foregrounds the idea of a connected and highly public space.

This contrasts sharply with those online spaces and communities that have been the focus of previous qualitative and critical social research. In many previous cases, research has dealt with ethical dilemmas of privacy and publicity in online spaces that were not designed with the same kind of predisposition to publicity and openness as Twitter (Trevisan & Reilly, 2014). Twitter is not structured as a private network for support or a safe space for the expression of marginalized identities, although there are undoubtedly a minority of people who use it in this capacity. The users that I have featured were not members of discreet Internet forums, but people openly producing and reproducing often hateful discourse in an extremely public medium to a potentially huge audience in a way that constitutes a public issue. Given these unique features of communication on Twitter, and the differences in how the communities and connectivity it fosters when compared to other online platforms, I argue that future critical research of Twitter is likely to negotiate similar ethical problems and should endeavor to push for treating the initial publication of Tweets as consent to republish in and of itself.

Reflections on Respect, Beneficence, and Justice
When Archiving and Sharing Data

Since completing my research project, my data has been subject to various forms of sharing. I have engaged in various kinds of formal and informal sharing through presenting my data excerpts at conferences, workshops, and other events as well as with colleagues. The sharing of my data raises

issues in terms of the aforementioned ethical principles of respect, beneficence, and justice.

In terms of the principle of respect, my research has been structured by
the COSMOS Risk Assessment with regard for the potential privacy concerns of participants firmly in mind: regardless of what is stated in Twitter's
user agreement, participants' content was not treated as public material.
When it comes to critical research of hate speech, this position is problematic. While it shows respect for participants, it inflexibly prioritizes participants' interests above respect for the condition and experiences of those
who are subject to hate speech. When considering respect for participants
with regard to archiving of data, consideration should be given to how this
principle affects those who, while not direct participants, are still highly
involved in the topic of study in different but extremely important ways.

My research was quite strongly linked to the principle of beneficence:
as a critical researcher with an explicit political stance toward my topic
of study, I have been motivated by a goal to critique and highlight hate
speech and problematic discourse for the public good. While the archiving
and dissemination of this data has the potential to be harmful or compromising to my participants, I argue that this still poses far less risk than
is found in the normal use of Twitter. Users' tweets are highly searchable
even without the use of specialist data collection tools, and even a cursory
search for the correct terms will reveal many users and groups engaged
in the production of hateful or sensitive discourse. In this sense, Twitter
itself represents a far larger and more open archive of potentially harmful
data, with far less attention paid to the principle of beneficence than my
own research and data sharing.

Finally, my research and data present complex issues in terms of the
principles of justice. Fundamentally, my research highlights the com-
promises critical researchers may be forced to make when collaborating
with Twitter in data collection. By the terms of the Twitter Developer
Agreement, tweets cannot be edited when presented by researchers,
which has the effect of putting special considerations on researchers
who approach the field with qualitative methods, and do not aggregate
the data they collect. Similarly, even when data is collected during, or
archived after the research process, researchers are obliged to follow up
on any deletions made by users to their tweets. Given the potential for
critical researchers to focus on hate speech, this has troubling implications for methodological integrity in archiving and sharing. These and
other factors may present serious dilemmas for critical research.

The ethical issues I have encountered and elaborated on leave the critical social media researcher with an uncomfortable dilemma: publishing data in full without consent means going against the interests of participants, anonymizing data means going against Twitter's Developer Agreement and risking the loss of academic access, withholding data from publication goes against principles of research integrity, and bypassing Twitter's developer agreement entirely precludes access to innovative collection methods. In the face of dilemmas, the standards set by the COSMOS Risk Assessment appear to be a fair and effective compromise, but this produces its own dilemmas: adhering to Twitter's standards while seeking affirmative consent from participants who produce hate speech risks compromising the principles of critical social research both in its effect of protecting these users and their speech from scrutiny, and in how it in forces critical researchers to adhere to the standards set by social media entities, the critique of whom may be another goal of the critical researcher.

The archiving and sharing of this kind of data extend these issues: archiving tweets that may be subject to deletion based on future actions of participants potentially harms the methodological integrity necessary for qualitative research, while the sharing and dissemination of unanonymized data puts identifiable users into a context that is likely very different from the original context of their discourse. In addition, the nuanced issues related to archiving and sharing are well beyond what can be communicated with a 140-character consent form. Given these issues, any further research of this type will likely need to develop more appropriate methods for gaining informed consent.

This case demonstrates the kind of flexible and reflexive moral reasoning that is required when engaging with new forms of data, such as social media. On the issue of consent, SDSL's defense of opt-in consent is well-grounded. The SDSL explicitly chose to not rely on the 'already public' defense. Online sites, they argue, blur the public/private boundary, and this is true even for Twitter, which is among the most explicit in its design and use as a publication and broadcast forum. Moreover, they drew on empirical evidence from the specific population of Twitter users to better understand their views and expectations. Their research showed that users have widely varied views about whether terms and conditions are fair, and do not believe their data should be available for other purposes. For a significant share of users, this is true even when data are to be used for research, and especially if users could be identified. In studies, 80 percent or more of Twitter users expected to be asked for consent if their data was being used in research (Williams et al., 2017b, this volume).

Gray acknowledges these strong claims and followed the recommended protocol by applying a strong form of opt-in consent. Yet, in doing so, he makes clear the underlying assumptions of this model: it privileges participants' interests above other claims, even victims of hate speech. Furthermore, he raises a very challenging question as to what level of protection 'public speech' deserves, when that speech is both inciting hate and (in some cases) protected by anonymized Twitter accounts. Finally, as in the first case, the publication of unanonymized tweets demonstrates that social research practice is shaped, even constrained, by terms and conditions of private entities holding the data. The implications of such constraints will need continuing ethical consideration.

CASE 3 – FACEBOOK'S EMOTION CONTAGION – RESEARCH AND DATA

In 2010, researchers at Facebook and Cornell University published research that provided evidence that online social networks can transmit large-scale emotional contagion, where the emotions of one person are transmitted to others (Kramer, Guillory, & Hancock, 2014). The experiment, based on a sample size of 689,003 users, demonstrated that reducing positive inputs to users' feeds resulted in users posting fewer positive, and more negative posts, and the reverse. Kramer et al. emphasized the meaning of their findings: emotional contagion had been shown to occur without face-to-face and nonverbal cues.

The import of the findings was swamped by the ensuing public outcry about the methodology, in particular, the manipulation of users' news feeds, and hence emotions, without their consent (boyd, 2015). This was seen as surprising by some, given that such testing of two different versions of a website (A/B testing) is common in marketing, software testing, and academic research (boyd, 2015; Metcalf et al., 2016).

While the main outcry focused on manipulation, consent' and ethics review, we want to use this Facebook case to highlight a slightly different facet of sharing social media data, namely, the responsibilities of the researcher *using* data that has been made available by another entity (Bishop, 2016).

One question that emerged was had the project been subjected to any formal, ethical review, and if not, why not? An Editorial Expression of Concern

(2014) from the publishing journal stated that Cornell had confirmed that the research did not fall under the purview of their Human Research Protection Program because the experiment had been done at Facebook and not Cornell. Furthermore, because the research was not federally funded, it was not required to go through an institutional review board.

When the authors prepared their paper for publication in PNAS, they stated that: 'Because this experiment was conducted by Facebook, Inc. for internal purposes, the Cornell University IRB [Institutional Review Board] determined that the project did not fall under Cornell's Human Research Protection Program.' This statement has since been confirmed by Cornell University. (Editorial Expression of Concern, 2014)

Moreover, the editors pointed out that: 'as a private company Facebook was under no obligation to conform to the provisions of the Common Rule when it collected the data used by the authors' (Editorial Expression of Concern, 2014).

Because of the differential treatment of private companies and academic research, the affiliations of the three authors also came under scrutiny. A press release from Cornell University (Carberry, 2014) attempted to clarify:

Cornell University Professor of Communication and Information Science Jeffrey Hancock and Jamie Guillory, a Cornell doctoral student at the time (now at University of California San Francisco) analysed results from previously conducted research by Facebook into emotional contagion among its users. Professor Hancock and Dr. Guillory did not participate in data collection and did not have access to user data. Their work was limited to initial discussions, analyzing the research results and working with colleagues from Facebook to prepare the peer-reviewed paper...

Because the research was conducted independently by Facebook and Professor Hancock had access only to results – and not to any individual, identifiable data at any time – Cornell University's Institutional Review Board concluded that he was not directly engaged in human research and that no review by the Cornell Human Research Protection Program was required.

The transparency of this statement is open to challenge on at least two counts. First, what definition of 'analyzing' is being used that does not entail any access to user data. Second, the distinction between analyzing data versus analyzing results is used to exempt the Cornell researchers, and university, from responsibility.

To simplify, the argument for the research being exempt from IRB review (and hence questions of informed consent) evolved as follows. First, there was denial of the experiment involving 'human subjects' at all. If only 'results' were used, then there were no new human subjects. Even if there were human subjects, the data collection was done at Facebook, an exempt institution.

And even if Cornell staff were involved, it was only in aspects of the research that, strategically, avoided any direct contact with 'user data.'

Regardless of this rather tortured episode, what most definitely did not happen was a proactive acceptance, by everyone connected with this paper, of responsibility for understanding the history, provenance, and conditions of collection – including presence or absence of informed consent – of the data they all collectively relied upon to write a paper and publish it in a highly regarded journal. Such partnerships raise challenging ethical questions as others have noted:

> To what extent should academic researchers partner with researchers within private enterprises that have troves of data collected under conditions that do not rise to the level of informed consent? (Metcalf et al., 2016, p. 9)

We think it is precisely this expanded responsibility for data that researchers (and repositories) have to acknowledge as part of the price of having access to 'wild' data.

CONCLUSION

We are skeptical of arguments that 'everything is new' and thus none of the existing writing and thinking about ethics in general, research ethics, and research integrity is relevant to big data and social media in particular. That said, there is no doubt we live in challenging times (data and its problems may be the least of our worries). And it is very clear that far too little is being learned from previous work on these subjects (Iphofen, Series Introduction, 2017). Regulations and other legal remedies, while essential, are almost always lagging in their effect. The General Data Protection Regulation will be crucially influential, not least because it will enforce greater consistently across Europe and because potential sanctions are more financially punitive. But it has taken many years to conclude and gaps remain in its coverage.

The way forward needs to proceed on two fronts: one individual, the other structural. Absent consensus in the law or ethics review bodies, researchers handling wild data must assume a broader range of responsibilities – to ask where data come from, what were the conditions of its collection, what expectations do its providers have about its future use, and so on.

There are already good resources available, and more being produced, so again, the challenge is finding and sharing the best available. Some examples include the SDSL Risk Assessment discussed here and the Twitter flowchart for publishing Twitter posts (Fig. 4). More general resources are provided

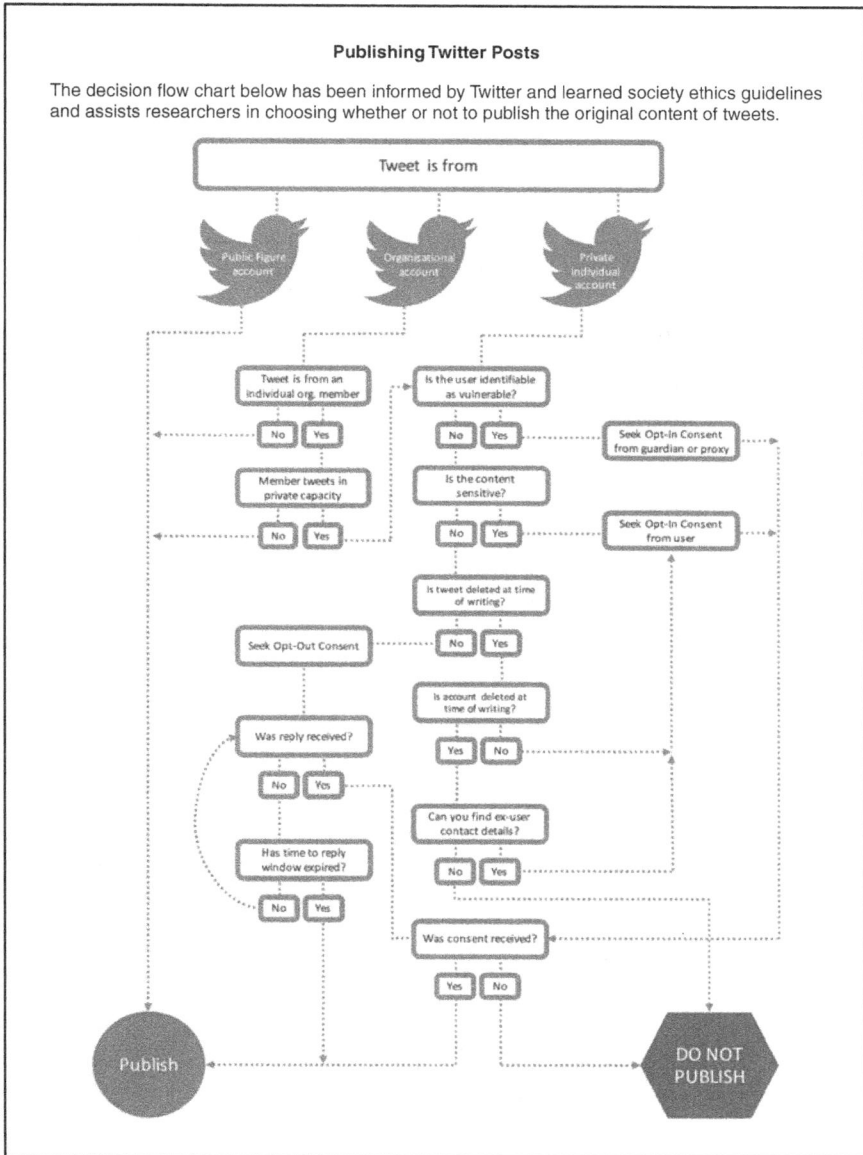

Publishing Twitter Posts

The decision flow chart below has been informed by Twitter and learned society ethics guidelines and assists researchers in choosing whether or not to publish the original content of tweets.

Fig. 4.   Flowchart for Publishing Twitter Posts (Social Data Science Lab). http://
socialdatalab.net/wp-content/uploads/2016/08/EthicsSM-SRA-Workshop.pdf

by UK Cabinet Office-Data Science Ethical Framework (2016) and guidance being produced by Web Observatories (Wilson, 2016).

Despite the existence of much training, what is still called for is training specific to big data, research ethics, and research integrity. The OECD (2016) has recommended proper development of training for researchers requesting access to personal data and the Council for Big Data, Ethics and Society calls for ethics training to be interdisciplinary and to be 'a cornerstone of big data education' (Metcalf et al., 2016). Experience from other domains such as health care has shown that applied ethics training should be practical, case-based, and interactive (Tolich, 2016, in Iphofen, Series Introduction, 2017). Embedding training in problem-solving events, such as data clinics, may be preferable.

However, this focus on individuals can be only half of the story. Too much emphasis on individual responsibility risks letting institutions off the hook. As with researchers, institutions – public or private – must be good stewards of the data under their control. Fortunately, good examples are emerging, notably the very recent archiving of geotagged tweets at GESIS. The curation of this test data demonstrates practical steps for balancing compliance with Twitter's conditions, lowering barriers to data reuse by supplying syntax and other documentation, and protecting privacy by regulating access to the data collection (Kinder-Kurlanda, et al., forthcoming). It is clear that while ethical challenges of sharing social media may seem daunting, they can be negotiated successfully.

REFERENCES

Acquisti, A., Brandimarte, L., & Loewenstein, G. (2015). Privacy and human behavior in the age of information. *Science, 347*(6221), 509–514. doi:10.1126/science.aaa1465

Barocas, S., & Nissenbaum, H. (2014). Big data's end run around anonymity and consent. In J. Lane, V. Stodden, S. Bender, & H. Nissenbaum (Eds.), *Privacy, big data and the public good* (pp. 44–75). Cambridge, UK: Cambridge University Press.

Bishop, L. (2016). Facebook's responsibilities to research subjects. *3 Quarks Daily*. Retrieved from http://www.3quarksdaily.com/3quarksdaily/2016/08/by-libby-bishop-amid-the-latest-privacy-kerfuffle-in-which-whatsapp-agreed-to-sell-users-data-to-its-parent-face-book.html#sthash.CxgomRgP.dpuf

Borgman, C. L. (2012). The conundrum of sharing research data. *Journal of the American Society for Information Science and Technology, 63*(6), 1059–1078.

Borgman, C. (2016). *Big data, little data, no data*. Cambridge, MA: MIT Press.

boyd, d., & Crawford, K. (2012). Critical questions for Big Data: Provocations for a cultural, technological, and scholarly phenomenon. *Information, Communication & Society, 15*(5), 662–679. doi:http://doi.org/10.1080/1369118X.2012.678878

boyd, d. (2015). Untangling research and practice: What Facebook's 'emotional contagion' study teaches us. *Research Ethics, 12*(1), 4–13.

Carberry, J. (2014). Media statement on Cornell University's role in Facebook 'emotional contagion' research. Retrieved from http://mediarelations.cornell.edu/2014/06/30/media-statement-on-cornell-universitys-role-in-facebook-emotional-contagion-research/

Concordat on Open Research Data. (2016). Retrieved from http://www.rcuk.ac.uk/documents/documents/concordatonopenresearchdata-pdf/

Driscoll, K. and Walker, S. (2014). Big Data, Big Questions: Working Within a Black Box: Transparency in the Collection and Production of Big Twitter Data. *International Journal of Communication, 8,* 1745–1764. Retrieved from http://ijoc.org/index.php/ijoc/article/view/2171

Edley, N., & Wetherell, M. (2001). Jekyll and Hyde: Men's constructions of feminism and feminists. *Feminism and Psychology, 11*(4), 439–457.

Editorial Expression of Concern. (2014). Experimental evidence of massive scale emotional contagion through social networks. *PNAS, 111*(29), 10779; doi:10.1073/pnas.1412469111

Evans, H., Ginnis, S., & Bartlett, J. (2015). *#SocialEthics: A guide to embedding ethics in social media research*. London: Ipsos MORI.

Giglietto, F., Rossi, L., & Bennato, D. (2012). The OpenLaboratory: Limits and possibilities of using Facebook, Twitter, and YouTube as a research data source. *Journal of Technology in Human Services, 30*(3–4), 145–159. doi:10.1080/15228835.2012.743797

Gray, D. (September 2015). *Talking about women: Misogyny on Twitter*. Master of Science Dissertation, Cardiff University, Wales, UK:.

Halford, S. (2017). The Ethical Disruptions of Social Media Data: Tales from the Field. In K. Woodfield (ed.), *The Ethics of Online Research (Advances in Research Ethics and Integrity, Volume 2)* (pp. 13–25). Emerald Publishing Limited.

Iphofen, R. (ed.) (2017). Background to the series: Advances in research ethics and integrity. In *Finding Common Ground: Consensus in Research Ethics Across the Social Sciences (Advances in Research Ethics and Integrity, Volume 1)* (pp. xi–xxv). Emerald Publishing Limited.

Iphofen, R., & Tolich, M. (eds) (2018 – forthcoming) *The SAGE handbook of qualitative research ethics.* London: SAGE.

Jane, E. A. (2014). 'YOU'RE A UGLY, WHORISH, SLUT': Understanding E-bile. *Feminist Media Studies, 14*(4), 531–546.

Kaczmirek, L. & Mayr, P. (2015). German Bundestag elections 2013: Twitter usage by electoral candidates. *GESIS Data Archive*, Cologne. DOI: 10.4232/1.12319

Kinder-Kurlanda, K., Pfeffer, J., Weller, K, Wolfgang Zenk-Möltgen, W., and Fred Morstatter, F. (Forthcoming). Archiving information from geotagged tweets to promote reproducibility and comparability in social media research. Big Data & Society.

Kramer, A. D. I., Guillory, J.E., & Hancock, J. T. (2014). Experimental evidence of massive-scale emotional contagion through social networks. *Proceedings of the National Academy of Sciences, 111*(24), 8788–8790.

Laney, D. (2001). 3D data management: Controlling data volume, velocity and variety. In Meta Group. Retrieved from http://blogs.gartner.com/doug-laney/files/2012/01/ad949-3D-Data-Management-Controlling-Data-Volume-Velocity-and-Variety.pdf

Maddock, J., Starbird, K., & Mason, R. (2015). Using historical Twitter data for research: Ethical challenges of tweet deletions. Presented at CSCW 2015 workshop on ethics at the 2015 Conference on Computer Supported Cooperative Work (CSCW 2015). Vancouver,

Canada. Retrieved from http://faculty.washington.edu/kstarbi/maddock_starbird_tweet_deletions.pdf

Markham, A. (2016). OKCupid data release fiasco. *Points*. Retrieved from https://points.datasociety.net/okcupid-data-release-fiasco-ba0388348cd#.nap8rybrv

Markham, A. & Buchanan, E. (2012). Ethical decision-making and internet research 2.0: recommendations from the AoIR Ethics Working Committee.

Mason, J. (2002). *Qualitative Researching*. London: SAGE.

Mayer-Schönberger, V., & Cukier, K. (2013). *Big Data*. NY: John Murray.

Metcalf, J., Keller, E. F., & boyd, d. (2016). Perspectives on big data, ethics, and society. *Council for Big Data, Ethics, and Society*. Accessed December 16, 2016. http://bdes.datasociety.net/council-output/perspectives-on-big-data-ethics-and-society/

Metzler, K., Kim, D., Allum, N., & Denman, A. (2016). Who is doing computational social science? Trends in big data research. Technical Report. London: SAGE.

OECD. (2016). Research ethics and new forms of data for social and economic research. *OECD Science, Technology and Industry Policy Papers*, No. 34, OECD Publishing, Paris. http://dx.doi.org/10.1787/5jln7vnpxs32-en.

Salon.com. (2013). *Justine Sacco's aftermath: The cost of Twitter outrage*. Retrieved from http://www.salon.com/2013/12/23/justine_saccos_aftermath_the_cost_of_twitter_outrage/

Schneier, B. (2015). *Data and Goliath*. New York, NY: W. W. Norton and Co.

Schroeder, R. (2014). Big data and the brave new world of social media. *Big Data and Society*, *I*(2), 1–11. DOI: 10.1177/2053951714563194.

Shilton, K. & Sayles, S. (2016). 'We aren't all going to be on the same page about ethics:' Ethical practices and challenges in research on digital and social media. In *Proceedings of the 49th Hawaii International Conference on System Sciences* (HICSS 2016). Kauai, HI: IEEE

Sloan, L. & Morgan, J. (2015) Who Tweets with their location? Understanding the relationship between demographic characteristics and the use of geoservices and geotagging on Twitter. *PLoS ONE*, *10*(11), e0142209. doi:10.1371/journal.pone.0142209.

Social Data Science Lab. (2017). Lab Ethics Statement. Retrieved from http://socialdatalab.net/ethics

Thomson, S. D. (2016) Preserving Social Media, Digital Preservation Centre Tech Watch Report 16–01. Retrieved from http://dpconline.org/publications/technology-watch-reports

Tolich, M. (Ed.). (2016). *Qualitative ethics in practice*. Walnut Creek, CA: Left Coast Press.

Trevisan, F. & Reilly, P. (2014). Ethical dilemmas in researching sensitive issues online: lessons from the study of British disability dissent networks. *Information, Communication & Society*, *17*(9), 1131–1146.

Twitter, Inc. (2017). Developer Policy and Agreement. Retrieved from: https://dev.twitter.com/overview/terms

Twitter 2017, Policy Update Clarification, https://twittercommunity.com/t/policy-update-clarification-research-use-cases/87566

UK Cabinet Office-Data Science Ethical Framework. (2016). Retrieved from https://www.gov.uk/government/uploads/system/uploads/attachment_data/file/524298/Data_science_ethics_framework_v1.0_for_publication__1_.pdf

US Department of Health, Education and Welfare. (1978). The Belmont Report: Ethical Principles and Guidelines for the Protection of Human Subjects of Research. National Commission for the Protection of Human Subjects of Biomedical and Behavioural Research. Washington, DC: United States Government Printing Office.

Weller, K. (2015). Accepting the challenges of social media research. *Online Information Review*, *39*(3), 281–289. DOI: http://dx.doi.org/10.1108/OIR-03-2015-0069.

Weller, K., & Kinder-Kurlanda, K. (2015). Uncovering the challenges in collection, sharing and documentation: the hidden data of social media research? *Standards and Practices in Large-Scale Social Media Research: Papers from the 2015 ICWSM Workshop.*

Weller, K., and Kinder-Kurlanda, K. (Forthcoming). To Share or Not to Share? Ethical Challenges in Sharing Social Media-Based Research Data. In: M. Zimmer & K. Kinder-Kurlanda, K. (Eds.), *Internet Research Ethics for the Social Age: New Challenges, Cases, and Contexts* (pp. 115–129). Peter Lang.

Weller, K., & Kinder-Kurlanda, K. (2016). A manifesto for data sharing in social media research. *Proceedings of the 8th ACM Conference on Web Science, 166–172.*

Williams, M. L. & Burnap, P. (2015). Cyberhate on social media in the aftermath of Woolwich. *British Journal of Criminology*, *56*(2), 211–238. DOI: 10.1093/bjc/azv059

Williams, M., Burnap, P., & Sloan, L. (2017a). Towards an ethical framework for publishing Twitter data in social research: Taking into account users' views, online context and algorithmic estimation. *Sociology* (forthcoming). Retrieved from https://orca.cf.ac.uk/99642/1/Towards%20and%20Ethical%20Framework%20Social%20Media.pdf

Williams, M. L., Burnap, P., Sloan, L., Jessop, C., & Lepps, H. (2017b). Users' view of ethics in social media research: Informed consent, anonymity and harm, Chapter 2 this volume.

Wilson, C., Tiropanis, T., Rowland-Campbell, A. and Fry, L. (2016). Ethical and legal support for innovation on Web Observatories. *Proceedings from the Workshop on Data-Driven Innovation on the Web (DDI '16)*, Hanover, Germany: ACM.

Woodfield, K., Morrell, G., Metzler, K., & Blank, G. (2013). Blurring the boundaries? NCRM Methodological Review paper. Retrieved from http://eprints.ncrm.ac.uk/3168/1/blurring_boundaries.pdf

Van den Eynden, V., & Bishop, L. (2014). *Sowing the seed: Incentives and motivations for sharing research data, a researcher's perspective* (Research Report). Retrieved from http://www.data-archive.ac.uk/media/492924/ke_report-incentives-for-sharing-research-data.pdf

Zimmer, M. (2010). 'But the data is already public': On the ethics of research in Facebook. *Ethics and Information Technology, (12)*, 313–325.

CHAPTER 8

THE ETHICS OF USING SOCIAL MEDIA DATA IN RESEARCH: A NEW FRAMEWORK

Leanne Townsend and Claire Wallace

ABSTRACT

Over the past decade, the number of people engaging with social media has grown rapidly. This means that social media platforms such as Twitter and Facebook are potentially good sources of rich, naturally occurring data. As a result, a growing number of researchers are utilizing these platforms for the collection of data on any number of topics. To date, no consistent approach to the ethics of using social media data has been provided to researchers in this sphere. This chapter presents research that has developed an ethics framework for the use of researchers working with social media data. The chapter also presents the framework itself and guidance on how to use the framework when conducting social media research. A full report can be accessed on: http://www.abdn.ac.uk/socsci/research/new-europe-centre/information-societies-projects-225.php

Keywords: Social media; data; ethics; privacy; anonymity; informed consent; sensitivity; risk

The Ethics of Online Research
Advances in Research Ethics and Integrity, Volume 2, 189–207
Copyright © 2018 by Emerald Publishing Limited
All rights of reproduction in any form reserved
ISSN: 2398-6018/doi:10.1108/S2398-601820180000002008

1. INTRODUCTION

In recent years, the number of people engaging with social media has grown rapidly. Social media platforms are now utilized as tools for networking, socializing, and for reflecting on all aspects of everyday life. Such online spaces are, therefore, rich sources of naturally occurring data on any number of topics, from consumer behaviors, to attitudes toward pro-environmental policies, to political views and preferences. This provides researchers with opportunities to gather data sets that would otherwise have taken much more time and resource to obtain (NatCen, 2014). Yet this opportunity is accompanied by a responsibility to ensure that how we obtain and reuse such data is done to the highest possible ethical standards. The ethics of using data obtained online have been under consideration for some time (Johns & Jon, 2004; Orton-Johnson, 2010), though previous work tends to refer to email, discussion forums, and personal messaging services being written before the explosion of use of social media platforms such as Twitter and Facebook. Traditional ethics frameworks can inform social media research ethics to some extent, but social media data brings new contextual challenges that the more traditional approaches are not equipped to deal with (McKee, 2013). This calls for a new consideration of best practice in this domain.

This chapter results from research and workshop activities carried out by researchers at the University of Aberdeen on the UK Economic and Social Research Council (ESRC)-funded project 'Social Media – Developing, Understanding, Infrastructure and Engagement (Social Media Engagement).' The purpose of this project was threefold – (1) to carry out research into approaches taken by researchers and ethics committees to ensure ethical approaches; (2) to understand user perceptions and expectations in regards to the use of their social media data for research; and (3) to produce a set of ethics guidelines for use by researchers, students, ethics committees, and anyone else with an interest in the ethics of online research methodologies. It is the third aim of the project – the production of ethics guidelines for social media research – which is the focus of this chapter. The framework was coproduced by participants at a two-day workshop that was held in February 2016, in Aberdeen, Scotland. The participants were some of the key thinkers in this area in the UK, and they are acknowledged for their contributions and feedback at the end of this chapter. This framework is intended to assist individuals in making informed decisions about the most ethical approach for their research. In addition to a diagrammatic framework, we have provided additional guidance on each area covered in the framework. We have also provided fictional case studies that can further help to clarify the best approach in the different social media contexts that researchers may find themselves working. The case studies were generated at the workshop and were discussed there. The solutions suggested are ones that emerged from the discussion.

In the next section, the key areas of consideration in social media research ethics are mapped out. Following this, we describe our methodology for the production of a new ethics framework that is tailored to the use of social media data in research. We then present the framework along with explanatory text and case studies to guide the reader in using the framework. We conclude with recommendations for future research directions in this sphere. In this chapter, the term *social media* can describe social media platforms such as Facebook and Twitter as well as referring to discussion forums, chat rooms, and other online networks.

1.2. Social Media, Research, and Ethics

Social media – that is, online spaces and platforms, that facilitate social interactions between users (encompassing social media platforms and online fora) – are growing phenomena in contemporary society. Social media platforms offer their users an easy way to access and develop networks of friends, family, and relevant professionals. Online communities of interest can be found to suit the interests of almost anyone. Social media platforms are increasingly used by many as a means of communication, sharing information, and – importantly for this chapter – the sharing of attitudes and behaviors on a huge breadth of topics. It is this user-generated content that presents such a valuable opportunity to researchers, whereas before, researchers gathered information on attitudes and behaviors through a variety of methods such as questionnaires, in-depth interviews, and observation, such data are often now accessible at the mere 'touch of a button' (or more accurately, typing a few search terms into a platform's search bar). Such data, found on social media platforms, online discussion forums, and blogs (to name a few) are typically rich, numerous, and naturally occurring (NatCen, 2014). Not surprisingly then, social media platforms such as Twitter are becoming popular field sites for data collection by researchers across diverse disciplines. Other social media sites might include Snapchat, WhatsApp, or Facebook as well as chatrooms and blogs. The most commonly researched platforms are Facebook and Twitter. However, the rapidly emerging nature of this field means that new platforms might already be in use by the time this chapter and volume is published. What these media have in common is that, together with others what are known as Web 2.0 applications, they allow participants to share information publicly – either to a general public or to a smaller group of followers.

As with other forms of data collection, the use of social media data in research poses important ethical concerns – the key concerns are explored in more detail later in the chapter. Indeed, given the relatively new and emerging context of social media platforms as research sites, there is as yet no clear ethical framework for researchers entering this field. By ethics we refer to the use of social media data that might involve harm to those producing it or to the general public and the issues of informed consent and privacy in the reuse of material. There have been some notable contributions in the form of guidance in recent years (e.g., see Association of Internet Researchers, 2012; British Psychological Society, 2013; NatCen, 2014), yet these are often conflicting (Evans, Ginnis, & Bartlett, 2015). This chapter, therefore, aims to support researchers with a framework that will help them to navigate the complex ethical concerns of working with social media data.

2. KEY AREAS OF CONCERN WITHIN SOCIAL MEDIA RESEARCH

The following sections outline the key areas of ethical concern in terms of social media data that are typically discussed in the existing literature.

2.1. Private Versus Public?

One of the biggest areas of concern with social media data is the extent to whether such data should be considered public or private data. Key to this argument is the standpoint that social media users have all agreed to a set of terms and conditions for each social media platform that they use, and within these terms and conditions, there are often contained clauses on how one's data may be accessed by third parties, including researchers. Surely, if users have agreed to these terms, the data can be considered in the public domain. In our interviews with researchers, a number of responses indicated such a view, for example, 'it's public data, people know that when they sign up. So I can use that data however I like.' But according to boyd and Crawford, 'it is problematic for researchers to justify their actions as ethical simply because the data are accessible… The process of evaluating the research ethics cannot be ignored simply because the data are seemingly public'

(2012, p. 672). Questions of whether online postings are public or private are determined to some extent by the online setting itself, and whether there is a reasonable expectation of privacy on behalf of the social media user (British Psychological Society, 2013) – for example, a password-protected 'private' Facebook group might be considered private, whereas an open discussion on Twitter in which people broadcast their opinions using a hashtag (in order to associate their thoughts on a subject with others' thoughts on the same subject) might be considered public. Questions of whether the data is public or private relate to the extent to which we are ethically bound to seek informed consent from social media users (see next section).[1] There is also the issue of social media data, containing data from people from broader networks, as in the case of people commenting on a social media user's post. Therefore, there is the problem that if informed consent is obtained from the primary participant; does this extend to their wider network?

2.2. Informed Consent

Informed consent is a critical component of the ethics of all types of research. In more traditional research approaches, informed consent is usually built in to the research design, for example, in the form of consent forms or boxes to be ticked and signed on questionnaires. Social media-based research, on the other hand, presents problems concerning the informed consent of participants. In many cases, a social media user's data are accessed and analyzed without informed consent having first been sought (NatCen, 2014). 'Participants' in such research are rarely aware of their participation. Acquiring informed consent becomes more problematic, the larger the data set, and can seem virtually impossible in aggregate data containing thousands or even hundreds of thousands of data units. Further, it is tempting to conflate a social media user having agreed to the terms of conditions of the platform (many of which include clauses on the accessing and reuse of data by third parties) with informed consent in research (Salmons, 2014) – problematic especially given that many social media users report not having read the terms and conditions properly. Important aspects of informed consent, such as the right to withdraw, are made more complicated in social media research (British Psychological Society, 2013) – for example, does deleting a post or an account equate with a withdrawal from research, and is a researcher aware when this happens? When working with social media data, there are some conditions in which researchers will be more ethically bound to seek informed consent, such as when accessing data which social media users expect to be private (see above section). Social media users are not always aware of what is public and what is private in their postings, as they may not remember the agreements they signed up to when first entering the platform.

2.3. Anonymity

Anonymity is a key consideration in research ethics, particularly in qualitative research practices or when data sets are shared outside of the original research team. The use of geotagging and time stamps makes this especially problematical as even people who post anonymously or through pseudonyms can be easily traced. Concerns over anonymity and online data are not new – Kleinberg highlighted the potential for anonymity breaches with social network data in 2007. With traditional forms of research, it is generally straightforward to anonymize data so that research participants cannot be identified. When working with social media data, however, anonymizing data is more complex – anonymization procedures are still evolving for aggregated or big data, and it is difficult to anonymize individual data extracts (such as Tweets) when these are reproduced in publications and during presentations (Narayanan & Shmatikov, 2008, 2009). This is further complicated when some platforms insist on units of data being republished only in their original form and attributed to the original poster. Thus, when quoting text directly from a tweet in an academic publication or presentation, even if the identity of the tweeter is changed or not included, it can be traced back directly to the original Twitter participant electronically, so anonymity is compromised. Different issues arise for different types of data too – the information contained within a text-based unit of data is different to what can be gleaned from images, audio- and video-format social media data. Given that social media companies tend to store data and meta-data for long periods, and that much of this data is searchable, anonymization in secondary use of data in some cases becomes challenging. Further problems arise when data sets are exported to external coders and research partners. Issues of anonymization become more critical in cases where data sets or individual units of data are published – for example, online, in journal papers, and at academic conferences. Protecting the identity of unwitting participants becomes even more crucial when the data accessed refer to sensitive subject matter, particularly when exposing such data in new contexts and to new audiences may place the social media users at potential risk.

2.4. Risk of Harm

Related to concerns over identity breaches is the risk of harm that researchers potentially place on their research subjects. The Association of Internet Researchers (2012) suggest that a researcher's responsibility toward his or her participants increases with the increased risk of harm to those participants, or increased vulnerability of individuals or groups online. This risk of harm is most likely where a social media user's privacy and anonymity have been breached and is also greater when dealing with more sensitive data that when revealed to new audiences might expose a social media user to the risk of embarrassment, reputational damage, or prosecution (to name a few examples). This, of course, must be balanced with a duty of care on the part of the researcher to report concerns such as abusive or threatening behavior online to the appropriate channels. It is not always clear to the researcher whether or not the data they have accessed, collected, analyzed, or reused can be retraced in its original online context, or what the repercussions of such retracing might be. Of particular concern is the republishing of quotes that have been taken from social media platforms and republished verbatim, as these can lead us, via search engines, straight back to their original location, often then exposing the identity and profile of the social media user they originate from (British Psychological Society, 2013). There may be issues in verifying information such as whether a participant is a child, or of a sound enough mind, to understand the easily accessible nature of their data. This becomes of increased importance when dealing with sensitive or potentially embarrassing data. Therefore, where data deals with very sensitive topics, it becomes important to revisit the other concerns, ensuring that confidentiality and anonymity has been fully protected, and to consider whether or not to seek informed consent. Risk of harm might not be present in all instances in which a researcher wishes to cite social media data, for example, when such data is shared by public bodies or organizations, or when the social media user is clearly aiming for broad readership (e.g., by using hashtags in Twitter).

2.5. Methods

The work reported in this article was carried out during a workshop held in Aberdeen in February 2016. The workshop attracted 12 participants (four male and eight female). Eleven of these participants were academics representing a range of expertise in social media ethics; one participant represented one of the UK-based funding councils and had expertise in social media ethics. These participants are all acknowledged at the end of the chapter. The workshop was carried out over 2 days, and adopted participatory mapping as a technique for reaching consensus on the coproduction of the ethics framework (Kindon, Pain, & Kesby, 2007). The two days were spent discussing the key issues relating to social media data ethics, and considering different routes to 'good ethics' relating to each of these. Working in smaller groups as well as the larger group, mapping exercises were employed to help the group reach consensus on the most ethical solutions to each problem area. The group then worked together to produce the framework which is presented in the next section.

3. FRAMEWORK FOR ETHICAL RESEARCH WITH SOCIAL MEDIA DATA

The framework presented here is the result of the workshop outlined in the previous section. We have also obtained extensive feedback on the framework through delegates at workshops that we have held at relevant conferences (Academy of Social Sciences Social Media Ethics Conference, March 2016; Media, Communication and Cultural Studies conference, January 2016;) and through members of the New Social Media, New Social Science (#NSMNSS) network.

The framework represents guidelines as opposed to rules, recognizing that principles need to remain flexible in order to respond to the varied social media contexts (i.e., platform used, the target population, the topic of focus, the methodology employed, and the type of data collected – text, images, video, etc.). It is designed in such a way that a researcher may use it to guide and support their own decisions, rather than providing definitive answers or a 'one size fits all' approach (Association of Internet Researchers, 2012). This ultimately does leave the responsibility with the researcher, along with his or her corresponding ethics committee. For further support with social media research ethics, we suggest researchers consult the 'New Social Media, New Social Science?' (NSMNSS) online network, as a place to pose questions to a community of social media researchers.[2] The framework itself is presented in Fig. 1, and further guidance is offered to readers in the subsequent sections.

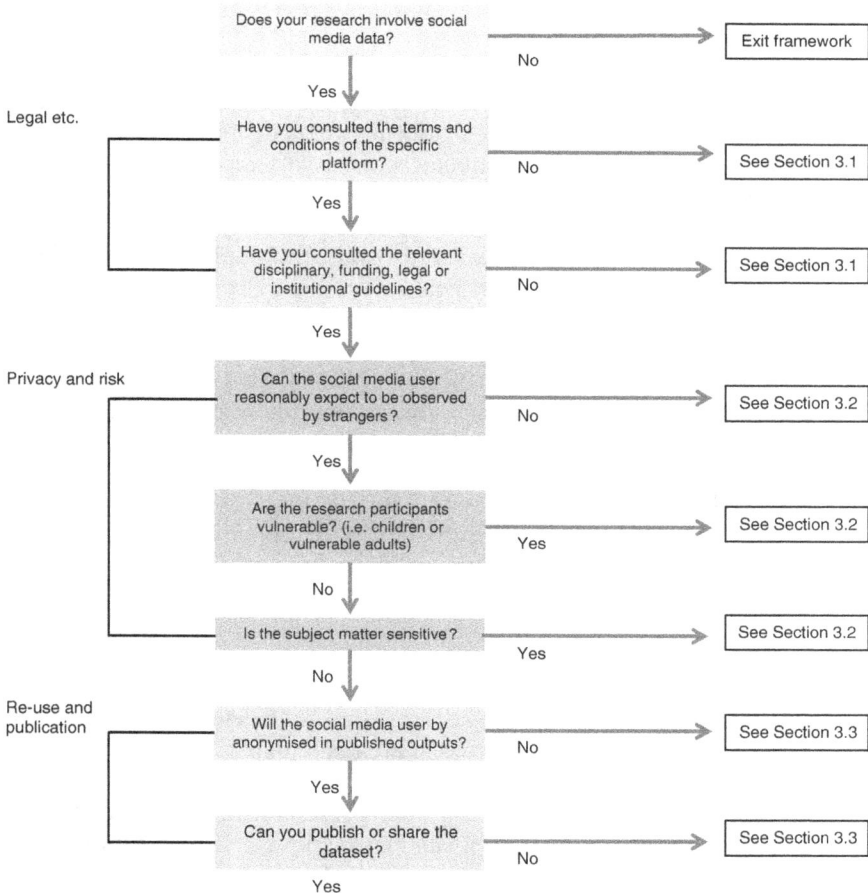

Fig. 1. Social Media Ethics Framework.

3.1. Terms, Conditions and Legalities

Before considering other aspects of the ethics of a social media project, it is important to consult with all other relevant terms, conditions, and guidelines. First, the researcher should carefully read through all of the relevant terms and conditions of the platform(s) that he or she will be using to obtain data. These terms and conditions will include those aimed at users, and might also include those aimed at third parties wishing to access data from the platform. Even if the researcher has read the terms and conditions of a specific platform at some point, it is worth bearing in mind that the terms and conditions of social media platforms change regularly in accordance with changes made to the platform, or changes in how the platform owners wish to make profit from the platform. Reading these documents may seem tedious – indeed, many platform users do not read them, and inadvertently agree to things they do not realize they have agreed to (such as use of their data by third parties!). But being familiar with the most current terms and conditions will help to make researchers more aware of potential legal action should he or she violate them.

The researcher must also ensure that he or she is compliant with all terms and conditions relevant to their university or their research organization (e.g., on the university webpage or guidance provided by the relevant ethics committee); external funding bodies that are funding the research (either in the documentation from the funding body, or on their website), and any disciplinary guidance provided either through one's own university or through major disciplinary bodies such as the British Psychological Society, the British Sociological Association, or the Social Research Association. Many such associations provide basic ethics guidance on their websites.

Privacy and Risk

The next task in working through the framework is to determine whether the data that the researcher wishes to access are really public, and if it is not, to decide how – or indeed if – to proceed. The question as to whether to consider social media data as private or public comes down, to some extent, to whether or not the social media user can reasonably expect to be observed by strangers (British Psychological Society, 2013; Fuchs, forthcoming). Things to consider here are the following: Are the data you wish to access on an open forum or a platform (such as on Twitter), or are they located within a closed or a private group (e.g., within Facebook) or a closed discussion forum? Is the group or the forum password protected? Would platform users expect other visitors to have similar interests or issues to themselves? Does the group have a gatekeeper (or admin) that you could turn to for approval and advice? How have users set up their security settings? Data accessed from open and public online locations such as Twitter present less ethical issues than data that are found in closed or private online spaces. Similarly, data posted by public figures such as politicians, musicians, and sportspeople on their public social media pages are less likely to be problematic because these data are intended to reach as wide an audience as possible. If the data that the researcher wishes to access are held within a group for which one would need to gain membership approval, or if the group is password protected, there are more ethical issues to take into consideration. Additional factors to take into consideration are the following: first, the researcher must take into account the potential for harm, if this is a safe space, then will their actions jeopardize that space. If so how will they mediate that risk? Second, the researcher might want to seek the group's approval and give participants the right to opt out, which is important to take into consideration.

The first port of call should be to make contact with the site or the group administrator. They will have an understanding of the social dynamics of the group and will decide how to proceed. They may wish the researcher to seek consent from individual group members in order to access their data, or offer group members the option to 'opt out' of the research (therefore, one could use peoples' data unless they specify otherwise). Will the researcher be asking questions of social media users in order to produce new data on a given subject? If so, it is vital that the researcher is transparent about their own identity (such as – a researcher in a university) and that responses will be used as data in their research.

CASE STUDY 1

Context: The researcher wishes to study support mechanisms between members of a discussion forum that deals with mental health issues such as depression and feelings of suicide. The forum is a closed forum that is password protected, and registration must be approved by a gate-keeper (a site admin).

Concerns: The researcher is aware that this data is private – there is a high expectation of privacy on behalf of the users who feel it is a safe space where they will only be conversing with other people in the same situation. This raises questions about the ethics of accessing the data, and how to report the findings of the data if it is accessed.

Solution: The researcher needs to treat this data as private and sensitive. In order to access the data, the researcher should consider seeking consent from the gatekeeper of the community (site admin), who might seek the approval of the group more widely before deciding. Once consent has been

> *granted the researcher might wish to make themselves known to the community, and give participants the right to opt out (so that their data is not republished or analyzed). The gatekeeper might grant the researcher access to a certain area of the site, and retain a 'safe' space to accommodate community members who are not comfortable with the researcher's presence. If the researcher wishes to republish certain units of data in order to illustrate their research findings, it is ethical to seek informed consent from each forum user whose data will be republished. Community members should be fully anonymized in any research outputs.*

The 'blurring of boundaries' between researcher and participant is a further consideration – the researcher's own social media activity (or that of people they know) may be part of the dataset that he or she is researching, which is potentially problematic. In this case, care needs to be given to how such research methodologies and findings are reported. Also, the researcher themselves might become searchable by participants, meaning that they should pay attention to their own online identity and privacy.

Another consideration here is whether or not the researcher might be dealing with young or vulnerable participants. They must ensure that they have taken all possible precautions to rule out the use of data by vulnerable adults (in the UK, the definition extends to all those who through disability, age, or illness might be unable to protect themselves) or children (or in the case of children, seeking parental consent). Social media can often make it difficult to identify such individuals, not least because people often shield their true identities on social media platforms and discussion forums. Importantly, if data are suspected to originate from young or vulnerable individuals, informed consent cannot reliably be given so these data should be eliminated from the research.

A final consideration is whether the data are potentially sensitive. Are the data about fairly mundane daily activities or opinion, or is there the potential to cause harm to social media users should their data be exposed to new audiences? Less sensitive data might include postings about, for example, the weather, recipes, or consumer preferences. More sensitive data includes postings about, for example, criminal activity such as driving offences or the use of illegal drugs; financial problems; mental health issues and feelings of suicide; extramarital sexual activity; controversial political opinions and activism. It is the researcher's responsibility to decide whether the content is sensitive, in consultation with participants, and if so to determine an ethical way of working with the data.[3] If there is risk of harm to individuals whose data you are using, you must either (a) paraphrase all data that is republished in research outputs, having taken steps to ensure that the paraphrased data does not lead interested parties to the individual's online profile; (b) seek informed consent from each person, should you wish to (or need to) use their data in its original form in research outputs or (c) consider using a more traditional research approach where consent and confidentiality can be more safely ensured. It is also important to take these things into consideration in terms of whether one can share data sets (covered in more detail in Section 3.3). There might be cases where it is not straightforward to seek consent. Conducting critical discourse analysis of harmful or ideological social media content (such as found in Neo-Nazi online groups) is one such example (for one thing, it might be dangerous for a researcher to get in touch with these social media users). We could argue for such material as being exempt from the seeking of informed consent, in order to both protect the safety of the researcher, and to ensure that social media research ethics does not result in an indirect censorship of critical research. Here though we would advise paraphrasing quotes, not least to protect the researcher from being targeted, and to ensure an ethical approach.

CASE STUDY 2

Context: A researcher wishes to study prolegalization narratives on marijuana use. The data will be collected from Twitter, so it is open public data. The researcher will gather data over the last 7 days posted with the hashtags *#cannabis, #legalize* and *#ismokeit.*

Concerns: First, the subject matter is sensitive because it refers to an activity that is still illegal in the UK. Second, there may be users under the age of 18 contributing to the debate. Therefore, the researcher must work out how to handle the data in terms of protecting anonymity.

Solution: the researcher decides that the data is public because it is posted on Twitter, a platform on which the default setting for posts is public; most profiles are set to public and can be viewed and followed by anyone. Furthermore, the use of hashtags implies that platform users are keen to contribute to a community or a debate and therefore expect an even greater number of people to see their data. The subject matter is sensitive though, and there could be children contributing data, so there is considerable risk of harm. The researcher decides it is ok to access the data and present results from aggregate data, but it is not ok to publish a data set (prohibited by Twitter anyhow) or republish direct quotes that will lead interested parties to the user's profile, hence compromising anonymity. The researcher will therefore present paraphrased quotes (removing ID handles) to reflect the themes that emerge, and provide details on how interested parties might recreate the data search for themselves. Some direct quotes may be used with informed consent from the platform user, but the researcher knows he must take steps to ensure that the user is over the age of 18.

CASE STUDY 3

Context: A researcher wishes to study public interactions on a dating platform such as Tinder. Although the posts under scrutiny are public, rather than through private messaging, she needs to sign up to Tinder to view them. By signing up, she has to fill in a registration form including questions such as 'I am a woman looking for a man/woman,' etc. It is therefore reasonable to think that users of the platform expect that other people viewing their profile might be doing so for similar (dating) reasons. The researcher is also aware that there may be people under the age of 18 using the platform. The users of the platform are aware that there is a very large number of people using the platform and potentially able to access their profile.

Concerns: First, can the researcher ethically access and re-publish this data, given that the users of the platform have a reasonable expectation that people seeing their data are like-minded (i.e. using the platform for similar reasons)? Second, is there a chance that vulnerable people (such as children) could be using the platform? Thirdly, is the data likely to be sensitive?

Solution: the researcher decides that, although the platform users may expect others viewing their profile to be like-minded, they will be expecting strangers to view their profile – so the data is not private. There is, however, a chance that children could be using the platform, and the data is potentially sensitive

> *(e.g., underage children engaging in sexual talk or activity, people looking to engage in extra-marital relationships, etc.). The researcher, therefore, can access and analyze the data, but needs to be careful with republishing. She does not publish the data set, and when writing up her results she only uses quotes that are paraphrased (and she is sure cannot be used to identify the platform user). Consent to use data is problematic here because the platform is popular with those under the age of 18, who may be dishonest about their age or use a misleading photograph. Furthermore, it is often impossible to know what the age or competence of the poster might be.*

3.3. Reuse and Republication

There are different types of reuse or republication to be taken into consideration when working with social media data. The researcher may wish to publish research results in a number of different formats, for example, online blog posts; journal papers; conference presentations (including the submission of papers to conference proceedings); book chapters; articles online such as in *The Conversation*. When reporting findings, do you want to use units of data (such as individual tweets or Facebook postings, or Instagram images with corresponding text) to illustrate the themes that have arisen in the data? If so, you need to refer to the framework outlined above in deciding whether it is ethically sound to do so. The researcher may feel the need to either paraphrase the data or seek informed consent from individual platform users before doing this. One should also give consideration to the format of the data – if the data is in photographic, audio, or video formats, are there copyright issues to be considered when republishing? Can such data compromise the anonymity of individuals or groups?

Sharing data sets is another consideration and something that is increasingly expected, for example, by external funding bodies wishing to encourage a transparent and replicable research process. The researcher should consider whether it is ethically sound to share the data set, as well as checking the platform terms and conditions to determine whether they allow or prohibit it. If it contains data that could cause harm if republished, then either the sensitive data should be removed or paraphrased, or the data set should not be shared at all. In cases of aggregate data where the individual units (or postings) are no longer discernible, it is generally safe to share the data set. If the data set does not contain sensitive data, or if it is not possible to identify individuals based on the data set, it is also safe to share.

Special consideration needs to be given to the anonymization of social media users. In almost all cases, it is important to ensure that users are anonymized in research outputs. There are some exceptions to the rule, for example, public figures and organizations seeking to share their data as widely as possible. Arguably, data that is not in any way sensitive (such as postings about the weather or the consumer preferences) are unlikely to cause harm to individuals; therefore, it can be argued that it is unnecessary to anonymize content of this nature.

3. CONCLUDING COMMENTS

CASE STUDY 4

Context: A researcher is studying viewpoints on a public health campaign. The Twitter data is accessed via a paid-for search service. Hundreds of thousands of Tweets are collected, and a computer-programmed analysis method called 'sentiment analysis' is used to present the results of the data. This means that the data is aggregated and no individual Tweets are republished or even maintained in the data set. Instead, the data set is composed of chunks of data that no longer resemble individual Tweets.

Concerns: Can the data be collected and analyzed in this way? How is privacy and anonymity protected for each Twitter user?

Solution: The data is posted on a public site (Twitter), and although it could be sensitive in some cases, anonymity and privacy is maintained because the data is aggregated and individual Tweets are not republished or presented in the data set. Twitter handles (profile names) should be removed from the data set (but check the current API T&C of Twitter to ensure that it is ok to share a data set of aggregated data, with Twitter handles removed – T&Cs change regularly).

As argued by the Association of Internet Researchers (2012), no set of Internet research guidelines can be static because technologies and the way that technologies are used are constantly changing, and the authors are unable to predict what new ethical dilemmas may arise in future social media platforms (or future versions of those we are already familiar with).

Consequently, conversations on ethical standards in social media research need to be dynamic too. The ethical issues highlighted were illustrated using five case studies. These should be seen as examples of what might constitute good ethical practice; that is not to say that solutions to such ethical scenarios are unproblematic or that they should be seen as the final word. Therefore, this set of guidelines should be considered flexible; we hope to see new frameworks emerge as changes to the nature and uses of social media make this necessary. Ultimately, the responsibility lies with the researcher and his or her corresponding ethics committee to ensure an ethical approach is taken to the collection, analysis, and reuse of data collected from social media platforms. This framework, or any framework that supersedes it, cannot be prescriptive. Each social media research context is unique, having a unique set of characteristics and ethical challenges. We hope that this framework will provide researchers with the decision-making tools they require to take the most sensible and ethical approach to their social media research.

CASE STUDY 5

Context: A researcher conducts a critical discourse analysis of a dataset of tweets using the hashtags #DonaldTrump; #TrumpTrain; #VoteTrump2016; #AlwaysTrump; #MakeAmericaGreatAgain or #Trum2016. These are analyzed in order to find out how Trump supporters argue for their candidate on Twitter.

Concerns: Can we consider this data public? Are there any issues of sensitivity or risk of harm? Do we need to seek informed consent before quoting these tweets directly?

Solution: Trump supporters use these hashtags in order to reach a broad public and convince other people to vote for Trump. It is therefore reasonable to assume that such tweets have public character: the authors expect and want to be observed by strangers in order to make a political point that they want others to read. The researcher can therefore directly quote such tweets without having to obtain informed consent. It is, however, good practice to delete the user IDs of everyday users, who are not themselves public figures. Furthermore, since Twitter data usage regulations change over time, it is important to be aware of the current versions.

NOTES

1. This could have implications for how and if the Data Protection Act is applied, see: https://ico.org.uk/media/for-organisations/documents/1541/big-data-and-data-protection.pdf
2. http://nsmnss.blogspot.co.uk
3. It is essential to refer to the EU Data Protection Reform, which legally sets out what can be considered sensitive data: http://europa.eu/rapid/press-release_MEMO-15-6385_en.htm

ACKNOWLEDGMENTS

This work was supported by the Economic and Social Research Council [grant number ES/M001628/1] and was carried out at the University of Aberdeen. With contributions and feedback from: Christian Fuchs, University of Westminster; Curtis Jessop, NatCen; Dave Harte, Birmingham City University; Elvira Perez Vallejos, University of Nottingham; Hayley Lepps, NatCen; Jennifer Holden, University of Aberdeen; Kate Orton-Johnston, University of Edinburgh; Luke Sloan, Cardiff University; Michael Smith, University of Aberdeen; Samantha McGregor, Economic and Social Research Council; Suzanna Hall, University of Roehampton.

REFERENCES

Association of Internet Research. (2012). *Ethical Decision-Making and Internet Research.* Retrieved from http://aoir.org/reports/ethics2.pdf

boyd, D. & Crawford, K. (2012). Critical questions for big data. *Information, Communication and Society, 15*(5), 662–679.

British Psychological Society. (2013). *Ethics guidelines for internet-mediated research.* Report Retrieved from http://www.bps.org.uk/system/files/Public%20files/inf206-guidelines-for-internet-mediated-research.pdf

CASRO. (2011). *Social media research guidelines.* Retrieved from http://c.ymcdn.com/sites/www.casro.org/resource/resmgr/docs/social_media_research_guidel.pdf

Collaborative Online Social Media Observatory (COSMOS). *Ethics resource guide.* Retrieved from https://www.cs.cf.ac.uk/cosmos/ethics-resource-guide/

ESOMAR (2011). *Esomar guideline on social media research.* Retrieved from https://www.esomar.org/uploads/public/knowledge-and-standards/codes-and-guidelines/ESOMAR-Guideline-on-Social-Media-Research.pdf

Evans, H., Ginnis, S., & Bartlett, J. (2015). *#SocialEthics: a guide to embedding ethics in social media research.* Report Retrieved from https://www.ipsos-mori.com/Assets/Docs/Publications/im-demos-social-ethics-in-social-media-research-summary.pdf

Fossheim, H., & Ingierd, H. (2015). *Internet research ethics.* Retrieved from https://press.nordic openaccess.no/index.php/noasp/catalog/view/3/1/9-1

Fuchs, C. (2014) *Social media: A critical introduction.* London: Sage.

Johns, M. D., & Jon H. G. (2004). *Online social research: methods, issues & ethics*

Jones, C. (2011). *Ethical issues in online research.* British Educational Research Association on-line resource. Retrieved from https://www.bera.ac.uk/wp-content/uploads/2014/03/ Ethical-issues-in-online-research.pdf?noredirect=1

Kindon, S., Pain, R., & Kesby, M. (Eds.). (2007) *Participatory action research approaches and methods: Connecting people, participation and place.* London and New York, NY: Routledge.

Kleinberg, J. M. (2007). *Challenges in mining social network data: processes, privacy and para-doxes.* Proceedings of the 13th ACM SIGKDD international conference on Knowledge discovery and data mining, New York.

McKee R. (2013). Ethical issues in using social media for health and health care research. *Health Policy, 110,* 298–301.

Narayanan, A., & Shmatikov, V. (2008). *Robust de-anonymization of large sparse datasets (How to break anonymity of the Netflix prize dataset.).* IEEE Symposium on Security & Privacy, Oakland, CA. Retrieved from http://arxiv.org/pdf/cs/0610105v2.pdf

Narayanan, A., & Shmatikov, V. (2009). *De-anonymizing social networks.* IEEE Symposium on Security & Privacy, Oakland, CA. Retrieved from http://www.cs.utexas.edu/~shmat/ shmat_oak09.pdf

NatCen. (2014). *Research using social media: users' views.* Retrieved from http://www.natcen. ac.uk/media/282288/p0639-research-using-social-media-report-final-190214.pdf

Orton-Johnson, K. (2010). Ethics in online research: Evaluating the ESRC framework for research ethics categorisation of risk. *Sociological Research Online, 15*(4), 13.

Salmons, J. (2014). *New social media, new social science ... and new ethical issues!* Report Retrieved from https://drive.google.com/file/d/0B1-gmLw9jo6fLTQ5X0oyE1aRjQ/edit

CHAPTER 9

WHERE NEXT FOR #SOCIALETHICS?

Steven Ginnis

ABSTRACT

Social media provides researchers with easy access to rich, real-time data that offers insight into both public opinion and the role of social media in public life. However, to date, good practice in analyzing social media has been led by what is technically possible and commercially viable. This chapter seeks to reverse that trend and is the result of a year-long study 'Wisdom of the Crowd' by Ipsos MORI, Demos, the University of Sussex and CASM Consulting to examine the ethical landscape surrounding aggregated social media research. Based on a review of the legal and market research regulatory landscape in the UK and a program of primary research with experts, members of the public and social media users, this chapter provides a series of constructive and practical recommendations on how to improve ethical standards in this field. Drawing on the context of public ethics, the recommendations provide advice to researchers, regulators, and social media organizations on how they can help to restore trust in social media research and better safeguard social media users.

Keywords: Social media; good practice; public ethics; consent, anonymization, data protection; data minimization

The Ethics of Online Research
Advances in Research Ethics and Integrity, Volume 2, 209–236
Copyright © 2018 by Emerald Publishing Limited
All rights of reproduction in any form reserved
ISSN: 2398-6018/doi:10.1108/S2398-601820180000002009

THE NEED FOR CHANGE

Social media analysis is increasingly becoming a valid and important research methodology. Similar to any other methodology, it is not well suited to all research questions; moreover, it should not be used as a cheap and accessible proxy for drawing conclusions on the general population. Nonetheless, there is immense value in delivering insight from research into the content, engagement, and relationships generated by social media itself. Notable examples of the value of social media analysis include using Twitter to predict outbreaks of Norovirus and to explore the role of social media in the 2011 UK Riots.[1]

While social media analysis is conducted by a wide pool of professions and organizations (including in market research, academia, marketing, journalism, and the civil service, each of whom have their own ethical structures), the professional market research industry and academic sector are particularly proud to ensure that all research is conducted in accordance with legal and regulatory principles that underpin both industries. These principles include core standards in ethics. Within social media analysis, this requires standards of data collection, analysis, and reporting that are distinctly different from an individual accessing publicly available social media data to draw their own conclusions. However, currently, not all researchers and social media analytics tools are adhering to these standards, and ethical frameworks are often struggling to keep up with the pace of technological change; as such, research methodology is being led by what is technically possible, not always by what is ethically appropriate.

Although there is a fair and lawful process for analyzing social media data on a quantitative scale, this is not synonymous with user consent to be included in a research project. By signing up to the terms and conditions of some social media sites, users are technically agreeing to social media research taking place; however, this is not the same principle as informed consent applied to more traditional research methodologies. Each individual social media project, therefore, needs to take appropriate action to consider the rights and expectations of social media users during the collection, analysis, and reporting of social media content.

Yet, there is a lack of clarity in the guidelines for researchers to follow. Social researchers and social science researchers already operate in a context of sector and organization-led codes of ethics, often within regulatory mechanisms. However, as outlined elsewhere in this book, there has been no coherent approach to address a number of specific challenges in social media analysis if it is to uphold these ethical principles. These include how researchers should consider research with privately shared data presented at an aggregated and anonymous level; what constitutes 'personal data'; how to treat sensitive personal data; and whether it is possible to fully anonymize social media data. Furthermore, there is also currently no guidance on how research should be conducted to mitigate the fact that those under-16 years of age are highly likely to be included in the data.[2] While the ethics of traditional forms of research have stricter safeguards on research with young people,[3] this has largely been ignored or, at best neglected, within social media research. Finally, there is a direct contradiction between some guidelines and the practice of conducting social media research. Most notably the following:

- Do market research and social science principles to limit the processing of personal data and publish anonymous findings prevent research identifying key authors or networks?
- How should researchers mask social media contributions and still adhere to the brand guidelines of social media organizations? Is there a need to differentiate publication of social media content between individuals and companies or organizations?
- To what extent can and should personal data be processed to enrich the data with key demographics to help identify the profile of the data and differences between users?

In addition, the structure of social media data presents a number of unique challenges that make it harder to navigate conventional standards. First, there can be no guarantee that personal data will not be collected during social media research. By its very nature, social media data are largely open text, unstructured data. Even if attempts are made to withhold metadata fields (such as author, age, or gender) from analysis, it is highly likely that data personal to the author or another individual will be present in open text content. It should, therefore, be assumed that personal data will be processed during the project, and, therefore, subject to the relevant data protection legislation – such as the Data Protection Act (DPA) in the UK. This applies to the collection, processing, and storage of social media data.

Second, there can be no guarantee of full anonymity within social media research. Even though it is possible to report at an aggregate and anonymous level, it is not possible to present raw anonymous content to the analyst, the client, or the reader. If the author field is removed, it would still be possible to search for the content online; moreover, it is unlikely that 'masking' content can fully guarantee that the author cannot be identified.

In light of the need for better clarity on how to navigate these challenges, the Wisdom of Crowd project sought to develop a series of recommendations for how best to embed ethics into social media research.

OVERVIEW OF THE *WISDOM OF THE CROWD* PROJECT

This Wisdom of the Crowd project was sponsored by Innovate UK, the UK's innovation agency,[4] with funding contributions from the Technology Strategy Board, the Engineering and Physical Science Research Council, and the Economic and Social Research Council. The collaboration – between Ipsos MORI, Demos, CASM Consulting LLP, and the University of Sussex – sought to critically examine the commercial possibilities for social media research, and address the technical and ethical issues caused by the huge growth in social media data. Its vision was to place nontechnical researchers at the center of the data exploration process and equip them with the tools, guidance, and experience necessary to undertake robust social media analysis.

An important part of this process is ensuring that the tools and the processes behind any social media research application meet the high standards demanded by the market research industry and the wider social research community, as well as the required legal obligations. By ensuring social media research is carried out ethically, researchers safeguard the reputation of their sector and industry as well as safeguarding the public. It is also important for researchers to step back and consider the views of the people behind the data used in social media research – while the technology in social media research is fast moving, public attitudes toward data do not always move in step with new technology.

A key strand of the Wisdom of the Crowd project, therefore, sought to investigate ethical uses of personal data on social media and review how organizations can balance uses of information with people's right to privacy. In recent years, there has been greater clarity in guidelines for conducting ethnographic and co-creational-based social media[5]; the project, therefore, intentionally sought to address the current gaps and contradictions in guidelines for conducting ethical large-scale social media analysis.

The ethical review of the project consisted of both a scoping review and a program of primary research. Secondary research included a review of the current literature around social media research and its ethical, legal, and regulatory implications. The primary research involved three stages:

1. An online quantitative survey of 1,250 adults aged 16–75 in the UK asking about people's attitudes toward possible uses of their social media data, and specifically, the value of social media research.

2. Three qualitative workshops in which participants discussed use of social media content and the principles of ethical social media research. Two of these groups were carried out with adults, and one was carried out with 13–15-year olds.

3. Statistical analysis (conjoint analysis) undertaken as part of the survey, during which respondents were asked to imagine they were on an ethics board and mark whether they would be likely to approve a series of hypothetical social media research projects with different features.

All fieldwork took place in July and August 2015.

The project culminated in a series of recommendations for improving ethical standards in social media research. The specific recommendations for improving ethical standards were set within the context of the market research industry in the UK, and thus under the regulation of the Market Research Society (MRS) and the DPA. However, wherever possible, the project sought to consider the legal and regulatory frameworks outside of the UK, and ethical guidelines from other disciplines outside of market research. It is thus hoped that the suggestions put forward here will also have a wider positive impact on other organizations and individuals conducting social media analysis – including academics, social scientists, journalists, communications and marketing staff, and policy-makers.

GROUNDING IN PUBLIC ETHICS

The primary research pointed to a number of core attitudes held by members of the public that help build the context on which an ethical approach to social media research should be based.

Awareness and Appetite for Social Media Analysis

First, awareness and appetite for Social Media Analysis was low. Among the survey, fewer than two in five people (38 percent) said that they thought sharing social media data with third parties for the purposes of research currently happens under the terms and conditions they sign up to on social media sites. As well as a lack of awareness, research with social media data was also one of the least popular activities on the list. When asked to select activities that they thought should not happen, a majority (60 percent) thought that data should not be shared with third parties for research purposes under the format of terms and conditions. Furthermore, a third of people thought that sharing overall aggregate numbers (i. e., not linked to individuals) for the purposes of research should not happen (32 percent; Figs. 1 and 2).

These fears were also voiced in our workshops with users, where the concerns of participants were often based in a fear that they had lost control over their data. They saw their data being used for research as *just another thing* that people wanted to do with their data, although they were often unable to articulate exactly why they did not want their social media information being analyzed. Important factors that could make participants more comfortable included a transparency with what their data was being used for, a beneficial end purpose, and the application of an opt-in/opt-out mechanism.

Furthermore, the public were comforted by attempts to apply data minimization wherever possible. Nearly three-quarters of adults (74 percent) would prefer to remain anonymous if their social media content was published – just 10 percent of people would like their participation to be attributed. Moreover, the majority (54 percent) also agreed that all social media accounts should be given the same rights to anonymity regardless of whether it's a public institution, company, or high-profile institution.

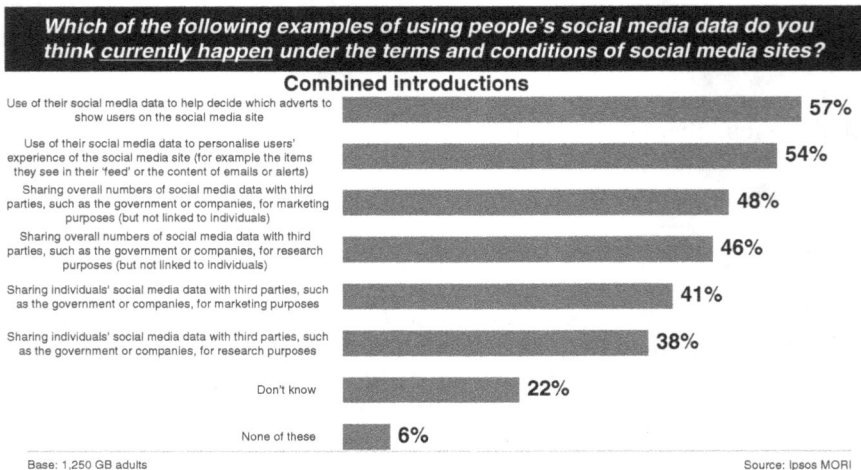

Fig. 1. Awareness of different uses of social media data. *Source:* Ginnis (2017).

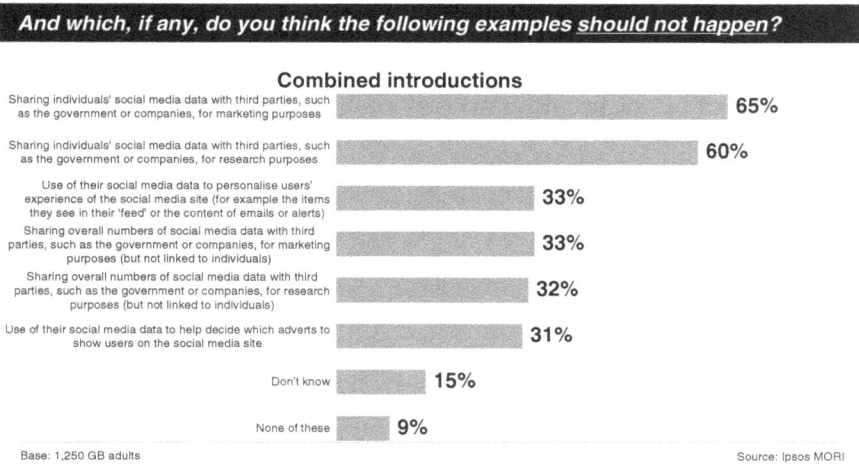

Fig. 2. Preference for different uses of social media data. *Source:* Ginnis (2017).

Conjoint Analysis

In addition to capturing core levels of awareness and explicit attitudes toward social media research, 'conjoint analysis' was conducted in order to identify the different principles that are most important in deciding whether social media research projects are likely to meet the approval of members of the public. This analysis involved asking respondents to imagine themselves as a member of an ethics board with the power to approve or reject research projects. Respondents were then presented with six scenarios, each with eight different attributes that might shape their opinion on the scenario. Respondents rated on a scale of 1–10 how likely they would be to approve that project. The attributes were randomly rotated meaning each of the possible scenarios was seen by a substantial proportion of the sample. The subsequent analysis determined which attributes are the most important in the decision-making process and, within that, which variables impact that attribute the most.

This analysis was intended to provide an understanding on two levels. First, what broad factors (attributes) were the most important when evaluating whether a project was permissible; and second, what levels within each attribute were the biggest drivers of acceptability (both positively and negatively).

The attributes for the conjoint, and their respective levels, were drafted based on findings from the literature review and the interviews to ensure the task asked about the most pertinent contexts for a research project. These were then tested in six cognitive interviews with members of the public to ensure that the exercise was manageable and that there were no important factors missing from people's concerns about using social media data for research. The attributes and levels were adjusted as a result of this. As a final check, the scenarios were presented as an additional probe to participants in the workshop, who undertook this exercise themselves.

While the conjoint was designed to give relative, rather than absolute, scores of likely approval, there was an average score across all participants – overall, levels of approval were low. On a scale of 1–10, where 1 is 'would definitely not approve' and 10 is 'would definitely approve,' the average score across all scenarios was 5.02. However, this misrepresents the range of views held by respondents: just 26 percent of respondents were around the midpoint of 5–6, 41 percent gave an average score of 4 or below (broadly a proxy for unlikely to approve), 33 percent gave an average score of 7–10 (broadly a proxy for likely to approve). This shows that there was a spread of results, with many people clustering their scores around the bottom of the scale, and another cluster at around 7–8 approvability.

Table 1 lays out the relative utilities of the different attributes that comprised every scenario. Within these attributes are different levels that are randomly selected for each scenario – for instance 'Who is the project for?' might appear with 'A central government department' or it might be 'A private company' as two examples.

Table 1.   The Relative Utilities of the Different Attributes that Comprised Every Scenario.

Attribute	Relative Importance of Attribute in Driving Approvability (percent)
Who the project is for?	16.8
Why are they doing the project?	4.7
Who could be included?	3.1
Has permission been given?	11.8
Is the social media data publicly available?	22.0
What kind of content would be looked at?	4.7
What personal information would be used?	16.7
How anonymous is the data?	20.2

Source: Ginnis (2017).

The conjoint analysis suggests that the biggest factor in the likelihood to approve a research project is whether the social media data is already publically available prior to inclusion in the research project. This factor explains about a quarter of the variation in approval seen for different combinations. The level of anonymity was also a big part of these decisions, along with who the project is for and how personal the information that is being used is.

However, there is much more nuance between the levels within each attribute. Looking at the data like this can tell us whether or not the importance of the attribute is driven by a constant improvement between attributes, or whether the importance is marked by a significant jump between two levels within the attribute.

For example, though 'Is the social media data publicly available?' is the most important attribute, this is mainly driven by a large disapproval for projects that would analyze private messages. Once private messages are removed from the proposal, there is less of a distinction between the other three levels within the attribute. Equally, there is little difference in likelihood of a project being approved between whether the project is commissioned by a government department, public service, university, or charity; however, there is considerable drop in likelihood of the project being approved if it has been commissioned by a private company.

Table 2 represents the *least* and *most* acceptable scenarios, based on choosing each of the least acceptable levels for each attribute. Under the least acceptable scenario, just 15 percent of the public would be likely to approve the project. In contrast, 50 percent of the public would approve the most acceptable scenario. This is driven mainly by the opt-in mechanism, the fact that posts have already been made public prior to publication and that no raw content will be published.

As part of the conjoint analysis, social media users were also presented with a number of similar scenarios that asked for permission to use their own personal social media data as part of a research project. In most cases, users were less likely to approve a project if it was to include their own data than somebody else's. Moreover, the higher-end users of social media – both in terms of frequency of use and diversity of use – showed minimal variation and were more open that others to use of their own data or someone else's. This suggests that the more engagement you have with a social media platform, the more lax you become about sharing data. Though, conversely, it may mean that if you do not share data on social media, you may be doing so precisely out of an increased privacy concern.

Table 2. The *Least* and *Most* Acceptable Scenarios Based on Choosing Each of the Least Acceptable Levels for Each Attribute.

	Least Acceptable Scenario	Most Acceptable Scenario
Who the project is for?	A private company	Researchers in universities and similar organizations
Why are they doing the project?	To identify the most active or most well-connected social media users in a network	To review or act on comments about a product or service they deliver
Who could be included?	Anyone on social media who has been identified as visiting a broad location relevant to the project	Anyone on social media who has used a word, hashtag, or phrase relevant to the project
Has permission been given?	All those who have agreed to the general terms and conditions of the social media site when they first signed up	Only those who have opted in to their data being used for this specific project
Is the social media data publically available?	Collecting all types of public and private posts, including private messages between individuals.	Collecting posts that have already been made public on a site where anyone can see contributions regardless of whether they have an account
What kind of content would be looked at?	Purchasing habits, or information on the products or brands people like	Health behaviors
What personal information would be used?	Sensitive personal information (e.g., sexuality and political affiliation) which is relevant to the project shall be used	Age, gender, and broad location will be used to compare different groups of people
How anonymous is the data?	Individual-level posts will be seen by researchers, individual social media posts will be published unedited (including author name and any other details posted by the author)	The researcher will not see names/locations and IDs during analysis; no posts will be published.
AVERAGE SCORE ON 1–10 SCALE (%)	3.55	6.28
Percentage giving 1–4 score of likelihood to approve (%)	64	23
Percentage giving 5–6 score of likelihood to approve (%)	21	28
Percentage giving 7–10 score of likelihood to approve (%)	15	50

Source: Ginnis (2017). Wisdom of the Crowd conjoint analysis, Base: 1,250 GB adults.

Towards an Ethical Framework

The variation levels of acceptability shown through the conjoint exercise challenged some of the earlier survey findings and demonstrated that there is no clear, universal public opinion toward the use of social media for research. Rather, that the composite components of how social media is collected and analyzed do make a difference as to whether it is something that the public would support. This finding is supported by a similar exercise undertaken by Ipsos MORI as part of research with members of the public to inform the development of the UK Data Science Ethics Framework within government.[6]

As part of an online survey, respondents were asked to imagine themselves as a part of a team in government responsible for solving problems using data science techniques. Respondents were then presented with two randomly generated data science projects of different scenarios where data science could take place. The selection of preferred data science approaches during the conjoint exercise was driven largely by the type of data that would be used – this accounted for 27 percent of variation in selection. This was followed by whether or not individuals could be identified in the data, which accounted for 19 percent of variation.

More broadly, once the public benefit and value of data science had been established, opportunities for data science were evaluated by the public based on a nuanced risk assessment of the entire proposed project and methodology. This assessment balanced three considerations: Is there a privacy concern? Is the approach effective in achieving the intended policy goal? What are the intended and unintended consequences of potential error?

The project found that there were no overall red-lines of acceptability with reference to which methods should or should not be used by the government for data science projects; instead, concerns about risk, consequence and efficacy were measured against the specifics of the policy aim to judge the merits of a data science project. Here, small changes in the features of a data science project, within the context of a specific policy, could alter the overall assessment of acceptability. Some features had a higher baseline of acceptability than others, but all were considered in the context of the original policy objectives and intended outcomes. For example, although social media were generally viewed less positively than other data sources, it was seen as a viable and appropriate methodology to use where the outcome had a clear public benefit and data was being used in aggregated and anonymized format.

In the broader context of clear skepticism among the public about the value of using social media for research, it is evident that they do see value in its methodology; however, it is also evident that the way in which social media research is conducted does matter, and that the nuance of methodology is crucial to securing public support for the approach. Researchers, therefore, require a framework from which they can review the ethics of individual projects on a case by case basis.

CONCLUSIONS AND RECOMMENDATIONS

Researchers seeking to conduct ethical social media research face a number of substantial challenges: both in navigating the conflicting guidelines that govern best practice and in grounding their methodology in the expectations of users. In light of the low level of awareness and trust in social media research among social media users, and the clear priorities for how best to improve the acceptability of social media research projects, the Wisdom of the Crowd project developed 19 recommendations to researchers, regulators, and social media organizations. The ethical principles discussed here are not new; however, these recommendations are intended to offer a series of sensible, positive, and practical suggestions for improving ethical standards in social media research, and as such seek to improve the congruence with ethical practice conducted in other forms of more traditional research methods.

These recommendations are intentionally aimed at the market research profession in the UK, and thus at companies practicing social media research under the regulation of the Market Research Society (MRS) and the UK Data Protection Act at least. However, it is hoped that the suggestions put forward in this report will also have a wider positive impact on market research agencies conducting social media research outside of the UK, and on organizations using social media data outside market research. This includes those working in academia, government, journalism, and technology, and in particular companies providing social media analytics in the UK but outside of MRS membership.

Most of the recommendations outlined in this chapter provide researchers with guidance on how they can improve their ethical practice; however, it is also acknowledged that some principles require additional action from regulators (or professional bodies) and social media organizations to support researchers in this endeavor and realize the full potential of social media research. Moreover, in some areas, it is possible to offer recommendations of best practice that should be conducted as standard; however, other areas require a new set of starting principles, from which exemptions should be made on a project-by-project basis under an internal ethics review. All appropriate steps should be taken to meet these principles and to mitigate against risks; yet the extent to which they are applicable may depend on the objectives of the research.

Awareness of Social Media Research

It is clear that the benefits of research on social media data are not widely understood and that the idea is not currently trusted. The survey conducted for this study found that under two-fifths of adults (38 percent) think that sharing individuals' social media data with companies for research purposes currently does happen; over half of adults (58 percent) believe that it should not take place at all. Researchers should, therefore, adopt transparent practices to ensure that awareness is bolstered and that negative perceptions are challenged.

Based on the discussions of the ethical challenges of social media research with legislators and regulators, it was clear that the best way of ensuring an ethical and legally compliant best practice is to maintain transparency. Any attempt to be as transparent as possible about what is being done with the data is likely to be perceived by regulators as a desire to be compliant.

The qualitative groups with the public reinforced this message that awareness of uses of social media is low among the public. Focus group participants were concerned that things were happening with their data that they were not aware of. Many participants in the groups were not aware that third parties are able to undertake research using their social media data, and this contributed to the overall feeling of a loss of control. It was expressed that other organizations and companies do too much with their data without their knowledge and that transparency was one way to counter this. It was stressed by some participants that while suspicious generally, and if researchers were more transparent, then this would help to build trust.

The findings from the conjoint analysis also demonstrated that context of methodology is vital for improving the acceptability of a research project. Particularly, knowing if the project is for a charitable or a public sector commissioner, and whether the data is in the public domain can have a big impact on the level of acceptability.

It was also apparent from the scoping report that there are significant concerns regarding the terms and conditions of social media websites. Specifically, whether terms and conditions provide a sufficient basis for research to take place without any further contact with the user? The law and the industry regulations accept that it does provide such a basis, but concerns remain among both users and stakeholders about the transparency of terms and conditions.

These concerns were also voiced in the groups with the public. The large majority of participants said they had not even tried to read the terms and conditions of the social media sites they used. A culture has been built up regarding all privacy policies as dull and too long to contemplate. Participants admitted that they would probably still not read the terms and conditions even if they were far shorter than currently.

There also appears to be a heavily entrenched view that privacy policies exist to baffle users rather than to help them, and this means that most users will not even try to engage with them. Steps social media organizations have made to shorten their privacy documents have not yet overcome the hurdle of people's preconceptions of the comprehensibility and length of such documents. As an end result, social media users are often unaware that the data they share on social media sites could be used for social and market research (Fig. 3).

Recommendations 1 and 2: Boost awareness to build trust

Recommendation for researchers

1.   Researchers should aim for transparency when conducting research projects that use social media analysis. Where possible, details of the project should be made available online, providing an explanation of whose data will be collected and for what purposes it is being used. With respect to commercially sensitive information and only with consent of the client, an abstract for each project should be made available online, including, where appropriate:

- the commissioner of the research;
- the purpose of the research;
- what kind of data will be collected and how; and
- whether the data will be published and in what format.

Recommendation for social media organizations

2.   Social media organizations now have a raft of preconceptions to overcome about the difficulties of reading privacy documents. Ethical research relies in part on people understanding how their data might be shared. Work has been done to simplify these documents and shorten them, but less has been done to advertise how their data might be used. It is recommended that social media organizations continue to review terms and conditions so that the possible uses of the data easier are easier to understand, including use of social media content for research purposes.

Fig. 3.   Recommendations for addressing low awareness of social media research. *Source:* Ginnis (2017).

Consent and Opting Out

During the fact-finding exercise with experts, it became clear that social media research with large datasets is distinct from other types of traditional research in that consent is simply not practicable. Regulators have made changes to allow social media research to take place, so long as the data are made public under the terms and conditions of the social media site.

Consent and permission were also important factors for the public. Even if they had not read the agreement in detail, participants in the qualitative workshops assumed that they were giving some level of permission for third party use of their data when agreeing to sign terms and conditions. They were most likely to cite use of their data for tailoring services to them or providing targeted advertising; in each of these examples, they perceived that users would get some direct benefit. However, they did not feel that technical agreement through terms and conditions was sufficient to be considered as consent for their data to be used in a research projects.

In the conjoint analysis, while *permission* was not one of the most important drivers of approving a project (5th of 8), the public were more likely to approve projects that had some form of opt-out or opt-in mechanism. Equally, they were least supportive of projects that relied purely on terms and conditions as permission to go ahead with social media research.

A system whereby an individual opts in to a specific research project was seen as the most ethical scenario, while opting out of specific projects had a good degree of approvability. Many participants in the workshops said that they would want to be contacted about specific research projects to ask for consent; however, others disagree and suggested that individuals might not want to be bothered each and every time a researcher was hoping to do social media research.

Participants also discussed the possibility of a tick box form of consent for research, which could be selected at the point of sign up or amended within profile settings at any time. While they thought that being approached for specific projects was fairer, there was an assumption that a tick box allowing people to opt out of their data being used for research purposes would be a more acceptable form of consent than simply allowing consent to come via the terms and conditions.

It is, therefore, clear that opt-out mechanisms for social media research warrant serious consideration for the market and social research industry. Google has recently put together an opt-out system for personalized advertisements.[7] The European Advertising Industry is also putting in place an opt-out system for behavioral advertisement – the practice of looking at internet browsing activity to target online ads at individuals[8] (Fig. 4).

Recommendations 3–5: The option to opt-out

Recommendation for researchers

3. Researchers should work to put in place systems to allow for users to opt-out from individual social media projects, or to opt out from all social media research conducted by that organization. Compliance teams already have similar systems in place for blacklisting numbers and email addresses for traditional research. At the very least, an email address should be provided for people to easily put their profile or account on a list that will be excluded from future social media research by that research organization.

It is acknowledged that researchers are only able to guarantee the execution of the opt-out when working with raw social media data. The full implementation of an opt-out mechanism requires the collaboration of social media analytics platforms, who often provide social media content to research organizations either as raw data or in an aggregated and anonymous format. One solution would be for research organizations to provide analytics platforms with a list of users to be removed prior to receiving either raw content or aggregated data.

Research organizations need to work with analytics platforms to ensure they understand the importance of giving the opportunity for privacy-conscious research subjects to remove themselves from analysis.

Recommendation for regulators

4. An opt-out for this kind of research being maintained by separate research organizations is over-complicated for members of the public. We call on regulators to look into creating an industry-wide opt-out mechanism that would work across the research organizations registered with them.

Recommendation for social media organizations

5. The final step would be to encourage social media organizations to build in an opt-out for research. We suggest that social media organizations explore ways of incorporating consent-for-research opt-out into their system. This might take place at sign-up, or be available in the account settings. While it is understood that such a system may not be technically desirable, it would likely be an unobtrusive and an effective means of building a broader consent basis for research.

Fig. 4. Recommendations for addressing challenges in gaining consent.
Source: Ginnis (2017).

Data Minimization

Another common theme among both stakeholders and members of the public was the amount of personal data collected during social media projects.

Regulators and legislators recommended a policy of 'data minimization' and only collecting the data that is required for a certain research aim. The UK Information Commissioner's Office (ICO) recommends data minimization as a policy of best practice when dealing with personal data and publishes a guide on the topic.[9] The primary aim of a policy of data minimization is to reduce the risk of harm to the research participant.

The groups with the public also illustrated that data minimization is a good course to follow. While there was a broad concern expressed in the groups that personal data could be used for malicious purposes, there was also a wish that any research that was done should only collect the data that was relevant to the study. Some participants maintained the belief that it must be possible to limit the *collection* of personal data, but admitted that, failing that, the information should be hidden from the researcher where possible.

The conjoint analysis reinforced the view that implementing a policy of data minimization would increase the likelihood that a social media research project would be approved. When asked to review a series of hypothetical projects, the type of personal information collected was a very important attribute and, within this, sensitive personal information was the characteristic most likely to prohibit a hypothetical project. Using age, gender, and broad location were the kinds of personal information that were more likely to drive acceptability.

While it can be tempting for researchers to collect as much detail as is possible, it is safer to try and limit the personal data that might be seen by the researchers. It is not always possible to limit *collecting* this data as the Application Programming Interface (API) of social media sites tend to either be *fully on* or *fully off*, but steps may be taken to ensure that the data the researcher has access to is limited. For example, this could include hiding meta data from researchers by default and/or masking the name of social media accounts.

The principles of data minimization should also be applied to deriving characteristics about individuals. Regulators recommended that the researcher ask themselves why it is that they need that data and whether or not it is possible to conduct the research without it before this was done. The quantitative study also suggested that deriving characteristics may be undesirable for the public, where less than a fifth (18 percent) thought it was acceptable for researchers to estimate personal details about an individual based on other information. This gives reason to take strict care of when and where inferred characteristics might be used.

Legal bodies, too, have concerns about derived characteristics, and we are looking carefully at what safeguards may need to be in place to ensure that such methods are fully compliant – for example, ensuring that these metrics are accurate and up to date. There are also restrictions on deriving characteristics classed as sensitive personal information. For these reasons, we advise researchers to be very careful when considering analysis using characteristics that are derived from other information a user has made public.

The use and interpretation of metadata can add value to a project, for example, looking at tweets that are geotagged in a certain location, which allows researchers to look at Twitter users only from within a broad geographic area. The qualitative work with the public, however, indicated that there appears to be little grasp of what kind of additional metadata is collected by social media organizations about them, nor of the potential variables that could be inferred from that data (Fig. 5).

Recommendations 6–7: minimizing unnecessary personal data collection

Recommendation for researchers

6.   Researchers should look to put in place restrictions on what the researcher can see in a social media analysis tool depending on the scope of the project. This will involve working with the designers of the technology to ensure that data can be removed if not required by the project. It is important to try and move toward a culture of questioning whether the data that is being collected is really necessary for a research project. Each project should be engaging in its own ethical review (see Recommendation 19) to establish potential harms to the data subjects, as well as what data is necessary to answer the research questions.

Examples of data minimization for a project might include, but is not limited to:

- removing the author's name and @tag from the researcher's sight;
- stripping out other data that is downloaded in the content of a social media post, such as named persons or place names;
- removing metadata that is not relevant for the purposes of a research project, such as GPS data that might be attached to the social media post;
- creating generalized groupings of data instead of analyzing specific data. For instance, generalizing locations by cities instead of exact street locations; and
- identifying where the need for creating derived characteristics is crucial to a project, and not running these algorithms as standard.

Recommendation for social media organizations

7.   We want to work with social media organizations to make the process of data minimization easier for researchers. Currently, downloading data from the API makes it impossible to avoid downloading data such as names, locations and other details, which are then immediately subject to conditions of 'further processing' under the DPA. For some of these fields, social media organizations should explore the possibility of limiting some of the fields of data that are downloaded.

Fig. 5.   Recommendations for addressing excessive data collection and analysis.
Source: Ginnis (2017).

Safeguarding Young People

The literature review conducted previously highlighted a gap in guidance relating to whether it is ethical to conduct research on social media given the fact that young people are openly using the services, but are not identifiable. The regulatory framework in traditional market and social research demands that researchers do not undertake research with under 16 years of age without prior parental consent,[10] and it was apparent from the interviews conducted here that regulators have not yet reached a decision on how to deal with this issue. This is an important safeguard to ensure that research is conducted within the best interests of young people under the age of 16.

The qualitative work with the public found that they were also concerned about this. Participants voiced fears that young people would not understand the extent of data that was being shared and would be left vulnerable to harm because of it. There was also a fear that the terms of use for social media services are even less likely to be read and understood by users aged under 16.

We also talked to 13–15-year olds as part of this study. This group is old enough to use most social media sites, but they are under the age that researchers would conduct research without a parent's consent. It was clear in these groups that their understanding of how much data, and how much personal data, they share on social media was fairly advanced and often more savvy than older participants; however, they had less awareness of the potential consequences of sharing this data. These young participants had not given much thought as to what might happen to their data once it had gone online, and the concept of social media research itself was somewhat alien.

When presented with information about different types of social media research, the response from young people was mixed. Many did not have a strong opinion on whether the research should or should not happen, while others asked whether it was right that researchers could look at their social media data without their consent.

While it is clear from talking to experts that there is the possibility for excluding 13–15-year olds from datasets by estimating their age, this will only ever be probabilistically correct. This means that estimating age will not be able to adequately avoid the fears of the adult workshop participants who did not feel that young people had a good enough understanding of how their data might be used to be a participant in research.

Currently, social media APIs do not allow for a selective download of data, or include a mechanism by which parental consent can be given for use of data – in the case of Twitter, the hose of Tweets is either on or off. This means that researchers who are conscious about downloading data from young people have no way of not downloading that data. Despite this, social media organizations do have this data available to them about users, so ethical researchers would appreciate a function that allowed a selective download of users (Fig. 6).

Republishing Social Media Content

One of the greatest areas of dispute surrounds the republication of social media content as part of a research project. Some argue that research agencies

---

Recommendations 8–10: removing under-16s from social media research

Recommendation for researchers

8.   Under-16s remain a particularly vulnerable group social media. In order to maintain this principle, researchers should make efforts to remove under-16s from the data. At the moment there is no way of excluding this group from the data collected from social media through their APIs. Until such a function is in place, the second best option is deriving the age of this group from the content they post. This will give an imperfect, probabilistic estimate of whether a user is under 16 so that a great deal of young people can be excluded from the research.

While this method appears to go against recommendation 3 - which asks researchers to question the need to derived characteristics – we would suggest it is acceptable to infer age for the specific purpose of removing a vulnerable group from the dataset.

There may be some very legitimate reasons to purposefully include or even target children under 16 in social media research – for example engagement in a wellbeing campaign or review of support services used on social media. However, these exceptions to the principle should be considered carefully and only undertaken if approved by an internal ethics review.

Recommendation for regulators

9.   There are currently no suggestions from regulators on how removing under-16s from the research can be done. Regulatory bodies need to provide details with the means to comply with the principle of avoiding conducting research with young people without parental consent.

Recommendation for social media organizations

10. Ethical researchers could be assisted by social media providers in this endeavour. Where aggregated and anonymous data is being provided (to either third party analytics platforms or directly to researchers), it should be possible to request that those known to be under 16 are removed from the dataset.

Fig. 6.   Recommendations for addressing potential risks to children and young people. *Source:* Ginnis (2017).

should be able to republish content that has already been made public. Others suggest that the principle of anonymity (on which consent for participation has traditionally taken place) should be upheld in social media research.

In order to adhere to anonymity, some industry regulators suggest masking social media posts, yet it is also accepted that this may not always provide a guarantee of anonymity. For example, for public Tweets, it would be possible to identify the author through using Internet search engines, even if the author had been masked in the publication of the research. This is complicated further by the brand guidelines of some social media organizations that govern the republishing of social media content. For Twitter, for example, there is a requirement to publish any tweets in full, including the user's @tag. In addition, any posts that are published must be deleted from the publication if they are deleted by the user from Twitter. Furthermore, it is also plausible that some people might actually wish to be attributed in the republication of social media posts.

However, there was a strong feeling from the focus groups that if given the choice participants would opt to remain anonymous in publication unless their consent is sought. Indeed, the quantitative research found that most people would opt for anonymity in publication (74 percent agreed with this, versus 10 percent who said they would want to be attributed).

While participants were happy to be republished by other social media users (where the comment remains in context), they are less comfortable with the principle that they will be attributed to content that has been processed and analyzed as part of a research project, where they perceive that the content will be judged to hold a particular opinion, attitude, behavior, and/or demographic. They were most concerned about the possibility of a comment being taken out of context and whether they would be held to account for things they said in the past that may no longer be true or where their views might have changed. This was particularly pertinent to examples cited where potential employers had used people's social media as a way of filtering out applicants for vacancies – a practice that some participants believed to be unfair.

Ethical consensus in this area already seems to be moving toward seeking consent where possible. Some journalists are starting to ask permission to reuse content from social media.[11] COSMOS – a social media research institution at the University of Cardiff – also practice seeking consent for all social media content that they wish to publish.[12] However, where the content of the post is not considered sensitive, COSMOS will still publish posts where they do not receive a response to their request for publication.

Ensuring the anonymity of participants/users during reporting the findings of social media analysis is still held highly by regulators. While researchers ought to make efforts to provide anonymity when undertaking many types of social media research, there are other times when this is either not practical or desirable. For example, network analysis identifies key individuals in a client's social media network. This type of research allows a client to understand which social media users play an important role in their network or helps map the flow of information between networks.

It is vital to this kind of research that individuals can be identified to the client, even if their specific posts are not published. Currently, the regulations would require anonymity and, therefore, erode the usefulness of this type of research.

However, social media are clearly very different to traditional forms of communication; there is currently a clear definition of when an individual on social media becomes a brand. Take analysis of the election, for example, while the official account of the Prime Minister (@Number10gov) would obviously count as a public organization, and thus not subject to the DPA, what about the account of the leader of the opposition, a parliamentary prospective candidate seeking election, or a journalist commenting on the campaign? Moreover, if a Twitter user is retweeting information about a communications campaign to several thousand followers, do they have a legitimate expectation of privacy about this fact? In addition, all social media users have the freedom to conduct their own kind of key influencer analysis simply by understanding who is sharing their content via social media platform plugins, and publically accessible tools such as Twitter Advanced Search can easily identify individuals within simple searches. Why should organizations not be allowed to undertake a more rigorous form of this kind of analysis?

The public groups did not have much to contribute when asked about this topic, although some did accept that individuals might at some point become a brand if they had a large enough base of followers. However, it was apparent that they, themselves, were content to 'have a nosy' at other people on social media who they might know through friends. In the quantitative survey, a small majority (54 percent) felt that institutions, organizations, and high-profile individuals have the same rights to anonymity as any other social media account.

The current guidelines for the display of tweets stipulate the following requirements, which are necessary for use of the API:

- Do: 'Show name, @username, unmodified Tweet text, profile picture (where possible), timestamp and the Twitter logo nearby'
- Don't: 'Modify the Tweet text with the exception of removing hyperlinks.'[13]

Both of these principles go against an ethical researcher's attempts to anonymize Tweets in the publication of them. Regulatory guidelines in place do not permit the identification of social media users at the point of publication, and so Twitter's limitations on anonymization of their content is problematic.

Brand guidelines force researchers to look for consent for each piece of content that is republished. It would be easier for the researcher and safer for the respondent if fully anonymized social media could be published, involving both de-authoring the content and masking it, by taking steps to reduce the risk of re-identification through modification of the social media content (Fig. 7).

Expectations of Users

The classification of social media data as either 'public' or 'private' has a number of important consequences for social media analysis, both in the extent to which users expect private content to by analyzed for research, and in the extent to which private sensitive personal information can be processed under the terms of the DPA.

The conjoint analysis demonstrated the public/private nature of the data is an important factor in determining the public acceptability of a research project. While use of public social media content was very likely to make a research project more acceptable, use of private data was considered fairly off-limits. As might be expected, research involving private messages was likely to eliminate all prospect of approving a project to go ahead.

Participants in the qualitative workshops were aware of privacy settings, and many had used these to tailor their account; however, they were uncertain how this aligned with what data was and was not available for social media research. Participants noted that everything on Twitter is public (unless an account is protected), but also held the expectation that Facebook data was viewable by all, unless they adjusted their privacy settings. They also noted that direct messages on Facebook, or similar applications like WhatsApp and Snapchat held greater implicit privacy; many participants suggested that these should therefore remain off-limits to researchers, and even social media organizations themselves.

The scoping report and subsequent interviews established that regulators would technically consider a forum like Facebook to be private, as it requires a password to view information. Private forums require explicit consent from members/users before research can take place compliantly within them. However, it was not clear whether Facebook can be seen as a great deal more private than

Recommendations 11–16: permission for publication

Recommendation for researchers

11. All social media research projects should question whether there is a need to publish verbatim content, and ask whether publication of aggregated and anonymous data would be sufficient to answer the research question. Any projects that wish to show verbatim text should first seek approval to do so through an internal ethical review. All steps should be taken to reduce the risk of harm to the participants.

12. If a project wishes to cite examples of content as illustration in a report or presentation, researchers should aim to contact social media users to ask them if they would be happy for their content to be cited. This would mirror existing good practices in other disciplines, as well as matching expectations of the public, who expect anonymity as standard. To adhere to brand guidelines, where consent has been given, researchers should keep the author next to any content, and avoid adjusting the text of the content.

13. Where a project wishes to show verbatim comment as part of an automated dashboard that provides a live stream of content on a certain topic, and often filtered cut by certain variables, the issue of anonymization is distinctly more difficult to implement. Where there is a clear need demonstrated from the client to include these which has been approved be an ethical review process, dashboards should be password-protected and deauthored as minimum to maintain some level of anonymity to the wider public.

14. In addition, where it is agreed that raw content will be seen by the client, researchers should consider putting in place an agreement with their client that they will not try to re-identify de-authored individuals' from the dashboard. There are models for these kinds of agreements in other kinds of research.

Recommendation for regulators

15. Regulators should attempt to form a clear definition for what constitutes a 'brand' on social media. For example, where social media accounts have a number of followers or friends that can be counted, is it reasonable to expect that those with a significantly large volume of followers expect less privacy than someone with fewer followers? Is it also reasonable to suggest that public accounts of prominent individuals, such as MPs or company CEOs, should be treated differently?

This definition of a brand can then be used to identify individuals in a network who are of special interest to a commissioner of research and that can be named in a report. We acknowledge that this might sometimes appear arbitrary, but regulators should focus on balancing expectation of privacy with genuine research interest in high-profile users.

Fig. 7. Recommendations for addressing challenges in publication and attribution. *Source:* Ginnis (2017).

Recommendations 11–16 continued

Recommendation for social media organizations

16. We would like to see social media organizations adopt developer guidelines that allows researchers the flexibility to make changes to the social media content they collect for the purpose of research. This would give researchers the ability to mask and anonymize content from individuals when republishing content in a research project. Care would be taken by researchers to uphold the meaning and content of the social media post, and attribution would be given to the platform brand. We also seek guidance from social media organizations as to what format they would ideally like these masked, modified social media posts in, and how they should look.

Fig. 7. (*Continued*)

Twitter – especially as the APIs do not have access requirements that restrict who can use the data at the back-end. It was clear from talking with legislators, that under the DPA, public forums are whenever the data has been made public under an agreement such as the terms and conditions of a website (Fig. 8). This has an important legal implication as sensitive personal data, such as

---

Recommendations 17–18: Defining 'private'

Recommendation for researchers

17. It is the responsibility of researchers to have a sound understanding of whether the data they have collected, analysed or enriched consists of public or private data. Analysis of private content should only be conducted with approval from an internal ethics review.

Recommendation for regulators

18. It is not clear from the primary research whether users are happy with data they share privately being used for research, even if new functionality allows this to be conducted at the aggregated and anonymized level. We recommend that regulators provide further clarification on extent to which this type of approach would comply with current research guidelines.

Fig. 8. Recommendations for addressing privacy concerns. *Source:* Ginnis (2017).

Seeking Ethics Approval as Standard

Interviews with experts in the field highlighted a fear that even though uses of social media data are safe, they can in some cases lead to a potential harm to participants. In all forms of research, regardless of whether it is market, social, or academic research, one of the fundamental principles is that of avoiding harm to participants. Where consent is not sought directly for a research project, the onus to avoid harm is, therefore, even stronger – although it is also clear that a participant having given consent does not remove the researcher's responsibility to protect participants from harm.

The conjoint analysis conducted for this project points to the importance of context in helping decide whether social media projects would gain approval from the majority of the public. Context is paramount both in terms of the purpose of the research and in the methodology used to conduct the project.

A number of the recommendations in this report suggest that approval from an ethical review process is required before it would be appropriate to proceed. This is particularly important where the project seeks to include data from those aged under 16, analyze aggregated and anonymous private data, or publish raw unedited verbatim content. An ethics review is also crucial to ensuring that the maximum amount of data minimization will be applied to the project (Fig. 9).

Social media analysis best practice should be continuously reviewed alongside changes in technology, legislation, and use expectations. As new social media platforms emerge and trends in social media change, so too should guidelines for how to conduct ethical social media analysis. For example, further work is needed to provide guidance on the analysis of images generated through social media, and on practices known as 'scraping' where data is collected without access to a formal API. It is also important to recognize that these changes will require trialing in order to ensure they are practicable and useful in ensuring an ethical best practice for social media research.

Recommendation 19 – establishing ethics reviews for social media research

Recommendation for researchers

19. Researchers should undertake an internal ethics review for all social media research projects that do not seek consent directly from research subjects. Researchers should assess the context of the research to try and understand where potential harm to participants may arise and identify what steps can be put in place to meet user expectations and protect users from harm.

Fig. 9.   Recommendations for addressing lack of coherent social media ethics.
Source: Ginnis (2017).

Implementing these recommendations will also need to be iterative, not least because digital communications develop extremely quickly. It is not assumed that all researchers will be able to adopt these recommendations wholesale, but it is hoped this chapter contributes to debates on this topic in related sectors, and that it encourages researchers to feel empowered to take positive steps to improve the ethical accountability of their social media research projects.

NOTES

1. Using Twitter to Predict Norovirus Outbreaks, Millison and Staff, NHS Choices Blog, 12/12/2016 http://blogs.nhs.uk/choices-blog/2016/02/12/guest-blog-using-twitter-to-predict-norovirus-outbreaks/ Reading the Riots, the Guardian, LSE, http://eprints.lse.ac.uk/46297/1/Reading%20the%20riots(published).pdf

2. For example, ESOMAR Guideline on social media research, and MRS Guidelines for online research remain ambiguous on some of these key issues.

3. For example the MRS Guidance for Research with Children and Young People: https://www.mrs.org.uk/pdf/2014-09-01Children%20and%20Young%20People%20 Research%20Guidelines.pdf and SRA Ethical Guidelines: http://the-sra.org.uk/wp-content/uploads/ethics03.pdf

4. Innovate UK is an executive non-departmental public body, sponsored by the Department for Business, Energy & Industrial Strategy.

5. Research where the researcher interacts with participants and consent can be collected; such as MRS Guidelines for Online Research https://www.mrs.org.uk/pdf/2014-09-01%20Online%20Research%20Guidelines.pdf

6. See further details on Open Data Blog: Ginnis, S. (2016, May 19). Engaging with the public on data science. Retrieved from https://data.blog.gov.uk/2016/05/19/engaging-with-the-public-on-data-science/

7. Google (2015), 'Opt Out,' https://support.google.com/ads/answer/2662922?hl= en-GB (accessed on 10/01/17).

8. Your online choices (2015), 'About' http://www.youronlinechoices.com/uk/about-behavioural-advertising (accessed on 10/01/17).

9. Information Commissioner's Office (July 2014), Big Data and Data Protection, https://ico.org.uk/media/for-organisations/documents/1541/big-data-and-data-protection.pdf (accessed on 15/09/15).

10. For example, the MRS Guidance for Research with Children and Young People: https://www.mrs.org.uk/pdf/2014-09-01Children%20and%20Young%20People%20 Research%20Guidelines.pdf or Social Research Association Ethical Guidelines http://the-sra.org.uk/wp-content/uploads/ethics03.pdf

11. See an example of best practice guidelines from the American Press Institute (September 2014), 'Practice ethical curation and attribution', https://www.american-pressinstitute.org/publications/reports/strategy-studies/ethical-curation-attribution/ (accessed on 15/09/15).

12. COSMOS, 'Ethical statement', http://www.cs.cf.ac.uk/cosmos/cosmos-ethics-statement/ (accessed on 15/09/15).

13. Twitter, 'Display Requirements' (accessed on 25/08/15), https://about.twitter.com/company/display-requirements

REFERENCES

ESOMAR. (July 2011). Guideline on social media research. Retrieved from https://www.eso-mar.org/uploads/public/knowledge-and-standards/codes-and-guidelines/ESOMAR-Guideline-on-Social-Media-Research.pdf

Ginnis, S. (May 19, 2016). Engaging with the public on data science. Retrieved from https://data.blog.gov.uk/2016/05/19/engaging-with-the-public-on-data-science/

Google. (2015). *Opt out.* Retrieved from https://support.google.com/ads/answer/2662922?hl=en-GB. Accessed on 10 January 2017.

Information Commissioner's Office. (July 2014). *Big data and data protection.* Retrieved from https://ico.org.uk/media/for-organisations/documents/1541/big-data-and-data-protection.pdf. Accessed on 15 September 2015.

Market Research Society. (2014). *Guidance for research with children and young people.* Retrieved from https://www.mrs.org.uk/pdf/2014-09-01Children%20and%20Young%20People%20Research%20Guidelines.pdf

Market Research Society. (2014). *Guidelines for online research.* Retrieved from https://www.mrs.org.uk/pdf/2014-09-01%20Online%20Research%20Guidelines.pdf

Market Research Society Research Board. (August 2011). *Online data collection and privacy: Discussion paper.* Retrieved from https://www.mrs.org.uk/pdf/2011-07-19%20Online%20data%20collection%20and%20privacy%202.pdf

Market Research Society Research Board. (August 2011). *Online data collection and privacy: response to submissions.* Retrieved from https://www.mrs.org.uk/pdf/2012-04-04%20Online%20data%20collection%20and%20privacy.pdf

Millson, D., & Staff, C. (December 12, 2016). *Using Twitter to predict Norovirus outbreaks.* Retrieved from http://blogs.nhs.uk/choices-blog/2016/02/12/guest-blog-using-twitter-to-predict-norovirus-outbreaks/

Social Research Association. (2003). *Ethical guidelines.* Retrieved from http://the-sra.org.uk/wp-content/uploads/ethics03.pdf

The Guardian & London School Economics and Political Science. (2012). *Reading the riots.* Retrieved from http://eprints.lse.ac.uk/46297/1/Reading%20the%20riots(published).pdf

Your Online Choices. (2015). *About.* Retrieved from http://www.youronlinechoices.com/uk/about-behavioural-advertising. Accessed on 10 January 2017.

CHAPTER 10

CONCLUSION: GUIDING THE ETHICS OF ONLINE SOCIAL MEDIA RESEARCH – ADAPTATION OR RENOVATION?

Ron Iphofen

Nobody could have guessed at just how rapidly online social media would develop. And nobody could have easily predicted the popularity across all sectors of the population these applications would become. What would have been predictable, however, was just how tempting these social activities would become to the modern researcher. If this is how people wish to engage social activities, to find and relate to each other and to share their thoughts, experiences and images – then this phenomenon was never going to be ignored by researchers.

It was also perhaps obvious that some observers would bemoan the threats to 'natural' social interactions and community-building that involve 'real' as opposed to 'virtual' social interactions. And others see online media as yet another globalizing threat to local life. It is impossible to know if, in the long term, such fears will be realized. But counter examples exist. Online media do provide for 'round-the-clock' operation, threatening to obliterate time as a function of a culture's sense of identity. Hongladarom (2002) in contrast uses the example of time to show how local cultures can resist the globalizing and

The Ethics of Online Research
Advances in Research Ethics and Integrity, Volume 2, 237–242
Copyright © 2018 by Emerald Publishing Limited
All rights of reproduction in any form reserved
ISSN: 2398-6018/doi:10.1108/S2398-601820180000002014

homogenizing tide. Local cultures find it hard to resist integrating themselves with the world through the Internet, but at the same time, they feel a real need to protect and to promote their identities. Hongladarom tries to show that local cultures find the Web an appropriate and effective medium for putting forward their own agenda; weaving together each time 'strand' to create a coherent pattern that is both global and local. In similar vein Wallace and Vincent (2016) also point to the way modern communications technology can in fact enhance community well-being rather than undermine it. So perhaps fears that threaten the 'local' by the 'global' may not have been realized. More importantly, for some, these online communities may be the only communities that have or can experience – all the more reason to take care with how they are researched.

All the chapters in this volume point up the particular ethical concerns that must be addressed in conducting research in online social media and networking and how necessary it will be to move beyond the established conventions of ethical principle. It is not that informed consent, anonymity, confidentiality, and privacy are not issues of concern – but the situated context of online research requires these principles are thought through in different ways.

The primary testing nature of this evolving research relationship relates to the status of the data. These are 'products' of the actions of people so what is up for study is not, directly, the people themselves, but their online products and, perhaps, the people *via* their online products. Some have even suggested this could be a way to evade the 'personal data' problem: Internet sources may not be 'human subjects' rather culturally produced textual material and so should be treated as such. So the debate is around whether online 'accounts' should be treated as human participants. In this respect it is not that much different from most social science research. The researcher/researched relationship is all too often 'mediated' via the 'products' of survey responses, interview transcripts, itemized questionnaire tick boxes, and so on. Direct observational research of social behavior is rarer since it is challenging in terms of access and resources. Conventional research faces the same fundamental existential, epistemological and ontological limitations as online studies – but the context presents a crucial difference and what the participants' expectations about that context actually are. The challenge of social science is that gap between what people think, feel, and do and, what they 'say' that they think, feel, and do. Inferences about 'real' thoughts and feeling have always been based on the products of people's actions and responses. The veracity and authenticity of an interview transcript, for example, is subject to its mediated quality. Ironically it may be that people feel 'safer' to disclose their thoughts and feelings in an online environment than they do face-to-face – placing the onus for responsibility in how those 'products' are exploited even more fully on the researcher.

This means that it is not enough to treat the online 'output' merely as 'text' – that is, not something that is not especially important, valued and significant to those that produced it. It is not enough to claim that is 'only the text' that is being researched and that problems only arise if the data are used to retrieve more personal insights. The text IS 'personal' if the user/producer thought it was – even if that is not what is technically meant by the data protection legislation.

The additional concern relates to the searchability of online data. Online materials are, by definition, 'secondary data' – produced for some other purpose than 'for research.' But the digital technology which carried them offers faster and more efficient retrieval options and so poses risks of access to more sensitive personal data. Once again, data protection legislation can be seen to apply once the use for which the data were intended is altered. So we are urged to find ways of limiting the risk of deductive disclosure by designing/using computer-mediated data collection tools that can manage these risks. This is what lies behind the move toward enhancing 'privacy by design.' The potential to retain even elements of treasured privacy will protect participants' personal interests a little more.

While most commentators recognize the difficulty of seeking informed consent, they also urge continuing to secure it. But if we disentangle the threads of this intricate process – one that has always been more complex than research ethics reviewers have acknowledged – we can see how even more convoluted it becomes in the online context. When should the 'information' be given and what information – in the terms and conditions (T&Cs) of the service provider? Providers may not be so keen to offer a 'generic research potential' clause and, as contributors to this volume have pointed out, users do not often read the T&Cs as carefully as would be required to ensure they were fully informed. Providers would be even less keen to add/modify such clauses for each proposed new research intervention.

Consent is particularly hard to seek from anonymous contributors to a chatroom, for example. Announcing that research is being conducted on a site may be ethically sound, but methodologically fundamentally alters the nature of the relationships involved – not just between researcher and researched but between 'legitimate' site users. Could 'seeking consent' create more harm than simply treating a public space as available for research? This represents a 'contamination of the field' problem – not for research purposes but for those perhaps seeking help from a help- or care-giving site. The research intervention might be considered intrusive enough to have undermined users' willingness to use the site. The mere announcement of research damaging users' opportunities to gain the help offered.

Further, how do we deal with the fact that people might change their minds? The attractiveness of much online research is the immediacy, the spontaneous, and the ephemeral nature of some aspects of human communication. The human problem with the 'real time,' almost instantaneous, online media is that it does not allow that participants might state a view rapidly without too much thought and then on reflection wish to change it later. One might confirm with the user that they had not changed their opinion since posting, but, if they have, what then? The data of interest were the spontaneous contributions, not their more durable, sustained reflection, opinions, views or thoughts – or, even, regrets. Both are worthy and interesting research topics in themselves – the spontaneous and the reflected. But they present researchers with different challenges: the conventional offer to participants for data withdrawal cannot apply to data that was delivered in the 'public' domain since its 'withdrawal' would undermine the analysis and understanding of all other products in that domain/research site. If the research focus was on the original online 'product,' then the withdrawal of even one element would affect the entire research project. Clearly, there should be an ethical response to participants' requests to clarify, amend or 'regret' a comment or contribution – but that might only be managed by an additional study reporting those concerns.

Whatever ethical practices are followed to collect data, there is little doubt that extra caution needs to be taken with how the data are protected. The European Union-based Article 29 Working Party (2009) has made recommendations consistent with existing data protection (DP) directives for social networking services (SNS), and those will have to be addressed again when any new regulations arrive. Some key elements are that SNS providers are considered to hold responsibility as data controllers and so should inform users of their identity, and provide comprehensive and clear information about the purposes and different ways in which they intend to process personal data. They should provide privacy-friendly default settings and information and adequate warning to users about privacy risks when they upload data onto the SNS. Pictures or information about other individuals should only be uploaded with the individual's consent. There should be access to an easy-to-use complaint handling procedure. There are many more DP points of recommendation and more should be expected as new regulations emerge.

There is not enough space in this volume to tease out all the issues that arise in such a rich, diverse, and growing field of interest. But the contributors to this volume have suggested a multiplicity of practical ways in which these issues can be addressed. It is hard to decide on 'first principles' when they often conflict or are in tension with each other. An overarching aim of research is to act in the public interest, but who decides what that is when it is 'the public' who are using online media and value at least some of their privacy? Observations of behavior in 'naturally occurring interactions' is the stuff of social science, but do the researchers' perceptions of what is private match those of the persons being studied in the setting? When evidence of harm is disclosed – whether in private or in public space – what should researchers do about it? How can anonymity be preserved by the researcher when it is not retained by the site user? Of course, researchers should be able to assess the extent of the potential harms due to uncontrolled disclosure and the extended dissemination of data and/or findings. But not even the most astute can anticipate all the possible risks involved. Can participants at least be made aware of risks as part of whatever form of consenting is adopted?

Using the advice offered in the preceding chapters, there is a good chance that online research of high quality that protects the interests of participants, researchers, and the communities involved can be accomplished. But occasionally, it is important to go back to some fundamentals, such as is this research really necessary? Is it necessary to 'intrude' upon this community of online users in order to 'discover' some matters of value to science and society – as well as to the users themselves? Is there any other way of gaining this information? And, ultimately to return to all the issues addressed in this Volume, can we gain these benefits without causing unnecessary harm? One aspect of concern that has not been adequately dealt with here relates to researcher safety. While there might be little risk of direct immediate physical harm coming to online researchers, they are certainly not immune to emotional or psychological harm. Researchers can find themselves subject to online bullying, emotional abuse and distress arising out of compassion they feel for those they are studying (see Granholm & Svedmark, 2018). The blurred lines that exist once you start researching online and being online as a researcher are incredibly important to recognize and consider when planning research of this nature. Internet trolling can be hugely damaging to victims and researchers need to think about their digital footprint, whether it should be personal or professional and what impact that might have on their studies or themselves. In each new research engagement, these questions must be teased out along the challenging route to research integrity.

The main lesson to learn from the rapid development of online media and the social networking it has promoted is that it is impossible to tell what lies around the corner. We can only guess that as robotics, artificial intelligence, nanotechnology, and the interconnectedness of digital communications grows, so too will the ethical challenges for us all – not just for researchers. There is an increased onus on the designers, engineers, and the systems providers to remain alert to the dangers of innovative technologies and for users to overcome complacency in their use of and engagement with attractive new apps and, not least, on researchers and their host institutions to help ensure that the risks, harms, and benefits are fully understood.

REFERENCES

Article 29 Working Party. (2009). *Opinion 5/2009 on online social networking, Directorate General Justice, Freedom and Security, B-1049*. Brussels: European Commission. Retrieved from http://ec.europa.eu/justice_home/fsj/privacy/index_en.htm

Granholm, C., & Svedmark, E. (2018 forthcoming). Research that hurts them and me: Ethical considerations when studying vulnerable populations online, In R. Iphofen & M. Tolich (Eds.), *The SAGE handbook of qualitative research ethics* (Ch. 33). London: SAGE.

Hongladarom, S. (2002). The web of time and the dilemma of globalization. *The Information Society, 18*, 241–249.

Wallace, C., & Vincent, K. (2016). Community well-being and information technology. In R. Phillips & C. Wong (Eds.), *Handbook of community wellbeing research*. Dordrecht: Springer.

INDEX